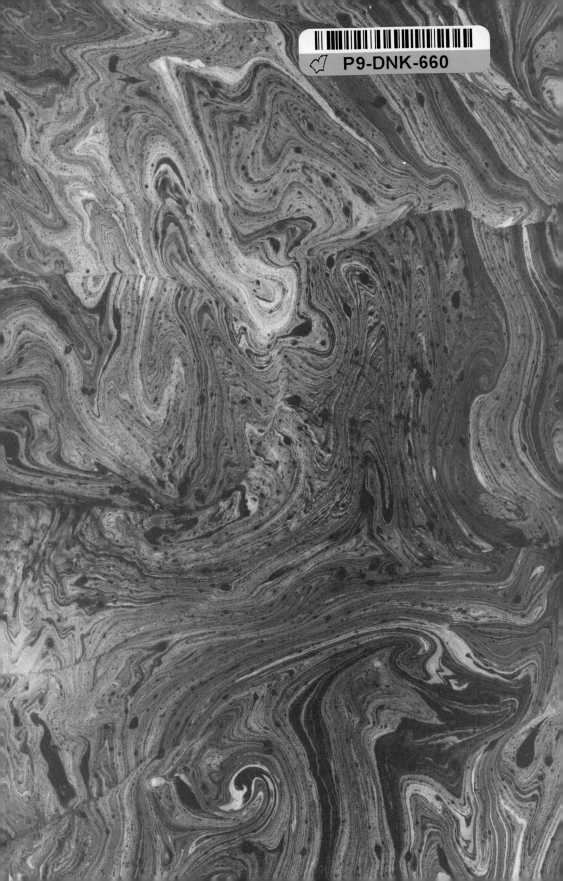

The Hotel

A WEEK IN THE LIFE OF

❧ THE PLAZA ❧

SONNY KLEINFIELD

S I M O N   A N D   S C H U S T E R

NEW YORK   LONDON   TORONTO   SYDNEY   TOKYO

Simon and Schuster

Simon & Schuster Building
Rockefeller Center
1230 Avenue of the Americas
New York, New York 10020

Copyright © 1989 by Sonny Kleinfield

Simon and Schuster and colophon are registered trademarks
of Simon & Schuster Inc.
Designed by Karolina Harris
Manufactured in the United States of America

1   3   5   7   9   10   8   6   4   2

Library of Congress Cataloging-in-Publication Data
Kleinfield, Sonny.
The hotel: a week in the life of the Plaza/Sonny Kleinfield.
p.   cm.
1. Milford Plaza Hotel (New York, N.Y.) I. Title.
TX941.M53K44   1989
647.94747'101—dc20   89-6200
CIP
ISBN 0-671-63541-7

for Samantha

THE HOTEL

PROLOGUE

HE crowd began to form in the approaching dawn, hours before anyone was expected to show up. The weather was good. It was a mild October day in 1907, a little windy, but not especially so for this time of year.

The first excitement came around seven in the morning. Clanging horse-drawn fire engines pulled up in front of the stately Fifth Avenue entrance and platoons of firemen sprinted into the hotel. There was, in fact, no blaze. It was just a last fire drill before the hotel finally opened to the public.

An hour or so later, the crowd had swelled into the hundreds. Police were all about, but it was a cordial, mannerly throng. The people had not come to be offensive, but only to look so they could return home and say, "My God, you'll never believe who I saw today." It had been rumored that there would be something of a competition to be the first to register, and there was an intense curiosity about who it would be. The answer came at nine o'clock, when a stubby black car drew up and out stepped Alfred Gwynne Vanderbilt, a top hat propped on his head. The crowd seemed to approve. After all, his father, Cornelius Vanderbilt, was reputed to be the richest man in the country. Looking pleased, the millionaire sportsman marched up to the front desk and signed the register in a sweeping scrawl: "Mr. and Mrs. Vanderbilt and servant." This signing of the register, a simple routine of a hotel's everyday life, was the only ceremony marking the opening. The new Plaza Hotel was a fancy place, to be sure, but it believed in tasteful and quiet elegance.

After Vanderbilt, the familiar names came apace. There was George Jay Gould, along with his wife and a well-behaved brood of children. Then Oliver Harriman. Then John Wanamaker from Philadelphia. They all moved through the doors with verve and deliberation. Understandably, the servants took it a little slower, and some of them were shining with sweat as they carried the seemingly endless line of steamer trunks and suitcases up the stairs and into the hotel. The onlookers craned their necks and studied them all enviously. A recognizable rhythm began to develop, rising or falling as notables arrived. There were appreciative grins when "Diamond Jim" Brady strutted up the steps with a cockeyed little smile, the actress Lillian Russell draped on his arm. Billie Burke appeared. And, a little later, Oscar Hammerstein came by. So did Mark Twain, then in his early seventies. He didn't wish a room, but just wanted to poke around and get a peek.

This was a day of some peculiarities, and as it happened, "auto-cabs" were making their first appearance in New York City. Their developer had chosen the hotel as a fitting place to station several of the bright red-and-green vehicles. A ride cost 30 cents for the first half-mile and then 10 cents for each additional quarter-mile. The owner, however, had shut off the meters. All guests of the hotel this day were being extended trips free of charge, and why not? The owner knew he would in time get plenty of money from these people.

As the graying evening set in, the crowd outside steadily began to dissolve, having squeezed all there was from the event. The day had delivered on its promise. "Looks like quite a place," a slightly rumpled onlooker remarked on leaving. "It must be really something to spend a night there."

• • •

MORE than three-quarters of a century later, the Plaza Hotel still goes about its business of providing beds and meals on the same site it has always occupied, a pretty remarkable feat in a city where many of even the grandest buildings have had an extremely brief street life. It's all the more remarkable considering that the southwest corner of Fifth Avenue and Fifty-ninth Street is possibly the most valuable parcel of real estate in Manhattan.

The landscape around the Plaza, however, has changed a great deal over the years. When it was built, the hotel stood prominently along "Millionaire's Mile," that famous stretch of Fifth Avenue dotted with the huge baroque mansions of the richest families in New York, the very clientele the Plaza hoped to attract. From an upper floor of the hotel, a guest looking southward could get a good view of the spires of St. Patrick's over the rooftops of these ostentatious homes, with their cramped attic cubicles for the servants and their far roomier basement spaces for horses.

In its original setting, the Plaza sounded a rather restrained note amid such a lavish display of wealth. Today, the private mansions have been razed or adapted to other purposes. The Plaza alone survives, dwarfed by encroaching walls of steel and glass. The horse-drawn carriages at curbside, for hire to take tourists for a spin around the park, are sad reminders of the smart transportation of the past. The Plaza has lived long enough to become something of an anachronism, a proud old dowager, seemingly oblivious to change.

There is an aura that always surrounds a *grand hôtel de luxe,* and the Plaza's long and colorful history is part of its unique aura. The continuous flow of rich and celebrated guests has added to its attractions. But from the day it opened, the hotel has stirred up fantasies, even among those who never stayed there, of elegant accommodations and discreet white-gloved service. For the earnest tourist or the exhausted businessman it somehow creates an atmosphere of unfolding possibilities, expectations of excitement or adventure, or at the very least a momentary break from the banality of day-to-day routines.

For a long time I have wondered about hotel life and hotel

people. To satisfy my curiosity, I spent a couple of years, off and on, visiting the Plaza and talking to the battery of managers, bellmen, bartenders, waiters, and doormen—the people who greet and serve its guests. I also met with the cooks, maids, plumbers, electricians, and hundreds of others whom few guests ever see. Then I picked one week in the spring of 1988 and spent all of my time there, talking to everyone who would talk to me and watching them at work. I followed them around from the basement to the rooftops. I managed to observe the inner workings of the Plaza and to discover firsthand many of the tricks of the luxury hotel trade.

So many things about hotels are deceptive and not at all what they seem to be. If the Plaza presents an air of ease and refinement, great chaos often prevails out of sight. That is true of every hotel. But the Plaza, I found out, has a lore and mystery all its own.

MONDAY

1

IN the early-morning light, a short, putty-faced man named Joe Szorentini took his normal position outside the main entrance of the Plaza Hotel. Nothing much stirred yet. The first hooded joggers were out and moving off in the direction of Central Park, and a distant police siren wailed, but that was about it. Szorentini bounced up and down on the balls of his feet. His eyes glanced from side to side. He was searching for arriving taxis or limousines. The landscape he saw never appreciably changed: taxis and limousines.

"Looks like a good day to be alive," the doorman said to me. "That means we ought to have some people."

Day after day, Szorentini scurried outside the big doors of the hotel like a vagrant pigeon, greeting the constant flow of guests. The work required fortitude, good cheer, and a willingness to be splashed by discourteous cars and jostled by people bearing packages and tennis racquets and hurrying to check in. While he waited for his first business, he rolled over in his mind the arrival and departure numbers he had picked up from the front desk. He always got the numbers first thing so he knew what to expect. It was a habit of mind that went with the job. Over time, ratios would present themselves. For instance, Szorentini knew to expect four or five cars for the garage for every hundred check-ins. Today would be fairly busy—281 check-ins, 304 checkouts. "Decent," he said.

The phone was ringing, and Szorentini moved quickly to answer it. There was a black phone booth in the left-hand corner of the entranceway. It had a direct line to the garage a couple of blocks away, allowing Szorentini to call for guests' cars, and any guest could call down to him from a room. "That was someone who wanted his chauffeur to pick up some clothing," he said to me when he returned from the booth. "You get all sorts of calls from guests who have instructions for their chauffeurs. A lot of times it's a shopping list. You're probably not going to believe this, but most of the time it's dog food they want. I get quite a few calls for dog food. So the chauffeur takes the limo and gets some Alpo or Gravy Train."

Nearby two birds were mating in the dirt of the flower beds. Szorentini cast a disapproving look at a spittle-dribbling bum wrapped in cardboard and newspapers who was camped just in front of the beds. Any violation of the decorum of the Plaza annoyed him. Lately Szorentini had been bothered by a flower thief. He knew exactly who it was: a grimy, addled man who he felt certain was on drugs. The thief pulled up the tulips, bulbs and all, from the beds in front of the hotel and then sold them unremorsefully to passersby a couple of blocks away. A few days before, the huckster had had the gall to attempt a theft in Szorentini's presence. The doorman was so maddened that he grabbed the man by the back of the neck and forced him to replant the flowers in the beds. Later on, after Szorentini had gone off duty, he returned and recaptured them.

The doorman was a lean man in his sixties, with gray hair, formidable eyebrows, prominent cheekbones, and a rather soothing aura. He wore a gold-and-fawn broadcloth uniform with collar and cuffs trimmed in gold braid—formal habiliments that suggested the hotel was not for just anyone. Around his neck dangled a silver whistle which he tweeted shrilly when someone needed a cab.

Presently a long black limousine sailed around the corner and slid to a stop in front of the entrance. Szorentini swung into action.

Deliberately, he tugged his coat into place. Straightening his cap, he bustled over to open the door for its passengers. Out stepped a stocky man with thinning hair, wearing a tweedy blue suit. On his arm was a towering beauty, heavily made-up, with hair dyed a copper red, and she was chattering away at a furious clip.

"Good morning," Szorentini said. "Welcome to the Plaza."

The man grumbled a curt hello, turned, thanked Szorentini, dug out a $1 bill, and put it in his palm.

Pleased with the reward, Szorentini smiled and patted his coat pocket.

The Plaza Hotel was just starting its day. There was a wedge of sunlight breaking through drifts of clouds. A crispness was in the air, and pedestrians turned up their coat collars against the razory wind. In the package room, two people were already sorting mail and bundles into the appropriate slots. Fresh linen was being readied by the maids. Just inside the gilt-and-marble lobby, two men on a ladder were delicately cleaning the massive chandelier that hung there, a chore they repeated once a month. The whole hotel, I was told, contained an extraordinary 1,650 chandeliers, enough to employ the two men full-time.

A lobby porter was making his way from one sand-filled ashtray to the next, collecting the most recent stubbed-out butts. He carried a small broom and a gold-colored dustpan on a wooden stick, and when he came to an ashtray, he raised the pan to its edge and then swept the butts into the pan. After smoothing out the sand with the broom as carefully as a caddy raking a bunker, he took out a squarish stamp and pressed it into the sand. When he removed it, there was an impression of the Plaza insignia—two Ps back to back enclosed in a crest. "There, that one's done," he said, and he shuffled off.

Szorentini lifted his head now and then to take a quick look at the skies. Inclement weather meant a scarcity of taxis and an abundance of guests who wanted them. If he worked hard, he could line his pockets with greenbacks. But bad weather could also ambush the body. In the summer, it was often too hot. In the winter, it was too cold. The hotel had thoughtfully installed a wide row of heating lamps under the marquee, and they helped to keep the flesh warm, but a doorman still had to spend a lot of his time away from their glow. Szorentini said he didn't much mind the weather conditions. "Listen, I'm used to it. You're out in these conditions enough years, your body becomes a fortress."

At various periods, starting in 1947, Szorentini had been a garbageman at the hotel, hauling bundled trash out to the sidewalk, an elevator operator, and a bellman. In 1952 he became a doorman. At first he was stationed at the entrance on Fifty-ninth Street, familiarly known as the Rookie Door. After three years, he worked his way to the Fifth Avenue entrance, which was where most of the guests entered; the doormen referred to it as the Big Door. "There's twice as much action at the Big Door," Szorentini explained. "All the limousines come here. All the private cars come here. The cabs from the airports come here. On Fifty-ninth, the police chase you away every couple of minutes. You can get fifty to a hundred people an hour at this door. It's definitely the door you want to work."

People were awake and much around. A cab stopped and a young blonde with big glasses hopped out. A dollar.

A shiny white limousine slowed to a halt and three Japanese men scrambled out of the backseat. Szorentini got their luggage and conducted them to the door. He was as protective of the arriving guests as a mother of an ill child. Two dollars.

He helped a man with electrified hair load up his BMW and got a $10 reward. As he snuck a look at the bill, he said, "Thank you very much. And have a very safe trip."

The busy pace at the Big Door inoculated Szorentini against the vagaries of idleness, for idleness can be destructive to a doorman. Szorentini's days were filled with friendly interchanges during which he acquired a good deal of social information. Conversation among the doormen seemed almost always to center around the hotel and hotel guests—oddities, irritations, famous arrivals, the latest from the gossip circuitry of the staff. "You know about the problem Cary Grant had with the English muffins, don't you?" he asked me. "Oh, yeah, Mr. Grant talked it over with me." He spoke as if it had happened yesterday, not several decades ago, for the good stories were told and retold with the reverence accorded legend. It seems that Grant had ordered English muffins for breakfast and had been served three halves. He wondered what had happened to the fourth. Unable to get a satisfactory answer, he called Conrad Hilton, then the Plaza's owner, untroubled by the fact that Hilton was traveling in Turkey. Hilton politely explained that an efficiency expert had determined that most people ate one and a half muffins. Grant expressed a low opinion of efficiency experts. His indignation got results, and the Plaza served two full muffins from then on. "I like that story," Szorentini said. "It shows that it's what the guest wants that counts."

Among the many kinds of people who came to the Plaza, Szorentini liked the celebrities best (though he had nothing against unknowns who tipped big). Those he had opened doors for many times he regarded as friends. Piled in his locker he kept a yellowed file of newspaper clippings having to do with his "friends." There was a lengthy spread from the *New York Post,* for instance, about Terence Cardinal Cooke. "Oh, yeah," Szorentini said, "Cardinal Cooke was a good friend. Whenever he came to a function here, I took care of him." Walter Brennan was another good friend. He used to take coffee in the mornings with Szorentini. The other doormen insisted that the reason was that Szorentini always grabbed the check. Szorentini said he had shaken hands with six U.S. presidents and just about everyone in the movie business ("Sinatra, Gleason, Jimmy Stewart, Clara Bow—the whole crowd"). He considered himself a minor star in his own right, for he had opened a door for Cary Grant in the movie *North by Northwest,* part of which was filmed at the Plaza. "Unfortunately," he said, "they didn't get my good side."

Szorentini thought I should know a story that was a favorite among the doormen. There was a little of the incredible about many hotel stories, and this was one of them. "See, there was this very attractive woman—I'd say in her late forties," he said. "She had this date with a man she was in love with. They were supposed to meet outside the Plaza one evening. She came and waited. The guy didn't show. The way I understand it, she never saw him again.

This sort of fried her circuits, and from then on, she kept coming back every week and acting as if she was greeting a man. She'd be talking to thin air. This went on for years. She was always well dressed, and she walked with her back very erect, just like a queen. But she had trouble upstairs. I used to say hello to her, but I couldn't ever figure out what she was talking about."

Terry Bertotti, one of the other doormen, said he had heard the woman owned a business that went bankrupt and that this was what had caused her to come unglued.

"I don't know anything about that," Szorentini said, frowning. "It was definitely a man."

He helped someone else now, a short, plump man with a craggy face and a dumb grin. Another dollar.

Szorentini credited success at the doors to giving a good greeting. "That's the key," he said. "A nice warm greeting. The newer people, though, are not as demanding as the old-timers were. The old-timers were very demanding. Rose Kennedy came here often, and she really put you through the mill. You had to have an umbrella ready if it was raining. You had to greet her properly— 'Good morning, Mrs. Kennedy,' or 'Good evening, Mrs. Kennedy.' If you didn't greet her, she'd get furious and she'd report you to management. Now you get these people who, when you say good morning, just say, 'Agggh.' They don't want to be bothered. Fine. I won't bother them."

He gave a knowing smile, looked out at the traffic, and nodded his head. "A big day I may get eighteen hundred people coming in and out of these doors. You can never tell. All manner of humanity goes through those doors over there. You get it all. Every last bit of it."

He started to say something else, but he had to stop. Another cab was drawing close.

2

THE Plaza Hotel was built as a monument to the new era of industrial wealth, as a magical place for people with an appetite for luxury and an aching to be part of high society. When it opened, it was an authentic wonder. Its first advertising campaign, in fact, described it as "The World's Most Luxurious Hotel." The owners actually feared it was so fancy that some of its prospective guests—no matter the depth of their pockets—might be intimidated. The day after the hotel opened, the uncertain manager ordered shellac applied atop the gold leaf decorating the lobby so that the guests would not be overly dazzled.

Though it has slipped somewhat from its early grandeur, the Plaza is still in many ways the quintessential luxury hotel. The place doesn't make you think of conventioneers with straw boaters and budget tourists in blue jeans but of chauffeured limousines, titles of nobility, and guests with eighteen pieces of luggage. The hotel stands on one of the most beautiful—and busiest—street corners in New York, Fifth Avenue and Fifty-ninth Street. It is a U-shaped, glazed-white-brick building of nineteen stories—a vast, grandiose place with a window-dotted facade, a copper-and-slate mansard roof, and abundant outcrops of balconies, loggias, and gables. It opened on October 1, 1907, and is one of the oldest hotels in New York City.

In its eighty-plus years, the Plaza has had seven owners. The United States Realty and Improvement Company, whose George A. Fuller construction subsidiary built it, owned it until 1943. Conrad Hilton then ran it until 1953. The Boston industrialist A. M. Sonnabend owned it up to 1958; then Lawrence Wien, a New York lawyer and realty investor, had it fleetingly before Sonnabend repurchased it. The Westin Hotels chain, the oldest operating hotel-management company in the country, took over the hotel in 1975 (at that time, Westin itself was a subsidiary of UAL, a diverse company which also owned United Airlines and Hertz Rent-A-Car). A partnership made up of the Robert M. Bass Group of Fort Worth, Texas, and the Aoki Corporation of Tokyo bought it in January 1988 for about $300 million but barely had time to take a get-acquainted tour of the place before agreeing to sell it for a quick and handsome profit to the casino operator and real estate wheeler-dealer Donald Trump, who paid a rather exorbitant $390 million.

There has been a flurry of interest in the hotel in recent years, in large part because of the possibility that vast sums of money could be realized by transforming a portion of the Plaza into high-priced condominiums or cooperative apartments, as has been done to a number of other classy New York hotels such as the Pierre and the Sherry Netherland. Trump, nonetheless, insisted that for the foreseeable future he would preserve the hotel as a hotel, and he signed a contract with Westin Hotels that retained Westin as the manager of the Plaza for a minimum of two years. Trump's first action was to appoint his statuesque wife, Ivana, a onetime alternate for the Czechoslovakian Olympic skiing team as well as a former model, as the president of the hotel for a supposed salary of "one dollar a year plus all the dresses she can buy."

There was actually once a smaller eight-story Plaza Hotel, which had occupied the site since 1890 and was demolished to make room for the present Plaza. The hotel that now stands was the vision of Ben Beinecke, a stocky former deliveryman for a New York butcher, who became a prosperous meat wholesaler and then a financier. He looked to invest in hotels, and he wanted to build a hotel that would be a sort of private club. He knew he alone couldn't afford the price, so he turned to Harry St. Francis Black, the chairman of United States Realty, which put up the bulk of the money, though Black also brought in as an investor John "Bet-a-Million" Gates, the barbed-wire king, who helped organize the United States Steel Corporation. Both Beinecke and Gates became directors of United States Realty. The construction took twenty-seven months, a speed record for building a hotel, and cost $12.5 million, which in those days was enough to found a bank.

The architect of the Plaza was Henry Janeway Hardenbergh, who had acquired a certain fame for designing the original Waldorf-Astoria, built on the current site of the Empire State Building, as well as the Dakota apartment building, which still stands on the corner of Central Park West and Seventy-second Street and is as grand and famous as the Plaza. He chose to build the Plaza in the French Renaissance style. Paul Goldberger, the architecture critic of the *New York Times,* would later describe it as "a French chateau blown up to the size of a small skyscraper and embellished with myriad classical details."

To furnish the hotel, linen was brought in from Ireland, crystal from France, lace curtains from Switzerland. Handwoven Savonnerie rugs adorned the lobbies. The order for the table linen, which cost more than $100,000, had to be placed over a year in advance. There were ten elevators, more than any other hotel in the world had, and five marble staircases. Each room boasted a clock controlled by a master clock located downstairs in the telephone room. (Years later, Enrico Caruso became so annoyed by the buzzing of the clock while he was practicing that he assaulted it with a knife and stopped time in every room in the hotel.) Water coming into the building was run through ten separate filters, and if it was to be drunk or used for cooking, it passed through yet another filter. The hotel featured a built-in vacuum cleaning system powered by steam, and seventeen thousand incandescent lights were kept burning by the Plaza's own dynamo. A terrace outside the Fifth Avenue entrance that came to be known as the Champagne Porch boasted oriental rugs and costly chandeliers; it was torn down in 1921.

On the day the hotel opened, every room was filled. Some 90 percent of the rooms were reserved for permanent tenants and just 10 percent for transients. The hotel even charged the permanent guests a higher price as a way to ward off undesirables contemplating long-term stays. Until the opening of the Plaza, hotel life on a permanent basis was pretty much unknown among people of wealth. When many families of position chose to move into the hotel, a new mode of living came into being. The most expensive suite was a thirteen-room beauty on the third floor that was rented to "Bet-a-Million" Gates for around $45,000 a year. He did get a private dumbwaiter to the kitchen. Gates was used to hotel life; he had moved to the Plaza from the Waldorf-Astoria. He had acquired his colorful nickname because of his willingness to bet on almost anything. One story has it that he wagered $1,000 on which of two raindrops dribbling down a window would reach the sill first, but no one seems to know if he won that one. Around the Plaza, he was famous for smacking his cane against the elevator door when there was no elevator available to take him down.

From the very beginning, the hotel developed a facility for making offbeat news that it has never lost. Just a month after the Plaza opened, on November 15, 1907, Mrs. Patrick Campbell, the famed actress, brazenly lit a cigarette in the Palm Court. Apparently she was the first woman to puff a cigarette in a public place in America. When the headwaiter spotted the offense, he dashed to the assistant manager and exclaimed, "Monsieur, it is a scandal! A lady, she smokes in the tearoom." He was instructed to calm himself and get her to desist. When he approached her, Mrs. Campbell nonchalantly blew a smoke ring in his face and said, "My dear fellow, I have been given to understand this is a free country. I intend to do nothing to alter its status."

In May of 1908, Hetty Green, the investor and loan shark who was known as "the witch of Wall Street" and was then the richest woman in America, checked into the Plaza for a month so she could search for a husband for her daughter. It was a painful adjustment for her. Despite her enormous wealth, she lived in a plain boarding-house in Hoboken, New Jersey, and ate graham crackers for a great many of her meals. She wore one black dress for so long that it turned brown and then green. When she checked out of the Plaza, having succeeded in her mission, she reportedly left only one tip, for the bell captain.

Over the years, the hotel experienced many ups and downs, and on several occasions it tottered on the brink. It almost went under during the Depression, when employees waited weeks to be paid. At the beginning of the 1960s, it had gone embarrassingly to seed. Guest rooms were dilapidated, occupancy was low, and the place had the reputation of being an old ladies' home. Some of the full-time residents used to stand in the lobby and openly discourage guests from checking in. Torn between whether just to unload the property or attempt to resuscitate it, the owners finally decided to spring for a complete renovation program.

Some inspired marketing helped the hotel ride out the rocky times. One of the most effective ideas was a droll advertising campaign directed at thirty thousand business executives, mainly those at companies boasting a net worth of at least $1 million, that consisted of chatty correspondence from a fictitious chambermaid named Mary O'Sullivan. Scores of businessmen wrote back to O'Sullivan. More important, many of them checked into the hotel. By the early 1970s, however, a stingy maintenance budget had once again let the hotel decline to a frightful state of disrepair. Cracks opened up in ceilings, wallpaper peeled off walls, faucets leaked, hot water was in short supply. A room at the Holiday Inn began to look good.

As the physical plant decayed, so did staff morale. Guests found themselves greeted by sullen, insolent employees who could take no pride in their hotel. Many regulars deserted the place and shifted their allegiance to the Pierre or the Waldorf. The hotel started losing money. Things got serious enough that the ritual of giving turkeys to employees on Thanksgiving was stopped and the annual employee Christmas party was canceled. Oddly enough, the hotel didn't lose as many guests as it probably should have. Because of the magic of its name and its illustrious history, many guests continued to check in and close their eyes to the cracks and the leaks, content just to be staying at the Plaza.

When Westin bought the hotel, another extensive renovation

began, in staggered fashion, portions of floors at a time. Between 1975 and early 1988, at a cost of $100 million, Westin managed to redo every room. Attention was given to the most minute details. Sixteen layers of paint were peeled from window frames to reveal the original copper. Not surprisingly, the mood of employees simultaneously began to pick up.

When Trump took over the hotel, he immediately mounted a crusade to raise the standards. His list of planned improvements included marble instead of tile in the bathrooms, new furniture to replace the rather bland pieces that filled the guest rooms, additional suites on the upper floors, and long-term leases to high-society types. And he was going to have page boys bring guests their messages on a silver tray, even if it was only Mom calling to see how the weather was. He also contemplated bringing back the Persian Room, the fabled Plaza supper club which had featured such entertainers as Hildegarde, Celeste Holm, Carol Channing, Genevieve, and Jane Morgan.

Trump could gaze out on the Plaza from his nearby office in Trump Tower, and he spoke about the hotel as "not a building, but a masterpiece. It's like the Mona Lisa." Trump may get decidedly mixed reviews for his taste—some consider him a fancier of ostentation and gaudiness—but he seemed to understand the quirks and expectations of those who patronize luxury hotels. Guest allegiances are fickle and can change for the most trivial reasons. The rule of thumb at the Plaza was to give people what they wanted and not bother to wonder what they wanted it for. People arrived with a huge freight of expectations and dreams. Even the overnight business traveler who really needed only a comfortable mattress and a prompt breakfast got a kick out of the thought that perhaps Clint Eastwood was snoring in the next room.

The clientele in recent years has been motley. It has included kings, presidents, movie stars, industrialists, race-car drivers, shopping-mall developers, salesmen, spoiled unemployed rich kids, oil-crats, big businessmen, and unknowns who happened to own the southeastern portion of Montana. The most famous Plaza guest was someone entirely fictitious. Eloise checked in in 1955, when she was six. She sprang out of the head of Kay Thompson, the singer and comedienne, who used the character in her act and then wrote a book about her. She was a spoiled brat who poured water down the mail chute, ordered room service to send up a raisin and seven spoons, and spent a fair amount of her time hunting for Shippordee the turtle and Weenie the dog, which looked like a cat and liked to have its back scratched with a wire coat hanger. Eloise was frightened of the dark, and whenever she experienced a particularly scary evening, she would apply cotton balls soaked in witch hazel on each toe. She became so famous that for a while the Plaza maintained a special Eloise room, where she supposedly lived. It had pink checked wallpaper, a yellow ceiling, a play table, a daybed, a pint-sized white upright piano, a pink ladder to reach high places, and a "Neat or Untidy" chart. There was even a love seat for Eloise's nanny to sit on while watching television. In 1988, all that remained was an oil painting of an impishly grinning Eloise that hung in the lobby.

Every president since Theodore Roosevelt is believed to have spent time in the hotel. Harry Truman used to meet his daughter, Margaret, for meals there. Richard Nixon, when he lived on Fifth Avenue, was a great frequenter of the Edwardian Room. The most attention was roused—enough that the mail room and the telephone room had their busiest week ever—when the mop-headed Beatles checked in for six days in February 1964. They took fifteen rooms, ordered lots of chocolates, and drank tremendous quantities of cola. Two enterprising teenage girls tried to get into their suite by having themselves concealed in boxes and presented at the front desk as gifts for the group. The deception failed.

I was told that despite the periodic famous faces, the backbone of the hotel's clientele was traveling businessmen on expense accounts. The category included several subcategories. Some of these men were chief executives of huge public companies. Others were entrepreneurs who owned small and relatively unknown firms. Still others were senior salesmen. Some of the guests stayed once at the hotel and, for one reason or another, never returned. Others had fanatical loyalties to the place. They were there practically every week and would never even think of another hotel. A judge from Louisiana came a couple of times a year to visit relatives. He got about with a walker. The hotel kept a walker on the premises and put it in his room when he was coming. A business executive came so often that he purchased an exercise machine for use while he was there. It was stored down in the housekeeping department and brought to his room when he checked in.

When I visited, the hotel had 808 rooms (or "keys," as they are known in the trade). When it opened, rooms cost $2.50 a day without a bath and $4 with a bath. The most expensive suite in the place was $25. In 1988 the cheapest room was an economy single at $175; a deluxe single with a view of Central Park was $390, and a one-bedroom Plaza suite was $1,100. However, people are willing to pay for service and for a hotel of distinction, especially today, in an age of look-alike chain hotels that may be clean and comfortable but are boring to stay in. You wake up in the morning and could be in any of a thousand cities.

Over the years, some legendary touches have been added to the Plaza. In 1913 Joseph Pulitzer left $50,000 in his will to build a fountain in the pigeon-frequented Grand Army Plaza out in front of the hotel; a statue of Pomona, goddess of abundance, crowned it. The fountain still stands and is probably best known for the drunken bath that F. Scott Fitzgerald and his wife, Zelda, took in it. Fitzgerald spent a lot of nights and consumed many gallons of alcohol at the hotel; he so loved it that Ernest Hemingway once advised him to will his liver to Princeton and his heart to the Plaza.

The centerpiece of the hotel's main floor, I saw, was the profusely green Palm Court, which the builders called the lounge and guests called the tearoom. It was modeled after the Winter Garden in London's Hotel Carlton but with its own special touches: the French-style mirrored rear wall, the arches supported by four marble caryatids representing the four seasons. The tearoom has become known as a famous courting place; more than a few men have proposed marriage there. The week the hotel opened, Count Lasio Szechenyl popped the question to Gladys Vanderbilt in the Palm Court, and ever since there has been a tradition that if you celebrate your betrothal there (with a cocktail), then you will have a happy marriage. A lot of smartly dressed women congregated at the tables there during the day, sat, gossiped, and drank gallons of tea. It was the best place for furtive people-watching.

Off to the right was the Edwardian Room, originally known as the Fifth Avenue Café and for a while in the 1970s, during a disastrous attempt to make the restaurant trendier and less formal, as the Green Tulip. It was a little stuffy but was regarded as one of the most romantic restaurants in New York. Then there was the somber, two-story Oak Room, which had the feel of a German cave, and the adjacent Oak Bar, which had started off as a private men's club. One of the unwritten rules was no discussion of business. Tenants in the hotel in 1988 included Cinema 3, a small movie theater in the basement where the old Plaza grillroom used to be. The Oyster Bar, which replaced a drugstore, was the last restaurant added, opening in 1969. It was designed to have the look of a turn-of-the-century pub, with etched-glass windows and a three-sided copper bar, and was a popular hangout for politicians and show people. Trader Vic's, a plastic Polynesian place that had no real business being part of the Plaza, nevertheless thrived there for a number of years before it was eased out early in 1988.

The ground floor was occupied by a varied group of quite expensive stores. In 1988 these included Shapero's Gift Shop, the Plaza Florist, Neuchâtel Chocolates, the Glemby Salon, Maison Mendessolle, the Plaza Art Gallery, James Hair Stylist for Men, and Black, Starr & Frost jewelers. Some of them had been around for a while, though they were a shifting population, subject to the whims of the current management of the hotel, which might at any time conclude that a shop had gotten a bit too sleazy for the Plaza and elect not to renew its lease.

Such is the nature of the hotel that it has become familiar to many people who have not only never stayed in it but have never even been to New York. That's because it has undoubtedly appeared in more movies than any other hotel in the world. Among the popular films that include scenes shot at the Plaza are *Plaza Suite*, *The Great Gatsby*, *North by Northwest*, *Funny Girl*, *Arthur*, and *Bare-*

foot in the Park. To shoot footage in the Plaza, I was told, the hotel charged $1,000 an hour ($500 an hour for still photography), fees that brought in about $50,000 a year. The money, of course, was insignificant next to the publicity value of the many movies. In the last couple of years, the hotel had noticed a significant pickup in business from Australia, to the extent that more foreign business now came from Australia than any other country (with Japan running a close second). The marketing people had been told by Australian travel agents that the reason was the popularity of *Crocodile Dundee* over there. The Plaza appeared prominently in the film, and so Australians figured it was the only place to stay.

The overriding interest of Donald Trump was to elevate the Plaza to a five-star hotel. For years, it had been awarded four stars by the *Mobil Travel Guide,* the hotel industry's most respected rating publication. In 1988 the guide evaluated more than 21,000 hotels and restaurants and awarded five stars to only thirty-one hotels. In New York City, the Carlyle Hotel alone won such distinction. In some years, the Plaza had in fact attained five-star status. It reached that peak from 1963 through 1966 and again from 1976 through 1978. But never in the last decade.

Mobil raters, checking into hotels incognito, follow lengthy checklists in order to arrive at their determinations. The guidelines suggest that to make a given number of stars a hotel must have certain specific features. But these are not hard-and-fast rules. To be awarded five stars, for instance, a hotel is supposed to have a swimming pool, but the Carlyle, like most New York hotels, does not. Beyond these requirements, subjectivity liberally enters the picture. "We have over one hundred criteria, from housekeeping to the paint on the wall," Pat Verde, a spokesperson for the guide, once explained to me. "Service is a big section. The idea is, with five stars you should remember your stay there. And five stars means that you should anticipate the guests' needs. They should never have to ask for anything. And if they do ask for something, the hotel will move mountains to get it. It's service, service, service."

Early in 1988, Hud Hinton, the manager of the Plaza, studied the Mobil criteria and drafted a memo suggesting deficiencies that the hotel might remedy in its pursuit of a fifth star. These included more lobby seating, a health club, central air conditioning rather than the individual wall units, fine artwork, fresh flowers, an uncluttered luggage-handling area, full-length mirrors in every room, medicine cabinets, transportation to and from the airports, some authentic antiques and fine reproductions in guest rooms, hair dryers and scales in all rooms, complimentary shoeshines, a swimming pool, and free limousine service to theaters and stores. Ivana Trump was also spending an appreciable amount of her time working at ideas for special touches. When I saw her one day, she told me, "Here's something I just heard about. At the Ritz in Paris, there's a little hook on the sides of the chairs in the restaurants for a woman to hang her purse. She doesn't have to worry whether she should sling it over the back or leave it on the floor. I think it's an absolutely terrific idea. It eases the guest's job."

3

UD Hinton bolted down a breakfast of coffee and a muffin in the employee cafeteria down in the hotel's basement, talked a bit with some of the department heads about boxing, then began his day, as he invariably did, by reviewing the front-office logbook. As the manager of the Plaza, Hinton hoped to keep at least rough track of what was happening in the hotel. That was never easy. The number of daily adventures that unfold in a large hotel is beyond calculation. Problems, crises, mishaps, breakdowns—they are continual. The logbook, however, always afforded Hinton a few good clues. The various assistant managers who manned the front office used the book to jot down any guest complaints or unorthodox happenings and what steps, if any, had been taken to handle them. Hinton always examined the prior day's entries to see if there was anything he ought to act on. When he finished, he signed his name beside the last entry. Problems were not necessarily cause for alarm. In the world of a hotel, every disaster presents an opportunity. One of Hinton's adages was "There is no more loyal guest than one who has a problem that gets fixed."

Hinton ran his eyes down the penned-in summaries, absorbing them with no signs of distress or amusement. A guest had taken a cab from the '21' Club to the hotel and informed the driver that he was going to buy something in the gift shop and would be right back. An hour and a half later, the man had not reappeared. The assistant manager had paid the cabdriver but had not been able to determine what had become of the man, who was probably not a guest at all.

Another guest had complained to the front desk that his room wasn't clean and that the Palm Court food was disagreeable. The assistant manager, as was proper form, had apologized and sent the man some wine and cheese.

A visitor from Chicago who had stayed in the hotel some weeks before had called to see if anything had been learned about the theft he had reported. According to his account, money had been removed from his wallet when he had left it in his room. The security chief had been asked to look into it.

Still another guest had insisted that a dinner roll served by room service contained a rock. Since it was almost always a bad idea to serve guests rocks, the head of food and beverage had been asked to investigate the matter.

The wife of the man who had complained about his dirty room had phoned to say that the couple had received no afternoon turndown service and so she had been forced to pick up dirty towels off the floor herself. She had received an apology and an amenity had been sent to her room. (In hotel parlance, an amenity is any small extra item—fruit, chocolates, toiletries, wine, and so on—provided to guests.)

Still another guest had complained that there was no hot water for his shower. The man had vowed to write to Donald Trump about the shortcoming. Hot-water shortages cause managers to flinch. It is drilled into hotel people to make sure there is always ample hot water. Complaints about icy showers are usually the most vociferous a hotel gets. People who will tolerate a lumpy mattress or spaghetti sauce on the carpet won't put up with cold water.

A man had reported that some of his personal belongings had been thrown out by housekeeping. The most "alarming" loss was a set of earplugs. The hotel had bought him a new set.

Yet another guest had complained that the mirror on the armoire had fallen off and conked him on the head, giving him a cut on the left side of his forehead. No medical attention, however, had been necessary. The hotel had picked up his room bill for a night and bought him dinner for two in one of its restaurants.

Two incidents bothered Hinton enough for him to follow up on them. The couple who had complained twice would merit a call to the head of housekeeping. Maintenance would receive an inquiry on the armoire. Those units were brand-new, and yet there had been a succession of problems with them, such as doors not opening properly. The falling mirror was further proof that something was wrong.

"All these are typical hotel complaints," Hinton said to me with a shrug. "A hot-water problem. Housekeeping throws something out. Someone didn't get turn-down service. It could be the guest put out a 'Do Not Disturb' sign and forgot about it. There are always guests who complain about something that never happened, knowing it's a sure way to weasel a free amenity or a free meal out of the hotel. You can almost spot those people if you meet them. They've got this mischievous look in their eyes."

Hinton took the elevator to the second floor, where the executive offices were. The hallways were empty and quiet, the guests already out or still abed. He entered his office, settled in behind his desk, and began his shift of running the hotel. He was a short, extremely tidy man with a thin mustache and thick brown hair. He was unemotional, pragmatic.

In his job, Hinton was primarily concerned with a multiplicity of day-to-day events. He reported to Jeffrey Flowers, who occupied the adjoining office and who carried the title of managing director. Flowers was entrusted with the strategic planning and overall direction of the hotel.

In 1988 the Plaza had a staff of just over thirteen hundred people —bellmen, maids, doormen, cooks, waiters, electricians, carpenters, painters, security guards, bathroom attendants, lobby assistant managers, bartenders, chicken boners, furniture cleaners, auditors, concierges, telephone operators, busboys, minibar attendants, night auditors, porters, payroll clerks, stewards, wine-cellar atten-

dants, and a seamstress. Upwards of 80 percent of the work force
was multilingual, and a total of thirty-five languages were spoken
by the employees collectively. All of the staff people were expected
to abide by very rigid rules of behavior, the most important of
which were always to be courteous and never to argue with a guest.
Management repeatedly implored employees to learn the names of
guests, so that they could address them personally whenever they
saw them. Plaza surveys had again and again revealed that guests
very much like being called by name. And whenever an employee
answered a ringing phone, he was expected to respond, "How may
I help you?"

In their essence, hotels are relatively uncomplicated businesses,
selling shelter. Flowers and Hinton were operating the Plaza for a
market composed of fickle travelers, who would change their pa-
tronage as a result of the smallest impertinence. Hinton was preoccupied with occupancy percentages—how many of the available
rooms were full. He was especially concerned with the number of
"rack"-rate guests—those who had paid the full advertised charge
for a room. He lived with the understanding that the commodity
he sold—a bed for the night—was perishable. If it was not sold on
a given night, it was as good as not there. It produced no money.

"Innkeeping has been around for a few thousand years, and it's
very simple," Hinton told me. "We give people a place to sleep for
the night and something to eat to keep their stomachs happy. Hotel
managers sometimes lose sight of the simplicity and let the business
become too complicated. They sometimes focus too much on the
minutiae and forget the basic intention of a hotel. Of course, in a
luxury hotel like this one you can't ever forget the details. It's the
details, after all, that separate the great hotels from all the others.

"Guest expectations have really changed," he went on. "Amenities in the room used to be a surprise. Now it's expected that you
have shampoo and a shoe mitt. But mostly guests want to check in
and out quickly and have a comfortable bed. It's really standard
now to have a desk in a guest room. You need a telephone on the
desk. You need a well-lighted area to work in. Quality in a hotel is
often a difficult concept to define, but I'll give you an example of

what it takes to make a hotel great. If you're supposed to have ten amenities in a room and we only got eight in—say the shampoo and the shoe mitt were missing—then our quality has just dropped a notch.

"One of the adages in this business is that if you manage the first and last impressions of a guest properly, then you'll have a happy guest. If the doorman is friendly and calls the guest by name, you've managed the first impression. People hate to stand in line to pay money, so if you check someone out quickly and thank them for the stay, you've managed the last impression. Then they'll forgive the chipped paint or even the lack of hot water. If there's a gruff greeting, they'll come into the hotel looking for other problems. They'll think, gee, if the doorman's snotty, what else is going to be wrong here?"

Hinton told me that hotels had been important to him since he was a teenager scrambling to make some spending money. He was born in Fort Bragg, North Carolina, the son of an Army man who necessarily moved often; he sometimes felt as if he had lived all over the South. When he was in high school, he landed a job as a dishwasher at the Safety Harbor Spa and Resort Hotel, an upscale establishment which drew people looking to shed truly significant amounts of themselves. After a short time, he was promoted to busboy, then room-service waiter. He worked there two seasons before going off to college at the University of South Florida in Tampa. In college, Hinton studied business, and to help with tuition bills, he found work as a night waiter in the banquet department at the Innisbrook Resort and Golf Club. He was moved to one of the restaurants and then to the gourmet restaurant. "I had a chance to wear a tuxedo and make Caesar salad and carve chateaubriand and bone Dover sole. I soon became a captain. I'm a sophomore in college and I'm a captain. I was captain for a year when the maître d' left for another hotel. I got his job. Then the owners decided to open a resort in Durango, Colorado, and wanted me to manage the gourmet restaurant there. I was twenty and missed a semester of school to go out there. I was too young to buy a drink. It was even illegal for me to pour wine and liquor, but I was doing it all the time. When I came back, Innisbrook offered me a job as director of food and beverage services. So I was overseeing four restaurants at this resort. Then they made me director of catering. I'm just graduating from college. I'm twenty-one. I'm planning banquets and parties. I was pretty wowed by all this. I did that for a couple of years. But I wanted further growth in the hotel business and decided I couldn't get it there. I needed to be in a chain operation. I'm making good money and figure this is a career. I interviewed with Westin and got a position as director of restaurants in the Detroit Plaza Hotel. I've been with Westin ever since, though, like all hotel people, I've been moved around a lot. A hotel man is often like a gypsy."

Much of his workday, Hinton didn't stick too close to his office but floated around the hotel, seeing how things were going, picking up crumpled trash off the floors that porters had missed, combing for problems. Watchfulness was an important trait of a hotel manager, he said. Managers who remained by their desks were doomed. I had heard about one well-regarded hotel which had three cash registers in the bar. Two were put there by the hotel. The third the bartenders installed themselves to ring up the money they were stealing. The manager thought there were only two registers, because he never bothered to walk around the hotel.

In his jacket pocket, Hinton packed a little pad for his journeys that he referred to as his "Ready Eddie." He told me there used to be a man who headed up Westin Hotels named Eddie Carlson and he carried around a leather pad on which to mark down offenses. It became known as the "Ready Eddie." So Hinton took up carrying one and scribbling notes to himself. This morning at breakfast, he had spotted a minibar waiter whose hair cascaded down over his collar in the back and so he had made a note to have the department head instruct him to cut it. After a lunch at the Palm Court, he wrote, "It looked like hell. The napkins were folded improperly. A few flicker bulbs were out. The mirrors were streaked."

Hinton tried to have a fair amount of guest contact. "Every day I talk to a couple of guests," he said. "I had a woman who called today and said she was here on a honeymoon, and though they had a great time and all, she was disappointed that she didn't get a bottle of champagne. If we do know that a couple are on a honeymoon, they get a congratulatory note from me and a bottle of champagne. So she lives in Long Island and I told her to come in and I'd give her a bottle. She should have gotten it, but it was one of those things that fell through the cracks. Another woman called to complain that the garbage trucks were noisy on Fifty-eighth Street. I told her we could control noise only so much. There's a very high expectation level here. A guest wrote that her shampoo bottle wasn't refilled promptly. I told her I don't expect that at the Plaza, either, and to let me know if it happens again. But you have to wonder that people are so concerned about such little things."

He chuckled at the thought. "I get a lot of dress-code complaints. Someone wrote me, 'When I used to eat with my grandfather in the Edwardian Room he had to be in black tie. I ate there the other day and the guy next to me was in a jogging suit.' I wrote back that this is a more relaxed era. I had a guy write from England that he couldn't believe that we let a person bring a coat and his briefcase into the restaurant."

It wasn't necessary to spend too much time with Hinton to realize that there are a lot of misconceptions about a hotel manager's routines. Hinton himself was often bemused by the way the hotel manager was pictured in movies and on television. "Did you ever see any of those shows about hotels?" he asked me. "They're not accurate. It's never the way they show it. I don't really get to know people or get to know intimate things about their lives and careers. I remember watching an episode of *Hotel* one night, and the manager saw this girl at the bar and she turned out to be a hooker. He felt this tremendous sympathy for her and got the idea that there was more to the girl. So he went on to devote days and days to trying to help put her back on a normal path. In the end, he made a rather dramatic change in her life and managed to cure her of hooking. I thought about how unrealistic that was. There's no way in the world I would even have the time to try to do something like that. Now I don't bother to watch the show."

Hinton picked up the phone and placed a call to a friend who worked at the Mayfair Regent. Several days ago, a guest had checked into the Plaza who claimed to be a major developer of hotels. Normally, he said, he stayed at the Mayfair, but his favorite suite there was in the midst of renovation and so he had decided to come to the Plaza. His bill was mounting up, and Hinton was beginning to suspect the man might be a con artist. Before he put on any pressure, Hinton wanted his friend at the Mayfair to find out if the man had indeed stayed there and paid his bill. Hinton didn't want to be too hasty in his judgment of the man. He had said he was developing two hotels in the Far East and was looking for a company to manage them, perhaps Westin. "He wears thousand-dollar suits," Hinton said. "He talks quite a good game. If he's a scam, he's a high-level scam."

After listening to the story, the Mayfair friend said he would happily look into it and call back. (When he did, he reported that the man usually paid, but he took his time.)

Hinton read some mail. There was a letter from a guest who said he had been given a gift certificate for the hotel that, he had been told, included dinner. When he got here, the front desk had said it didn't include a meal. When he checked out, he had had to pay tax on his room. That didn't sit well with him. Hinton forwarded the letter to the front desk.

The door opened and Jeff Flowers walked in. He was tall and dapper, with dark hair, and, like Hinton, he wore a mustache. Nothing was pressing; he just wanted to shoot the breeze. They discussed some special guests who would be arriving on Friday: the king and queen of Sweden. They were staying for two nights and would be honored on Saturday night at a banquet in the Grand Ballroom. For several months, the hotel staff had been looking forward to their appearance.

"We all set for the visit?" Flowers asked.

"I think so," Hinton said. "All the department heads are excited. For this hotel, though, a king and queen are no big deal."

"Mmm-hmm," Flowers said. "By the way, how are we doing on the flowers for the Palm Court?"

"I've got a proposal for two thousand dollars a month."

"Think we could hammer them a bit? Do it for a thousand dollars?"

"Maybe," Hinton said. "I've also got some literature on the palms."

"Oh, good," Flowers said. "We've got to get rid of those scrawny palms and put something dramatic there."

The hotel had had little luck getting palms to grow tall enough in the Palm Court. Hinton, checking around, had come across a company that embalmed plams, shooting them with a fluid that put them in a state of suspended animation. The palms cost $1,000 apiece, but never had to be replaced.

"I want to make sure they're tall enough," Hinton said. "If they aren't much bigger, there's no point."

Robert Bachofen, the food and beverage manager, came in to show Hinton a newly upholstered banquet chair in a white fabric. The banquet chairs were sorely in need of refurbishing, and Bachofen wanted to do them in this material. The cost, he explained, would be $100 a chair, as opposed to $200 to replace the chairs altogether.

Hinton felt the fabric, sat down in the chair, squirmed around a little, got up. "Okay," he said. "It looks good. But put some glop on it and make sure it cleans well first. We don't want something that's great until the first gravy hits it."

4

*T*HE front desk, an L-shaped affair with a pale marble top, seemed cramped, with not much space behind it. As I watched, the attendants kept excusing one another as they bumped their way from one side to the other. Hips took a beating. A queue was beginning to form— some early arrivals checking in, but mostly people checking out. A business-suited man was finishing his three-day stay. A young woman had been here for a single night. A family of four was winding up their weekend. The two children, in a sportive spirit, were engaged in a wrestling match on the lobby carpet. The boy ended the skirmish when he pulled a plastic pistol on his sister and she grudgingly surrendered. A middle-aged couple arrived, confessing that they would be having face-lifts together and would be recuperating in the hotel for several days. "We won't be out and about too much," the man said. "But that's okay. The rooms here are quite comfortable."

The desk attendants knew they would see only a portion of the departing guests. One of the oddities of the Plaza was that every day sixty or seventy people left the hotel without bothering to check out. They didn't forget. They just felt it was unnecessary. David Zeuske, who ran the front desk, explained it: "They figure they're staying in New York and at the Plaza and so they don't need to check out. They shouldn't have to bother." All hotels, he said, found that a certain number of guests behaved in the same thoughtless way, but it was rare to have more than eight or ten a day. The Plaza didn't lose any revenue from the practice; it already had credit-card imprints and could just fill in the final tally and send out the bills. What's more, the guests were usually pretty reliable about leaving their keys in their rooms. The difficulty was that the front desk had no way of knowing the rooms were vacant and therefore available to be cleaned and occupied by other guests until the one-o'clock checkout deadline had passed and someone was sent around to look. "It really screws us up when the house is full," Zeuske said. "But there's nothing we can do. That's just your Plaza guest for you."

Neat, odd, the front desk seemed really inadequate. It was too small, built for a hotel that might attract a small number of transients who would stay for an average of a week. "It was designed to accommodate about a hundred check-ins and checkouts a week," Zeuske said. "Today, the average length of stay is two days, and we get three hundred and seventy-five in and three hundred and seventy-five out on an average busy day."

The L shape was particularly bad for a busy hotel. The desk would have functioned much more efficiently if it had been straight. "People stand in front of an L-shaped desk and don't know where to go," Zeuske said. "Do they go to this side or do they go to that side? The truth is, they can go to either side. But they can't seem to figure that out. It's awful. So we have a lobby assistant manager whose big job is simply to direct people where to go."

A woman approached the desk. "Howell," she said. "You have a reservation for me."

"Okay, let's check this out," Roy Chaney said. He was a rolypoly, upbeat man, given to punctuating his comments with staccato laughs. For two and a half years he had been working as a Plaza desk attendant. I thought I would watch him for a while.

He glanced at the computer screen before him and nodded. "Here we are. You'll be with us for one night, ma'am?"

"That's right," the woman replied. "Unless things get delayed, the way they always do."

"Well, we'll see how it goes," Chaney said, and he handed her a small card to fill out and asked to take an imprint of her credit card.

Once she finished, he gave her two keys and explained, "Here's the key to your room, and here's the key to your refrigerator, in case you want some refreshment in the morning."

"Thank you," the woman said. "I might need a little nip right now, in fact."

A small, gnomish man came by and asked Chaney to cash four $100 traveler's checks. Chaney swiftly counted out twenty crisp $20 bills. The man took them and stuffed them into a money clip in the shape of a horseshoe.

Like the other attendants, Chaney was responsible for a "bank," in essence a cash drawer that at the beginning of each day contained $9,000. The money was used to make change and cash traveler's checks. "You need at least that much money during the day, because of all the financial transactions," Chaney explained to me. "Say a guest wants to pay his bill and it's nine hundred dollars and he gives me a thousand dollars in traveler's checks. I have to be able to give the person a hundred dollars. Some days you can walk out of here with five thousand dollars in cash. Some days you can walk out of here with fifteen. Some days it seems like everyone wants to pay you in cash. You just never know. Every once in a while, someone pays his entire bill in cash. I had one guy whose bill I had laid out on the counter. It was a mess of pages. He had nine thousand dollars approved on his Diners Club. The bill was seventy-four hundred. He looked at it and said, 'Gee, is that all?' I said, 'Yeah.' 'Well,' he said, 'then I'll pay you in cash.' And he gave me seventy-five brand-new hundred-dollar bills."

Chaney shook his head from side to side. "I check in some interesting people," he said. "I checked in James Brown, Milton Berle, Aretha Franklin, the Pointer Sisters, Tony Orlando, Ringo Starr, Margot Kidder. They pretty much check in and out like anyone else. When Margot Kidder checked out, though, she didn't want to put her phone number on the back of her check, the way you're supposed to, because she said a lot of crazy guys called her. I also had a run-in with Bo Derek. I wouldn't cash her traveler's checks because she wasn't a registered guest. She got mad and called the assistant manager, who apologized and cashed the checks. Hey, I went by the rules."

Chaney checked out a young Japanese man. The bill came to $1,156.02 for four nights. He dug out a fat roll of bills and peeled off the necessary amount. While Chaney prepared a receipt, the man lit up a cigarette and clamped it in tobacco-stained teeth. Hotel employees were forbidden to smoke anyplace where a guest might conceivably see them. Guests, of course, could puff without restriction.

"Did you enjoy your stay?" Chaney asked.

"It was okay," the man said.

"I can see that man was thrilled," Chaney told me after he had gone off. "You know the biggest complaint I get? Everybody wants to sit and look over the park. Everybody comes here and feels they have to see trees. Give me a break. We're responsible for guest comfort and guest service. But I can't give everyone trees. I tell people there are four sides to this building. They can't possibly all overlook the park. I also get people who come to check in and say, 'I want Room 332.' I say it's occupied. 'Well, move them,' they say. What am I supposed to do? Go to the room and grab the person by the neck and drag him out of there? People have their favorite rooms. Unfortunately, they're not always available."

I watched the credit cards and greenbacks pass back and forth as Chaney checked in and checked out several more people. He and the other desk attendants were supposed to create a warm atmosphere, so that a person's stay got off on the right note and finished the same way. A key requirement was that they make eye contact with all the guests and inquire about a departing guest's stay. "The management wants you to stand out here and say the same thing over and over," Chaney said. "But you know what? You turn into a robot. After I've checked in people for hours, Raquel Welch could be in the line and I'll look her in the eye and not say anything. I'm programmed. There can be ten people standing here. I'm supposed to go, 'How are you, sir? How was your stay? How are you, sir? How was your stay?' By the tenth time, how sincere is that going to sound? I think we should mix it up. All our guests aren't the same. They all don't make the same money or do the same thing. So why should I say the same thing over and over? So I go ahead and mix it up. Sometimes I don't even ask a guest how his stay was. You just look at him and you can tell."

A bristly-haired woman timidly approached Chaney. "Excuse me, I have one small question," she said. "My husband and I were just discussing this. Is there a rule of thumb as to how much tip we should leave for the maid?"

"Well, if it was good service, about a dollar or two dollars a day," Chaney said.

"Okay, fine, thank you."

Once she left, Chaney said, "People think we have all these rigid rules. 'Yes, at the Plaza we give two thirty-eight per day for the maid. And not a penny less.' "

Chaney checked in two pin-striped men and a pair of matronly women traveling together. Then the activity slackened. Chaney's face got an abstracted look on it. He said, "I figure over the years I've made a lot of people happy in this joint and I've made a lot of people unhappy. Because you can't please them all. Some people just kill me. They come here and they expect four rooms on the park, whirlpool, disco lights, Ping-Pong table, a piano in the room, and a couple of dancing bears. Give me a break."

5

T H E door to the Grand Ballroom opened onto a crowd of somber-suited men and women and a coffee urn. I walked in and sank into an empty chair. It was mid-afternoon. These were people seeking the peak of corporate success. Many of them had dazed, desperate expressions on their faces. The Marketing War College two-day seminar had resumed after a brief coffee break.

As the attendees settled in, there was a fair amount of coughing and chair-shuffling. In the morning, they had discussed "the strategic square," "the principles of defensive warfare," and "the principles of offensive warfare." Now a husky man stood up behind a podium, surveyed the assemblage, and launched into an energetic lecture. "We're ready to talk about flanking warfare," the speaker said. "Let's start with the Prince tennis racket. How much market was there for an oversized tennis racket before the Prince tennis racket? Zero. That is one of the key aspects of flanking warfare. Flanking, you see, requires you to visualize how a battle will unfold before it happens, much in the way that a chess player can visualize a game ten and twenty moves ahead."

This seminar, I learned from some literature lying near my seat, was the brainchild of Jack Trout and Al Ries, two former advertising guys who had switched to what they called the strategy business. Through some books they had written and innumerable speeches, they had established themselves as experts on how to position a product in the customers' perception so as to maximize sales.

Whenever I walked into one of the hotel's second-floor banquet and meeting suites, I never knew what I would find. Every day there were six or seven functions going on, and the makeup was pretty motley. There might be an annual meeting, a cocktail party to celebrate a new bra, an attempt to float a loan to Mexico, a sales conference of the Frito-Lay potato chip people. Marie Osmond unveiled her "Complexion Care Set" and "Marie Cologne for teenagers" at a Plaza conference. When Rubin "Hurricane" Carter was cleared of triple-murder charges against him after having spent twenty years in prison, the ex-boxer decided to celebrate at an affair held in the pink-colored Baroque Room. It was a nice change for him from death row in Trenton State Prison. *Playboy* set up Jessica Hahn in a comfortable suite so the press could interview her about her forthright appearance in the magazine. (Hud Hinton got her to autograph the cover of the magazine and had it as one of his souvenirs in his office.) Susan Butcher, the two-time winner of the Iditarod Trail Sled Dog Race across Alaska, came to the Plaza to get the Women's Sports Foundation's Professional Sportswoman of the Year Award and talked about Alaskan husky sled dogs and the rigors of Alaskan life. She told people she liked a day on a sled much more than a day at the Plaza Hotel.

A slide show began. On the screen appeared Flanking Principle Number One: "A flanking move is one made into an uncontested area."

This was followed by Flanking Principle Number Two: "Tactical surprise ought to be an important element of the plan."

Then came Flanking Principle Number Three: "The pursuit is just as critical as the attack itself."

The speaker explained some ways in which to flank. "Flanking with a low price is one common way," he said. "Take the Savin 755 copier. It costs less new than the Xerox 3100 costs old. Budget Rent-a-Car is another example."

The audience seemed to turn off to these thoughts, and I didn't blame them. How much money and prestige, after all, could there be in being the cheap guy?

The speaker cleared his throat and hurtled on. "But it's very difficult to flank with low price. Flanking with a high price, we think, has more longevity and is a much sounder approach." Now everyone perked up, as if the lecturer had beautifully recovered from a temporary brain spasm. "Jolly-Time popcorn is thirty-five cents," he said. "Who would have thought Orville Redenbacker could sell popcorn at ninety-nine cents? And Absolut Vodka has been very successful up on top of the vodka category by nailing down the high end of the vodka category. And we have Rusty's Hand Mades —'farm-fresh potato slices.' These are potato chips. They call them slices and they're very high-priced. But they're very successful. Joy perfume. The most expensive perfume in the world. You can use your price to establish yourself up on top of a category. Why is Passport the most expensive radar detector in the world? Here is using price proudly in the radar detector field to establish your identity."

As I listened to the lecturer breezing along, I was pretty amazed. Now he seemed to be saying that all that was necessary to become a zillionaire was to take an ordinary product and charge people through the teeth for it. I envisioned coming out with a Q-tip for $19.95 and seeing what happened.

The members of the Marketing War audience, most of them men and most of them with their jackets off, were sitting at long tables with white-covered booklets and were scribbling notes in their booklets and on pads. Things were being said that seemed to invite guffaws, but no one was laughing. Everyone listened with morbid intensity.

There was a pause while a new speaker took the podium. The audience wondered, waited.

I fell into a whispered conversation with a short, middle-aged man with sloe eyes. "People take this stuff awfully seriously," I said.

He nodded inscrutably. "Business is an extremely serious, extremely sophisticated field today," he told me. "We are in economic war every minute of every day. Our armies must be ready."

"Do you find you're getting much out of this?" I asked.

"Oh, sure," he announced with a righteous tone. "Yes, indeed. Aren't you?"

I said I was always suspicious of marketing schemes.

"Oh, no," he said. "These aren't schemes. This is a way of life. This is teaching you to practically breathe differently."

Then the man whispered that he had seen a great movie the other night all about giant spiders that were taking over the earth and gobbling up humans. He said it really made chills go up his spine and it was a terrific feeling. "Same way I feel when I get into a good marketing battle with one of my competitors," he said. "Hell of a sensation."

The conversation stalled, so we went back to listening to the lecture, which had advanced to the topic of the principles of guerrilla warfare, in which everything was upside down and the guerrilla was supposed to do the opposite of what the market leader was expected to do.

6

WATCHED Mike Skira search through the bag room for a violet suitcase. A French guest who was a regular at the Plaza had left it there while he got something to eat, and he watched, too. The poorly ventilated room was crammed with bags, shelves and shelves of them, more variety than I had ever seen in any luggage store. Skira was methodical. He picked through some alligator luggage, a bagful of stuffed giraffes and weasels, a couple of Saks Fifth Avenue shopping bags.

Finally he found what he was looking for. He smiled and patted the bag as if it were a favorite dog. The Frenchman grabbed hold of it, mumbled some appreciative words, and stuffed a folded $1 bill into Skira's palm.

Mike Skira, the day bell captain, was short in stature, tall in talk. He had a voice like creaky hinges, which he used often, and an angular, pocked face. He stood with feet planted wide apart, back straight as a stake. There was a spring of tension, an athlete's readiness to jump, in Skira. He lifted bags as easily as he breathed.

A taciturn, sad-eyed woman wearing metal-rimmed glasses wanted her suitcase and a taxi. "Yes, ma'am," Skira said. He ducked into the back room, produced her bag, carried it out to the curb, and flagged down a cab. Poker-faced, she gave him $2.

The business of carrying bags had occupied Skira for nearly twenty years. Throughout his career, he had undoubtedly lifted a hundred thousand bags. His strained, cynical eyes lit up whenever he thought of the thousands of tips he had earned. He came to America from England, where he had worked in the factories. His first job here was at the Plaza. He was an elevator operator, worked in the package room, and then became a bellman. For fifteen years he had presided over the bellmen at the Plaza.

Skira explained the job of bellman succinctly: "You lift bags and put them in the room."

There actually was more to it than that. He showed me the professional way to lift bags. "You have to bend the knees a little and nice and easy lift it up," he said, bending down and lifting a suitcase. "Don't go too fast. You gotta go smooth, like the way you make a golf swing. Then the bag won't hurt you. You don't just snatch it up. That's asking for a hernia. Some bags are light, but most are plenty heavy. Especially the ones the foreigners bring. I don't know if they've got bricks in there or what."

In a given day, Skira estimated, a Plaza bellman checked in nearly fifty guests, lugged upward of 150 suitcases, and dispensed countless bits of secondhand advice. If a guest wanted an errand run, the bellman was expected to run it. "Sometimes it's like searching for the Holy Grail," one of the men told me.

The work could extract a mean price on the body if you didn't take the proper precautions. Forced to be on their feet almost constantly, some bellmen changed their socks twice a day and wore padded shoes, thereby avoiding the corns and calluses that are bellmen's nightmares. Hernias, varicose veins, and backaches are other common afflictions. One man said the chiropractors got a lot of business from bellmen. Another man said he went in for yoga and found that it worked much better than any doctor.

"A lot of this job is the shoes," Skira said. "You got to buy the good shoes. You need the good support. You look at any bellman's feet and you'll see a good pair of shoes. Thick shoes. That way you don't go home with your feet screaming."

A trolley of luggage came in. There were some stuffed toys piled on it, and Skira picked up a penguin and fooled around with it. He made it talk for a couple of the other bellmen, who thought he was being funny, but not all that funny.

"I can't figure out who's the dummy," one of the bellmen said.

"You guys are just so jealous," Skira said.

Tips were all-important to the bellmen, since the salary was only about $210 a week, and the subject of tips always seemed to enter their conversation. They said they could intuit the size of a tip by taking a quick measure of the guest. His nationality could suggest his generosity. "The average tip is from a dollar up," Skira said. A few of the other bellmen who were standing around grunted in agreement. "You get some—the foreigners in particular—who give you a quarter. They pretend they don't know. They know. The Japanese are very cheap. They take the cake. Who knows why? They give you a quarter and think they're doing you a favor.

"You can get two dollars, three dollars, five dollars. Five dollars, in my book, is a good tip. Sometimes you get a ten-spot when a guest arrives with a load of bags and he sees you sweating. Not too often. The middle-class Americans are the best tippers. The rich people—you never see them. They've got all this security and managers, so you don't get a good tip. A movie star checks in— you don't see him. His people check him in and give you a lousy tip."

Some further tipping wisdom:

Men tip better than women. And a man with his mistress or girlfriend tips better than a man with his wife.

Women traveling alone tip more than women traveling in pairs.

Forget show-business stars and doctors. They skimp.

Clergymen are generous. Within this group, Catholic priests head the list, rabbis come next, and Protestant ministers are last.

Groups were charged flat rates at the Plaza. Each bag produced $1.40 in and $1.40 out. And each doorman got 62½ cents for each group member coming in and the same amount going out.

A bellman who merely allows the fates to determine his gratuity isn't a serious professional. As I hung around, I picked up some tried-and-tested techniques to extract the maximum reward from any given situation. For instance, you should always carry change for at least a $100 bill. Guests sometimes think they can avoid a tip by whipping out large bills and saying that they have nothing smaller. When being tipped by a man traveling with his wife, always try to block off the wife's view. No matter what the husband produces, the wife generally thinks it's too much. Don't linger overlong if a tip isn't forthcoming in the first few minutes after the guest has been shown his room. Face the fact that you've got a stiff on your hands, and head back to the lobby, where the prospects may be more promising.

Skira was stoical about rotten tips, seeing them as an unfortunate but unavoidable part of his job. He could be grimly amused by the stinginess of some guests. Guests, if they insisted, were allowed to check themselves in, but the bellmen were scornful of that option. From their perspective, it amounted to a flouting of the fundamental rules of being a good guest. "We don't like it," Skira said. "Even if all he has is an overnight bag, we like to do the work. He does it by himself and the bellman loses the gratuity. I don't mind if someone goes up to the room ahead of the luggage, if he's been here and knows the place. As long as we still bring the bags up. That way, we get the gratuity. My opinion is it doesn't look right if the guest carries his own bag. These are big shots who check in here. A big shot doesn't carry his own bags."

All the bellmen agreed that weekend duty was the least desirable, because that was when steep discount packages took effect and many guests not normally inclined to stay in a luxury hotel populated the Plaza. The less-senior bellmen got stuck working those hours. "Boy, do you see the caliber of guests change," Skira said. "These are the people who can't really afford this place but they want to tell their friends they stayed at the Plaza. That's fine, but I want to tell my family I got some tips today at the Plaza. They're the schmuck class, you know."

He nodded sagely and said, "It's a really junky, junky type of person. They look for us to tip them. They don't even eat here. They stay in the Plaza and they say, 'Excuse me, where's the nearest McDonald's?' It's unbelievable. I don't know where the hell these people come from. They don't belong here. Some of them put five or six in one room, with the cots and all. Come on. What are they doing in the Plaza? They never want a bellman. No way. They check themselves in and out. We don't need them. Believe me, we don't need them."

Skira assumed a spraddle-legged stance, like a fencer, and stared out at the lobby. Standing to his right, Nabil Haddad nibbled on a Life Saver and waited for his turn. The other bellmen called him Joe, because they couldn't pronounce his first name. Born in Egypt, the son of an appraiser for the Egyptian government, he had come to America in 1968. "You can make five hundred or six hundred a week in this job if you work," he confided. "But you've got to check in a lot of people. You have to be smart. Say a guest says he'd like some cigarettes. You don't say, 'Make two lefts and then a right and there's Shapero's. They carry them.' I go get them. The cigarettes are a dollar fifty. He may give me two dollars. He may give me five dollars. And in the future, he may ask for me. You build up steady customers. You see, I have the long vision."

Haddad was a small man with a moon face and thick tortoiseshell glasses. He spoke five languages: Italian, French, Arabic, Spanish, and English. He had been able to detect differences in tipping patterns among nationalities. "Sometimes you go up with six bags and you get a dollar," he said. "The Italians are the worst. They often give us nothing. They say they don't have change. Or they say they'll make change and tip you later. Then they forget. I assume they forget. But they may be cheap. The Americans are the best tippers, with the exception of doctors and lawyers. They are cheap, cheap, cheap. Americans bring lighter bags, but more of them. They believe in a little bit here, a little bit there. The Japanese bring very heavy bags; they always come with all these papers and books and cameras. The Australians bring one bag but it takes Hercules to lift it. It's the size of a trunk and they put their whole house in that bag.

"You know the worst thing?" he asked. "If you have to change someone's room. That costs you one or two check-ins. And you get several room changes every day. It's usually they don't like the room or they wanted a king-sized bed."

I asked about the image of the bellman as a procurer of prostitutes. Haddad said that was grossly exaggerated. Some of the others, however, told me that a few bellmen would hustle a broad if asked, or at least point the guest in the right direction.

Stories began to emerge. One of the bellmen told me a famous story about a recently departed member of the staff who made the mistake of substantially overstepping his responsibilities. As he later explained the events, he had finished taking some luggage to a room in advance of a guest's arrival. Then he went in to use the bathroom. He heard a key turn in the lock, and, fearing that the guest would be annoyed at finding him there, he made a fast move out the bathroom window and onto a ledge. He inched his way along an entire side of the building before he finally found an open window through which he could return to the hotel. It was the last open window he would crawl through. As he came in, a guest was using the bathroom. He was one of the top executives of Westin Hotels. He was not understanding. Of course, few employees who knew the story believed the bellman's version. They were convinced that he had probably been in bed with someone's wife when the key turned in the lock.

As their turn came up to room a guest, the bellmen followed a prescribed pattern for where they had to stand. The first man in line stood directly across from the front desk, his back to the daily function board. Number two stood to his right and across from him. Number three stood to the right of the revolving entrance door. Number four stood by the bell captain's desk around the corner and across the lobby. When the number-one man heard the command "Front," signifying that a guest needed a bellman, he would step forward to the front desk and the others would simultaneously shift to their new spots, as if playing some sort of peculiar party game. Guests, of course, had the prerogative of requesting a bellman they were familiar with from previous visits, even if he was back in the order. When that happened too often, the others would usually give him dirty looks as he passed by.

Moving up to the number-one spot now was Bobby Pantekas, a paunchy, bustling little man. The other bellmen were giving him a bit of a hard time because he was the coach of the employees' softball team and was trying to round up recruits. "You can hit," he told one of the bellmen. "I know you can hit. You know you can hit. So hit."

Tom Wagner, who got referred to as the "movie star" because he had a minor role in the picture *Arthur,* now stood in the number-two spot. He was the tallest member of the crew and had a funny streak. When a guest shrugged off assistance and said he would carry his own bags, Wagner would wait until he had turned around and then make a face and say, barely audibly, "I hope your room is occupied, sir. Have a good day."

"I'll tell you one of my weirdest experiences," he said. "When Billy Carter and some of the others from the Carter clan came, I took up Ruth Carter Stapleton—you know, the evangelist. The first thing she did was take out a picture of herself in a white robe —her arms spread wide—with a light behind her that made it look like a halo was over her head. She put that on the TV. First thing she did. That was pretty weird in my book."

Bellmen (they will tell you) have a rough job. They are always under time pressure. How fast a guest gets from the curb outside to his room is a key measure of service in a luxury hotel, and the bellmen have a lot of control over it. Hotel experts count on it to take no more than about seven to nine minutes. The Plaza had been averaging about five and a half to six, an impressive performance in a hotel its size. Once they got the guests to their rooms, the Plaza bellmen were expected to deliver a spiel telling newcomers about the remote control on the TV, the minibar, the closet safe, and all the restaurants and the hours during which they served.

"The whole thing is speed," Dominic Szorentini said. He was crusty. He had a right to be. He had been at the Plaza for thirty-three years (and was the brother of doorman Joe Szorentini). He said he normally took about five to eight minutes to check in a guest but sometimes got stuck with a guest with a lot of questions or someone who was fussy.

On more than one occasion, he said, something truly wacky had happened that had set the bellmen back for the whole day or maybe the whole week. He recalled the time that a king arrived accompanied by a substantial entourage. The bellmen had just finished hauling up the 250 bags of the entourage when one of the king's staff members inquired about his highness's luggage. "Coming up next," one of the bellmen responded. "Oh, that can't be," the man said despairingly. "The king's bags must be brought up first." The bellmen had to return all 250 bags to the lobby, take up the king's couple of suitcases, and then once again fetch the other luggage.

A curvaceous blonde in a very short skirt came off the elevator. "There you go, Mike," Szorentini said. "There's your lunch."

"Okay, I'll take her," Skira said.

Skira's phone rang. After he put down the receiver, he summoned a bellman. "I've got a live one," he said. That meant somebody who didn't like his room and wanted it changed. He was going from the seventh floor to the twelfth. "Ought to have a good view up there," Skira said. "Much better view."

A guy with a checkered aviation cap and a slight reek of liquor approached Skira. He wondered where the bags were that were supposed to have been put in his limousine. "I asked for the bags and I want the bags," he said. "I don't want them tomorrow; I don't want them next month; I want them now. So how about the bags? They didn't just walk off."

"Maybe he put them in the limousine already," Skira said promptly. He walked outside and checked the car. Nothing. No bags. "Drives you nuts here," he said, disappearing into the bag room, where the luggage still stood. "This place drives you absolutely nuts."

$$7$$

ATE in the afternoon, the lobby was fairly crowded, and as I watched the movement I had the sense of many narratives in the heads of all these people. Superficially, hotels weave together many disconnected stories, but few of them ever truly merge. Most of the people have things to do and places to go and no time to talk. But one man, who seemed in no particular hurry, paused to chat with me.

"The thing about this hotel is it really gets your imagination going in high gear," the man said. "That's a big part of why I come. I live in a nice place and all, but it's not something out of a magazine or anything. When I come here, I think I've just been made a prince. I must say I'm a bit of a hog about the services. I hit room service every day. I always ask for wake-up calls, because I love to have somebody call me and give me a big warm hello the first thing in the morning. Beats the hell out of an annoying buzz in your ear. I'm a big user of the concierge desk. They're the best for getting you tickets to the shows and reservations at the tough restaurants. And all the help is always calling you by your name. They name-call you to death here, and I eat that up. You know that show *Fantasy Island?* I feel like a guest on that show when I'm here. The only trouble, of course, is, no matter how long I'm here for, I've always got to go back to the real world. That's a pain."

The man was in his early forties, lived in Oregon, and described himself as fairly far along on the fast track of life. He was thin at the waist but so big in the chest that he looked inflated. Having checked in and settled into his room, he was heading out for a stroll.

He was a taxidermist. He said he had come to New York to meet some fellow taxidermists with whom he wanted to discuss new techniques. "Can't say too much about them to you," he said with a snort. "Don't need to have everyone knowing too much."

He paused to watch a couple of blondes walk by, and then mentioned that he had stuffed foxes, squirrels, weasels, cougars, elk. "You see a lot in my field," he said. "Believe me, I've known plenty of animals." If I wanted to, he said, I could come up to his room later, because he had brought photos of his work with him. He said you never knew when you might run into a potential customer. He also said he had brought along a portable videocassette player and a bunch of good tapes, in the event I wanted to watch any. "Westerns are my favorites," he said. "All this new adventure stuff, forget it. I'll always take a good, well-done western. That's a movie."

He added that the only thing he hated about coming to the Plaza was that he dreamed badly in hotels. "Last time I was here I dreamed I was being given shock treatments," he said. "I could almost feel the currents going through my head. What a trip that was. That wasn't the worst, though. One night in a Hyatt I dreamed I was being hanged for hijacking a plane. Never stayed in a Hyatt since."

Just then, two young men, conversing in low tones, drew near, and the taxidermist squeezed to one side to let them pass. One of the men, his hair wet and unkempt, was nervously lighting a cigarette. "I hate smokers," the taxidermist said once they had gone past. "I think people who smoke must have had demented childhoods."

He told me that I should feel free to be amused about what he did. He was immune to laughter about his work. "When I tell people what I do, they're either confused or start laughing," he said. "A lot of people think I drive a cab. I guess I can understand that."

The man said that taxidermy could be a fairly nice living once you had built up a reputation, though it was "not like law." It came out that he had been the beneficiary of a sizable inheritance, which allowed him to live beyond the means of most of his fellow professionals.

"Well," he said finally, "I don't suppose there's much use in my standing here. I'm going to see what's out there and let the city know I'm in town."

$$8$$

I FOUND that the most interesting place to go in the evening was the Oak Bar. The drinks there were strong, refreshing, and expensive. I sipped one and stared at the arriving patrons as they jockeyed for empty stools and tables. Two women moved past, wiggling their compact hips, their heels clicking and their heads held high, and they settled in for some serious drinking and gossiping at the far end of the room. A young woman whose hair wandered off in shocks greeted an older, tub-bellied man with a hug and a saucy smile, hopping onto a stool he had kept available beside him. Before she could say a word, the man hailed the bartender and had him put down a drink for the woman. Within a short time, there were people standing two and three deep around the bar. They snickered at one another's jokes and waved their hands when their glasses needed replenishing.

The bartender on duty, a placid, plainspoken man with a bulbous nose, was in the space of fifteen minutes able to give the same weather comments in the same modulated tone to four different patrons. Mostly, though, he didn't seem interested in conversation. He just listened and refilled glasses as rapidly as they were emptied.

"Give this man a vodka," someone hollered from the end of the bar. "He made one hell of a presentation today. Hell of a performance."

"Oh, Jack, cool it," the other man said. "Let's not make a production out of this."

The bartender smiled at the other man and poured him his drink.

The bartender, Mose Peracchio, was seventy-nine, and there wasn't a drink known that he couldn't mix. "If there is one," he told me, "nobody's ordered it yet." He had served drinks at a bar on the Riviera in his native Italy until, when he was thirty-nine, he decided to come to America to start a business. It didn't work out and was enough of a sore point that he wouldn't say a word about it. ("Next question is what I have to say about that.") He got a job as a bartender in the Plaza's banquet department, stayed there for thirteen years, and then moved to the Oak Bar, where he had been serving alcohol for the last twenty-seven years. He got to the hotel a little before five, went down and took his dinner in the employee cafeteria, worked on a crossword puzzle, walked over to the cashier to collect a tray with $200 in change, and crawled in behind the bar at five-thirty. He remained there until last call at one-thirty in the morning.

Peracchio hardly ever joked with the people who came in, and he said he didn't talk politics with the clientele because you could never tell when you were going to strike a nerve. He liked to stick to weather and sports. Rarely expansive, he didn't go out of his way to inquire about a customer's health. If somebody wanted to unload their woes on him, which didn't happen too often, he would patiently listen, but he didn't consider himself a prescribing bartender. "I don't start any conversations," he said. "There should be quiet in the bar is the way I see it. Most people want to be left alone and just sit by themselves and relax."

When he was not pouring drinks, Peracchio just planted his feet apart and stared moodily. He never sat down. His legs might cramp up. His eyes watched customers, seeing whether their heads lolled, studying how they walked when they went to the bathroom, whether they listed to one side. When signs showed that a customer had had too much, the customer was "eighty-sixed" and got no more to drink. If someone was insistent, Peracchio might pour him a straight club soda or something else free of alcohol and hope that would fool him. Often it would, but other times it would just make him sulk. If someone became a problem and was slobbering over other patrons, then Peracchio would draw a finger across his throat. That was the signal to the captain to toss him out.

He set up two glasses of wine, cracked open a beer, put out some peanuts. "We don't get too many regulars here," he told me. "You have to consider the prices. We're not really competitive. We get our share of complaints. Everyone tells me we're the highest. But don't get on my back about that, because I'm not the one who sets the prices."

The prices were pretty painful—$4.78 for a glass of the passable house wine (a French table variety), $6.44 for a scotch, $6.22 for a vodka, $3.78 to $4.71 for a beer, $3.72 for a soft drink—but the Oak Bar's atmosphere was worth paying for. Repose came easily in the bar. The place occupied a niche in the history of the hotel. Over the years, the spot to discuss business, personal or professional, had always been this dark oak-paneled room at the back of the hotel, decorated in the German Renaissance style. It was originally known as the barroom and had been an exclusively male bastion. Starting in the mid-1930s, rules were relaxed a little and women were allowed in for lunch on weekends and after the market closed on weekdays. Not until 1969, however, were they put on equal footing with men, able to come whenever they pleased.

Many years ago, the barroom boasted an electric fountain in the center, one of the first of its kind. To attract businessmen, there were six branch offices of stock brokerage houses located in the corridors between the bar and the main lobby. One of them had a mahogany stock board. When Prohibition arrived, the bar was taken out of the room and it was transformed into a brokerage office for E. F. Hutton. Drinking persisted; chauffeurs would drive up and hand bottles to the doormen, who would in turn hurriedly transport them to the maître d' for final delivery. In the early 1940s, Hutton moved upstairs and the place was restored and reopened as the Oak Bar.

The restoration added three murals by the American painter Everett Shinn. One was of the Vanderbilt mansion that stood across the street until it was torn down to make way for the Bergdorf Goodman store. A second showed Central Park as it would have looked from the hotel on a brittle winter night in 1907. The third, the one above the bar, was of the Pulitzer Fountain as it looked when it was first placed out in front of the Plaza. The murals still loomed there, soothing sights to dream upon. Until recently, each time the hotel was sold, the Shinn murals were not made part of the sale and had to be negotiated for separately. Westin Hotels, in fact, labored through fourteen months of discussions before managing to reach a satisfactory price of $500,000. A recent appraisal of the murals put their value at $1.2 million.

The northwest corner of the dining room adjacent to the Oak Bar was officially named the Cohan Corner, because George M. Cohan sat there in a booth almost every day, from about three-thirty or four on, to knock back a few, until his death in 1942. Before he came in, he followed a little ritual. He would walk around the reservoir in Central Park with a couple of rolls of quarters, handing them out to needy people as he passed them. The last thing he would do before coming in was to pick up the afternoon paper, mostly because he was a great sports fan and wanted to check the scores. The Yankees were his team, and he would often talk with the help about their prospects. His drink was a Gibson—a martini with an onion. Many days, George Jessel would drop in and sit with him, or else Ethel Merman or other theater people. Cohan usually hung around until about eight o'clock, by which time he would be well into his cups. These days, when Plaza managers were entertaining someone in the bar and wanted to impress him, they frequently chose the Cohan booth.

I didn't find too much high-toned talk in the bar, despite its sophisticated atmosphere. It seemed to attract staid customers who were, for the most part, well behaved. It was not a place where you heard wolf whistles. It was not the sort of place where you had to worry that some drunk would spill scotch on your shoes or that you might get a barstool busted over your head. One of the barmen, though, told me about a patron who liked to come in occasionally, get plastered, and start singing "Raindrops Keep Falling on My Head."

A real neighborhood tavern is always good for an occasional fistfight, but altercations, I was told, were extremely rare among the mannerly patrons of the Oak Bar. The way Peracchio figured it, people couldn't afford to get drunk enough to start slugging away at one another. "For the prices," he said, "you don't get drunk. The average person has two drinks, period. And if you can't hold two drinks, you got no business being in a bar." I did learn about one scuffle not long ago during a hard-drinking evening. Six people at one of the large tables were quietly planning their mother's funeral. Next to them sat another, similar-sized group intent on having a good time—no recent deaths in their families. For one reason or another, their neighbors became fed up with the mourners and started taunting them. The mourners took it only so long before one of them got up and popped one of the hecklers in the mouth. That did it. In the same chain reaction that can turn a hockey fight into an out-and-out brawl, the swing touched off a punching free-for-all. Some security men managed to maneuver the raging battle out to the lobby, where the punching continued until the police arrived and sent everybody sailing out into the street.

The tone of the bar did shift this way and that way from time to time. Back in the sixties, I had heard, the Oak Bar became something of a rarefied hangout for a number of the city's gay people. The rather unenlightened management at the time became troubled. Thus the bar was shut down for several weeks while things were thought out. When it was reopened, the managers hired a group of gorgeous models to come each evening and just sit at the bar and sip free drinks. The gays pretty much stopped coming and a lot of women-chasers showed up.

A family of four came in and took a table by the window. Tourists, for sure. The two small children were haggling over how many Cokes they could have and whether they were going to get hamburgers and French fries later on for dinner. "Let's just cool ourselves down," the father said firmly. "There is no reason to go off the deep end."

The standard drinks of the bar were beer, wine, and vodka. "That's all people want—beer, wine, and vodka," Peracchio said. "It used to be scotch, martinis, Manhattans, whiskey sours. It started to change about fifteen years ago. Now I can go a day without making a martini. Scotch has gone down in such a big way it's unbelievable. We used to have two cases of scotch gone in a day. Now maybe a couple of bottles. You used to have a bottle of vodka and you'd have it all year. No more. Tastes have changed. It's beer, wine, and vodka."

Peracchio said most of his customers were guests at the hotel; few were locals. That suited him fine. "I like the traveler and the businessman," he said. "That way you don't get involved. Here you don't get too many of the problems. Mostly, when they talk, they talk about sports."

Peracchio himself carried temperance to an extreme. Before he started his shift, he grabbed a bottle of Mountain Valley Water, and he quenched his thirst with that from time to time until he knocked off. "I'm not a drinker. I don't go for it. Water or iced tea suits me fine. When there's company at home, maybe I'll accept a glass of wine. When you work behind a bar, it's too easy to start drinking, and you abuse it. Before you know it, you're a prisoner of that bottle. It's just too easy."

A skinny fellow who looked to be in his late forties sat at the near end of the bar, engrossed in conversation with another, somewhat younger, somewhat chubbier man, who had his hands pushed deep into his pants pockets.

"Market stunk today," the skinny man said. "And do I mean stunk."

"Ah, it'll be roses tomorrow," his companion said, making a mock-sour face. "Market never smells the same two days in a row."

"I don't know about that. All I know is I'm fast on my way to becoming independently poor." The man consulted a small spiral notebook in which he had scribbled assorted stock prices. He grasped it delicately between his index finger and thumb, staring at it.

"You've been keeping that ridiculous little book for years," the chubby man said. "It never works." He acted as if he had more important things to do than listen to a simpering stock loser.

A couple of stools down from them, a fidgety man, loosened by the alcohol, was offering opinions on child-raising, birth control, nuclear war, Cajun cooking, the prospects for the Yankees, the trouble with Washington, and subzero refrigerators.

"C'mon," his companion was saying. "Subzero's not that important."

"I'm telling you," he said, "subzero can make an incredible difference in your life. It's absolutely vital. The ice you get is unbelievable."

"Look, are you for real, or what?"

Among the other customers in the bar were:

An aspiring actress having a drink with a less than overwhelmingly successful agent.

Two whiskey-eyed businessmen from Chicago in town for a sales conference.

A public-relations man who worked a couple of blocks away and who had just had a "godawful day, if there ever was one."

Two middle-aged, very expensively dressed women, downing drinks while they waited for their husbands to return from a business meeting.

An investment banker from Los Angeles, here on business that so far was not going especially well.

A retired shipping executive, red-faced from drink and hoarse from talk.

A mother with her teenage daughter, who had recently embarked on a modeling career.

A marketing vice-president whose suburban train had been delayed and who figured a drink was the best way to wait it out. "What the hell, so I miss dinner. I'll drink dinner."

I fell into conversation with a man with pepper-and-salt hair who was chewing audibly on cocktail peanuts and washing them down with beer. He was working a *New York Post* crossword puzzle. "Damned thing's too easy," he said, tossing it aside.

He sat quietly for a moment and looked at the mural behind the bar. "You know," he said, "I could become one hell of a drunk. Problem is, I don't have the time. Serious drinking really takes up your time." He ordered a second drink, a scotch this time, and began chewing on a swizzle stick. I noticed he had unlaced his shoes. "Done a lot of walking today," he said. "This town insists on maximum use of the feet."

I listened to the man as he dilated on several topics: some ups and downs with his marriage ("We're sort of wavering between up and down at the moment, meaning we're speaking, but it's usually in a very loud tone of voice"); the mating habits of the octopus ("They don't do it the way you'd think"); how he used to be a great ladies' man in college ("Dreamboat was my middle name"); what to do about roaches ("If you've got them bad, you've just got to set the place on fire"); how he was once so broke that he didn't turn on the lights in his house for a month to save some pennies ("Helped me develop a hell of a sense of feel"); and how the smartest kid in his college graduating class was now a long-distance truck driver ("Life's a mystery, all right").

I asked him what had brought him to the Plaza.

"A little of this, a little of that," the man said cryptically. "Actually, I'm looking to pull off a tremendous deal, just a tremendous deal. I do it and I've got it made. I have to have a drink at night just to calm me down about it, the thing's so goddam big."

"What is the tremendous deal?" I asked.

"Gophers," he said.

"Gophers?" I said, a little disappointed.

"That's right, gophers." He leaned forward in his chair and began to speak with more vigor. "You know how people's lawns get ripped apart by gophers. Well, I've got a device you stick in the ground and it makes these noises only gophers can hear. Drives them wild. There're others in this market, but I've got something that beats anything out there. Gophers can't live with my device around. They don't just get off your lawn. They move to another state."

"How's the thing work?" I asked.

He looked at me with squinting eyes. "Can't tell you," the man said, and he shook his head sharply from side to side. He grinned, showing uneven teeth. "Proprietary information. It's an unbelievable product, but I don't tell a soul about it. I don't tell my mother about it, you understand? That's how things go in the business world. Some innocent chap finds out about your product and the next morning he's got the damned thing on the market. No way I breathe a word. But I got people I'm talking to, and if they say the magic word—which is 'money'—then these things are going to be in lawns from here to Timbuktu."

I told the man it all sounded very interesting and wished him luck.

"Hey, nice talking to you," he said. He lurched to his feet, started to say something more, but instead just headed for the door.

TUESDAY

ARTHUR Hoyt stood under the shade of a spreading palm. He mopped his sweaty brow, then mashed his handkerchief in his hand and stuffed it back in the jacket of his dark blue suit. He shuffled around the perimeter of the Palm Court, where a resonant humming of business talk and gossip from breakfasters bounced off plants and tables. Hoyt had a stiff-legged walk, and as he walked his watery eyes swept over the lobby.

The director of security was thinking hard about a couple of cases that perplexed him—some American Express traveler's checks that had been filched from an issuing agent and were turning up in New York hotels, and a five-member team that had been very effectively lifting suitcases from hotel lobbies. He couldn't think too hard, however, because every few minutes a guest who mistook him for an assistant lobby manager or some other staff member would ask him for directions to one of the ballrooms or restaurants. Though thoroughly tired of answering the same questions over and over, Hoyt was invariably polite and would accompany his response with a welcoming grin.

"Most of our time is taken up by PR," he told me, a little sullenly. "In a hotel like this, I'd have to say that about seventy-five percent of our work is PR and only twenty-five percent is security. We're directing people to banquet rooms, assisting guests in one way or another. We also get a lot of folks from small towns who think that New York is such an unsafe city. So they're looking for safety tips. Well, I've got them. 'Don't show your wealth' is the first thing we tell people. We tell women to turn their rings over so the stones don't show. They should wear their jewelry inside their dress. They shouldn't carry more cash than they need. Use credit cards. Carry your wallet in your inside jacket pocket. Stay in congested areas. There really is safety in numbers. It's all pretty basic stuff, but people don't seem to know it."

Hoyt was a stout, edgy, gap-toothed man with straight gray hair, a retired New York City policeman. He had been in the police department for twenty-four years and had worked his way up to detective. His last assignment had been as a crime-prevention specialist. He would visit companies, undertake evaluations of their security, and, if he found it wanting, would provide advice on how to improve it. During his tenure on the police force, Hoyt was involved in thousands of arrests and received sixteen citations, yet what he was most proud of was the fact that he never had to shoot anybody. ("I was fired at once. When he missed, the guy surrendered immediately. I guess he knew what he was up against.") After leaving the force, Hoyt worked as the night manager at the Hyatt for a year and then spent five years as director of security at the Regency before coming to the Plaza in early 1986. Hotel work suited him. It wasn't too demanding, and despite all the inane questions he had to answer, there was a certain prestige to the job.

People flowed through the lobby in a rushing stream. Hoyt studied them, looking for telltale signs of dishonesty. When the hotel was crowded, the lobby could be teeming with five thousand to seven thousand people a day. The security staff, very discreetly, had to try to keep track of all of them and to become familiar with the lobby's habitués. In the old days, the popular conception of the "house dick" was that his prime responsibility was to make sure that unmarried people weren't twisted together in bedsheets. Most of the job today consisted of tireless hours patrolling the floors, guiding guests and searching for suspicious and shadowy characters.

"We get quite a variety of unsavory types here," Hoyt said after telling a middle-aged woman where she could buy face cream. "They're constant headaches. We'll never get rid of all of them. We try to deter them, but they always come back. They do their best to look like tourists. They hang cameras around their necks, carry shopping bags, ask about getting postcards. I've seen all the tricks."

As I followed him on his patrol of the hotel, Hoyt described the characters he had to worry about. The most common category of hotel thief was the "bag booster," who loitered around the check-in and checkout areas and stole bags. Quite often, he worked in collaboration with one or two colleagues, and sometimes as part of a gang of as many as half a dozen. When they operated in groups, they never spoke to one another once they got inside the hotel, but communicated exclusively by eye and hand signals, like mutes. One or two of them would try to distract a targeted guest, another would serve as lookout for security men, and still another would actually swipe the bag. Most of the boosters working the city's hotels these days, Hoyt said, were Colombians. They came to New York in the spring and fall, when the hotels were packed, and then repaired to resort areas in the winter and summer. "They actually follow the crowds around the world," Hoyt said. "They're jet-setter bag boosters."

The bag boosters were flexible in their modus operandi, Hoyt told me, but some of them favored certain techniques. One Plaza frequenter lugged around a black briefcase, and when he spied someone with a similar case, he trailed him, hoping that he would put it down to make a phone call or buy a newspaper. Then the booster would deftly switch briefcases.

The teams depended on distraction. Their most common trick was for one of the group to squirt some mustard or ketchup on the back of a target's coat, and then to tap the guest on the shoulder and point out that he had some gook on his back. As the person turned around to rub it off, one of the other thieves snatched his suitcase. "Ketchup and mustard are what they like to use the most," Hoyt said. "Sometimes they go with hot-chocolate powder.

They get these little packages from coffee shops or from the Korean fruit stands. Usually they don't even pay for them.

"There was a classic case the other day in a nearby hotel," Hoyt went on. "A woman took thirty thousand dollars' worth of jewels out of the safe-deposit box and went to the cashier to check out. She laid the bag of jewels on the desk. Someone approached her and said, 'Pardon me, you dropped something.' She looked down, and there was a hundred-dollar bill lying at her feet. She reached down and picked it up. When she stood up, her bag was gone. A little later, another person came by and said he was a guest and had dropped a hundred-dollar bill. The woman said, oh yes, she had found it, and dug it out of her purse and gave it to him. He was part of the team. So they even got their hundred dollars back."

For all the tales of big scores, bag boosting was a hit-or-miss business. Often all the thief would get was a suitcase jammed with clothing, usually not his size. "The Colombians know the luggage to go for," Hoyt said. "They want the carry-on bags. They know that's where the valuables are. The bags that are checked won't be the place where anyone puts jewels. They also hit the guests checking out, not those checking in. They know people don't usually bother to come back from some other city to file a complaint. They especially like the orientals, because they know they're not coming all the way back here to testify. If we catch these guys, even if we don't have anyone to file a complaint, we'll still charge them with criminal trespass, but that doesn't get them so much as a day in jail."

The other common pest Hoyt came up against was the pickpocket. Probably the most prevalent and effective technique used by pickpockets was the two-man revolving-door blockade. An appealing target would be identified and one man would fall into step in front of him and precede him through the door. Once the pigeon was about to enter, the crook would hold the door, giving the impression that it was jammed. The second man would bump into the victim; his guard was not likely to come up, since it was not uncommon to be jostled when a door had abruptly jammed. While the victim was being jostled, though, his wallet was also being snatched.

Besides the boosters and the pickpockets, there were occasional "prowlers," who would register as guests and then go roaming through the halls hunting for unlocked doors (it was astonishing how many people, despite hotel reminders, would go to bed with their doors unlocked or the key dangling from the keyhole) or locks that could be picked. Burglars who break into hotel rooms to seize loot, however, are a rather rare breed, simply because the locks have gotten better. The Plaza used Winfield locks, which could be reprogrammed in about fifteen seconds into any of 999,000 combinations. One of the locksmiths, who worked in a cramped outpost tucked away on the second floor of the hotel, told me, "I can reprogram the lock in fifteen seconds. The paperwork, though, takes three minutes." Four keys were issued for every room at the Plaza, and once three were missing (usually because guests had neglected to turn them in), the lock was reprogrammed. Enough keys vanished so that every Wednesday afternoon Mickey Pierce, a member of the security staff, devoted himself exclusively to reprogramming locks. Before he was through, he would have visited sixty or seventy rooms.

Shrewd burglars who did like to break into rooms were alert to successive spells of hot and cold weather, because they caused gaps to open up between the wooden doors and the sashes of some rooms, making them "loidable." That meant a credit card or a strip of celluloid could be slipped into the gap and manipulated to disengage the lock's bolt. Security made a point of inspecting as many doors as it could in the wake of such weather, and if it spotted gaps it asked the carpenters to come by and fill them.

The latest thing at hotels is electronic locks that operate with cards rather than keys. The locks record the precise time the door was opened and can determine who unlocked it—whether it was the card of a member of the housekeeping staff or a guest-relations person or a guest. The locks are able to keep track of the last ten times the door was opened. Many newer hotels, and quite a few older ones, have converted to these systems. The Plaza management had been scrutinizing them as well, but was biding its time, thinking the locks would improve in sophistication.

Despite the formidable barriers to working rooms, there was a fairly well known transvestite burglar at the Plaza. He would wander around the halls with a female accomplice, rap on doors until a man answered, and tell the occupant that they needed to use a phone. The woman would then start flirting with the man and pick his pocket. Meanwhile, the transvestite, while he feigned making a call, would scoop up whatever he found lying around. In five minutes, the guest would be cleaned out.

Other hotel pests included the flimflam men, who preyed on employees as well as guests. One of them who had been rather successfully working the hotel circuit was caught late in 1986 at the Plaza. He was a forty-year-old Yugoslavian national identified as Aldo Zenzerovia. His ruse was to approach Mexican immigrants when they showed up at hotels looking for low-level jobs and tell them he could get them a position in exchange for a fee of anywhere from $100 to $200. Once he got the cash, of course, Zenzerovia disappeared. There were no jobs. After he had swindled quite a few immigrants looking for work at several of the big New York hotels, a description of him was passed around to security forces, and one of the Plaza men nabbed him setting up another pigeon.

Jewel robberies are a constant source of worry to all hotel managers. The greatest headaches are guests who will not put their valuables in the safes provided for that purpose. The biggest, and most puzzling, jewel theft at the Plaza occurred in September 1925, when Jessie Woolworth Donahue, one of the heirs to the Woolworth fortune, had $683,000 worth of gems stolen from her suite. James Donahue, her husband, and the valet were both in other rooms of the suite at the time, but saw and heard nothing. Among the jewels was a necklace of rose pearls valued at $450,000. The insurance company offered a $65,000 reward. A few days later, the missing jewels were returned by a private investigator on a "no questions asked" basis. To this day, no one knows who the thief was.

There have been other sizable heists. In February 1964, when twenty policemen were in the hotel to guard the visiting Beatles, a thief took almost $23,000 worth of jewels from the room of a Florida couple. In November 1971, a retired Minnesota businessman and his wife had jewelry worth nearly $59,000 lifted from their fourteenth-floor room. The jewels had been carelessly left in a canvas travel bag on the bedroom dresser.

In May 1974, a Connecticut physician was slashed on his face and neck and his wife was pushed and punched by a knife-wielding assailant who forced his way into their second-floor room. However, he fled empty-handed. Just two days later, a man accompanied a California architect to his room and then, waving a double-edged razor blade, stole $2,000 and some jewelry from the architect and another man staying in the room. The thief tied up the two men with socks and shirts and escaped dressed in the architect's butter-scotch-colored suit. He left his own dungarees and white jacket behind.

On a Saturday evening in August 1987, three men and a woman, working as a team, trailed a couple into an elevator and rode with them to the seventh floor. They forced them into their room and took $400 in cash and $2,300 worth of jewelry, then tied the man and woman up before fleeing. To cap off the day, the team wandered over to the New York Hilton, six blocks away, and robbed a family of four of $1,500 in cash and jewelry valued at $25,000.

Hoyt told me he was always surprised at how neglectful people could be—and how incredibly lucky some of them were. Not long ago, a guest from South America, in New York because his daughter needed specialized medical care, forgot his flight bag in the trunk of the cab he had taken from the hospital to the hotel. It happened to contain $12,000 in cash. Hoyt had nothing to work on but a sketchy description of the cabdriver; he wasn't optimistic that the bag would ever be recovered. Miraculously, the driver showed up at the Plaza the next morning and handed it over. He had never opened it. Hoyt couldn't resist asking the driver if he would have brought it back had he known it was filled with all that money. He told Hoyt, "I wouldn't have been happy if I kept it." The guest gave the driver a reward of $500.

Another time a maid turned in a key-shaped diamond that was so big Hoyt couldn't believe it was real. It turned out to be thirty carats and worth about $80,000. Hoyt called the guest who had last been in the room. It was hers, all right. "I'm always forgetting that thing," she told Hoyt. "But it's always getting returned to me."

Jewels turned up all over. A string of priceless oriental pearls was found in a Plaza vacuum cleaner when it was emptied. A diamond bracelet was discovered in a Plaza elevator. One of the skills required of security officers was being able to find gems that their owners had hidden in odd places that they had then forgotten. Once a woman stuck a diamond ring in a cold-cream jar for safekeeping but couldn't remember its whereabouts. Security, familiar with cold-cream stashes, found it.

An older, mottled man approached Hoyt, clearing his throat. "Excuse me," he said. "There used to be a fish restaurant in the hotel."

"Yes, sir," Hoyt replied. "It's still here. The Oyster Bar. Around the corner to the right."

"Where's the main desk?" a young Frenchman asked.

"Make a left," Hoyt said.

I trailed Hoyt over to the front desk, where he paused and studied the check-ins for a while. A Japanese man was casually filling out a registration card at the desk. He had a flight bag hooked over his shoulder, and a leather suitcase stood at his feet. "Now, if you were a crook, which bag would you go after?" Hoyt asked me.

I didn't respond fast enough, and Hoyt said, "The flight bag, of course. The valuables are always in the bag the person holds on to. The suitcase on the ground is probably just plain old clothing."

A glint came into Hoyt's eye. "What I try to create for the people who are dishonest is an anxiety barrier. A guy who's going to think twice won't commit the crime. We want to convince him to go elsewhere, that it's not worth trying here. So the idea is to have security men visibly placed at all the key locations. A criminal is very good at picking out a security guard. Usually the earphone is the giveaway. Or the walkie-talkie. Or the way he's standing and watching the luggage or watching the door. If a thief isn't sure, he may test one of our men. He may make an overt move toward a bag and see if the security man positions himself to get a better view. We're not going to dig a moat around the hotel and fill it with alligators. But we want to make sure this seems like an impregnable fortress."

Hoyt himself knew as a boy that he could never go into crime. He said he wasn't ever able to get away with anything. "I used to do all the bad things kids do—steal cookies from the cookie jar and all that. My father always caught me. I asked him once how he knew. He said, 'Every time you did something, you came and stood in front of me with your hands behind your back, waiting. That was a dead giveaway.' So I got the hint early on that I was destined never to be a criminal."

A likely way for Hoyt to hear of a potential thief in the building was from one of the employees. Only the other day, a maid had called security to say that a suspicious-looking character was snooping around on her floor. Her antennae went up after she glanced at him, because he seemed surprised and hastily ducked into an elevator. Usually, a guest would nod or say hello. Security stopped the suspect and couldn't believe who they had—none other than "Champagne Johnson." He was one of the most prolific room thieves in town, and all the security men knew his face well. In a twenty-year career, he had lifted considerable sums of cash and jewels out of hotels. He had gotten his nickname because he was so smooth and polite. He always dressed impeccably. As Hoyt put it, "If you met him, you'd probably invite him over to dinner." Nobody knew how he managed to defeat seemingly impenetrable locks. When he interviewed Champagne, Hoyt looked him in the eye and asked him, "What are we going to do to make sure you don't come back to this hotel?"

Champagne gave a wry smile and replied, "Mr. Hoyt, I'm not sure it would be in my best interest if I answered that properly."

The hotel had him arrested on a charge of criminal trespass. In short order, he was back on the street, wandering with itchy fingers through the corridors of another hotel. Not long afterward, though, his string ran out. He was caught stealing in the Roosevelt Hotel and would be serving a couple of years behind bars. He had been arrested under fourteen different aliases for criminal trespass, but this was the first time he had been put away. Every hotel in the city sighed with relief.

It was Hoyt's supposition that Champagne had probably hit all the hotels at one time or another. He was the best the hotel security men had to face. He was a master at changing his appearance through subtle deceptions so that people wouldn't recognize him. At one moment, he would have his chin sunk on his chest; then he would jut out his jaw and look like another person. He could hunch his shoulders and manage to have people who saw him describe him as short; he could stand almost on his toes and convince anyone spotting him that he was tall.

He was a fast thinker, too. During one robbery attempt, the guest whose room he had broken into surprised him by returning before Champagne could escape. Calmly and convincingly, he explained that he was from the hotel's building staff and was checking the smoke detectors in all the rooms. And a good thing, he went on, because he had found that the battery was dead on the alarm in the guest's room. With that, he excused himself and said that a maintenance man would be up soon to remedy the situation. The guest was mildly suspicious, until a half hour later a maintenance person came by and replaced the battery in the smoke detector. Upon leaving the room, Champagne had picked up a house phone, called the building department, and reported a defective alarm. Not until the next morning did the guest notice that he had been robbed of all his cash and jewelry.

The corners of Hoyt's mouth turned down, and he said, "There's another professional who's worked in the industry for a while and is known at all the hotels. He's always well groomed, too. He picks up name tags, as if he were from a convention. His only intent is to steal luggage or pick pockets. He's damned good. He's slick."

Studying his security guards, Hoyt roamed around the Central Park South lobby, paying particular attention to where the men were positioned. He constantly reminded them to stand with their backs against a wall. That way, no one could creep up behind them and tap them on the shouder, causing them to turn around and perhaps miss a theft. Now and then, Hoyt would tiptoe up behind a guard who had drifted away from a wall and say, "Good morning." If the guard twirled around, Hoyt would give him a good dressing-down.

Done examining the lobby areas, Hoyt trudged downstairs to see what was happening at the dispatch center. The nerve center for the security department was a lonely glass-fronted enclosure in the basement of the hotel. It had a concrete floor and a desk that ran the length of the room, allowing someone to sit there and face out through the glass. Above the desk were twenty-two television sets —a TV junkie's paradise—each of which was connected to a video camera strategically mounted somewhere in the hotel. Cameras were installed in all of the elevators, at the check-in areas, at the different entrances to the restaurants, at the safe-deposit boxes, and at the hotel entrances. A camera also registered the activity, or lack of it, in the wine cellar, since the hotel kept hundreds of thousands of dollars' worth of alcoholic beverages down there. Each videotape ran for three days and remained on file for three months before being reused. At the moment, nothing suspicious was discernible on any of the screens.

An indispensable resource stored in the dispatch center was the Hotel Alert Book, which gave compact histories, including pictures, of criminals known to work hotels. Every member of the security staff was required to study its contents, familiarize himself with the faces, and then carry them in his head as if they were members of his own family. The book had the lowdown on about fifty or sixty current criminals and another 150 old-timers who hadn't been spotted in a while. Every so often, though, one of the veterans would strike again after a prolonged absence; it usually turned out that he had been away serving time.

Hoyt said, "We have about ten hotels in the area which assist each other through networking. If somebody is spotted and flees, we call one of the other hotels, and then they call another one until all ten have gotten the alert. If you deter somebody, he's not going to go home, take a shower, and go to sleep. He wants to commit the crime, and so he'll just move on to the next hotel. The Park

Lane. The St. Moritz. The Pierre. This is his job, so he's got to strike somewhere.

"Sometimes we get some good help from our guests. The last month, we've had a pickpocket working the streets outside the hotel. A man and wife who were staying here were walking along the sidewalk by the entrance and this woman approached the man. She was dressed like a hooker and began to come on to him, even though he was with his wife. Well, his wife thought this was just a riot, a hooker approaching her husband. She had a camera and decided to snap a picture. After the woman left, the guy noticed that his wallet was gone and his ring was half off his finger. So the wife came to us with the picture. When she told me she had taken a shot of him with the hooker, I sort of humored her, because I figured it would be useless. Her finger was probably over the lens or it was way out of focus. Boy, was I wrong. The picture was absolutely perfect." With the help of the photo, the hooker was caught.

Back in the lobby, Hoyt ran into John McHugh, the assistant security director, who told me that he was busy watching eyes. He had an eyebrow arched in perpetual scrutiny, and his back was ramrod-straight. "I try to watch what a guy's looking at," he said. "Is he looking at the floor, at bags? Is he looking at women or is he looking at their bags? Sometimes there'll be these absolutely gorgeous women parading by, and some guy won't even glance at their face or their legs. His eyes are glued on their handbags. He's trouble. In the winter, you want to watch the guy who walks around with an overcoat draped over his arm. He's picking a pocket with the hand under the overcoat. Our procedure is that if we see someone suspicious, we approach him and say, 'Can I help you?' He says, 'I'm just looking.' Then he knows he's been spotted. He knows now to go to another hotel. This work is standing and watching. At check-in time, there could be twenty bags belonging to ten people, and a good security man knows every bag and who it belongs to. It's concentration. The whole name of the game is concentration."

"Yeah, you can never let up with these clowns," Hoyt agreed.

"They're so good." He said he once watched a felon in the Palm Court. As he was bending over to pick up a scrap of paper he had dropped, he pushed his right foot backward, hooked a purse under a table behind him, and then kicked it over to a partner working the hotel with him. Hoyt apprehended both of them.

A good tip, he said, was to study fingernails, because pickpockets always kept their fingernails filed as sharp as razors. They didn't actually touch a wallet when they removed it. Rather, they grabbed the fabric of someone's pocket and nudged the wallet up through the cloth with their fingernails.

It was also worthwhile to take notice of people's attire, especially their shoes. "I tell my men to watch how clothes fit," Hoyt said. "Boosters have an opportunity to get a lot of nice clothing. But it doesn't always fit them that well. I tell them to look at the shoes. They don't often get shoes and they may have a beautiful suit on with an old, crummy pair of shoes."

Many of the people that the security staff came up against were completely harmless; they were nettlesome to management, though, because their presence violated the aesthetic consistency of the hotel. One legendary character was a brassy old woman who came to be known as the Spitter. She would materialize in the hotel almost every day, wandering around the lobby in ragged clothes, muttering to no one in particular. When a security man would attempt to get her to leave, she would curse loudly, kick the guard, and spit profusely in his face. Anyone who found himself forced to boot her out would draw disapproving frowns from patrons, who thought the old woman was being abused.

Hoyt's rules permitted no one on the Plaza security force to carry a gun, including himself. "There's nothing that could occur in a hotel that's worth taking a life over," he said. While Hoyt had been there, no one had ever shot a gun in the hotel, though there had been some tense moments. A short time ago, a man was browsing in one of the shops and his jacket was open; the salesperson noticed he was wearing a gun. The man left and disappeared into the Oak Bar. The salesperson immediately informed a security officer, who trailed him into the bar. He waited until the man had both his hands on the bar and then swiftly sat down beside him, identified himself, and asked if he had a permit to carry a gun. The man responded that he did, and that his permit was in his left jacket pocket. The security man gingerly slipped it out. The man was a dentist from Scarsdale who carried the gun for his own protection.

It was pretty unusual for someone to attempt a stickup, though Hoyt told me that the Parker Meridien had recently had one on the nineteenth floor; the guy had been armed with both a shotgun and a handgun. When gun-toting crooks were believed to be in the hotel, the police were called. "We had eight policemen once come into the hotel with their guns drawn," McHugh recollected. "This was in about 1984. There was a call that there was a guy up on the fourteenth floor waving a gun. The cops went through the hotel with their guns drawn, but they never found anyone. It was just a prank call."

There had been no murders in the Plaza, at least none that Hoyt knew of. Whenever there was a murder at one of the Manhattan hotels, though, it had its ripple effects at the other hotels. In September 1982, when a female bank executive was stabbed to death during a robbery attempt in a nineteenth-floor stairwell of the Waldorf-Astoria, the Plaza at once tightened its security, adding more patrols. For a number of weeks, any female guest who came in was offered an escort to her room. The Waldorf case was solved the following April, when a detective, working from a single blood-smudged fingerprint found on the woman's business card in her ransacked wallet, tracked down the murderer. Security was stepped up again in June 1986, after a Houston hotel company executive was shot dead in his room, once again at the Waldorf. That case has remained unsolved.

"Murder in a hotel, that's rare," Hoyt said. "There're a lot of better places to clip someone. This is not the place."

"Excuse me," a snowy-haired woman cut in. "Could you tell me where the ladies' room is?"

"Make two rights and you'll see it on your right-hand side," Hoyt said. "You can't miss it."

2

I WENT over to sit in on the weekly deliberations of the executive committee of the hotel. The committee was meeting in a small conference room adjacent to Jeffrey Flowers's austere office. Six executives had shown up —the head of human resources, the food and beverage director, the marketing director, the comptroller, Flowers, and Hud Hinton. The room was shaped like a shoe box, the oblong table in it so close to the side walls that the participants' backs almost touched them. A pot of coffee had been plopped down in the middle of the table, and a stack of Styrofoam cups stood next to it. Flowers, a tightly controlled man, slumped down at the head of the table. Behind him was a small window looking out over Central Park.

Without ado, Hilton cleared his throat and reminded the group that the king and queen of Sweden would be arriving Friday morning and that everyone should do his best to make sure all was in order for them. Nods came from around the table.

Flowers interrupted to ask, "Have we got the Swedish flag to hang out front for them?"

"Yes, we do," said Bob Yienger, the marketing director.

"Is it in good shape?"

"I'll have to check," Yienger said, and he wrote a note to himself on a yellow ledger pad.

"I saw the Norwegian flag out there the other day," Flowers said impatiently, "and it looked like shit."

"Okay, I'll check it," Yienger assured him.

Next, Flowers asked Yienger for a progress report on something the hotel was thinking of introducing: an amenity that would change every day and be left in the rooms during the afternoon turn-down service.

"Well, we've had some discussions about this," Yienger said. "We've discussed having a different message on a little card every night. They actually do that in Westin's Hawaii property. I think what they do there is use quotes from different authors. Uplifting sort of stuff. We're still working on something, but I've got nothing concrete yet."

Yienger then folded his arms and said, "By the way, I just saw the trailer for the new movie *Big Business*. There's a great full-front scene of the Plaza, and the trailer says it was filmed at the world-famous Plaza hotel. So we get a great plug."

"That's terrific," Flowers said.

Bob Bachofen, the food and beverage head, wanted to show the group a mock-up of a new house champagne. He passed a color photograph of it around the table. The label simply read "Plaza," though the champagne was made by Charles Heidsieck.

Flowers looked at it and made a frown. "Did we discuss this? The fact that a house label is thought of as inferior?"

"I think we're okay on champagne," Hinton put in. "And the Charles Heidsieck name appears on the glass. So we're okay."

Time passed, and Bill Reis's turn came. The comptroller handed out a recent analysis of American Express charges in the hotel, pointing out the surprisingly high percentages that foreigners accounted for.

Hinton gave a low whistle. "I never would have guessed that twenty-five percent of our American Express charges were foreign."

Flowers said, "And look at the average charge by foreigners: four hundred and twenty-five dollars. For Americans, it's one ninety. When the foreigners spend, they spend big."

Flowers rubbed at his nose and asked Hinton whether the new amenities for the guest rooms had arrived yet.

"They're in the rooms," Hinton said.

Bill Reis said, "One concern I have is they don't include tooth-paste and mouthwash."

"We can do the mouthwash," Hinton said. "But the belief is people travel with toothpaste and so it's not a good amenity."

"Well, why do I always forget it?" Reis said.

"That's something you'll have to deal with," Hinton said.

Flowers now wanted to show the group something he had been working on, a new gift that could be given to special guests. He reached into a large manila envelope and removed a woman's scarf. He spread it out on the table. It was light blue, with the Plaza's double-P insignia in the middle and red-and-gold trim around the outside.

The others seemed to think it was very nice. "My only question is, do we know what colors the ladies buy?" Hinton said.

"I showed it to my wife and she said you can wear it with anything," Flowers said.

"If you want to make some points," Reis said, "ask Ivana Trump."

"Bingo," Flowers said. "Got the answer on that."

The meeting was winding down when Yienger had a question. "One thing I was wondering about. Are we all supposed to punch in and out? Two people asked me that today."

Jeffrey Sablick, the stout, red-cheeked director of human resources, said, "The official policy is everyone punches. The practice is upper management doesn't."

"The problem," Flowers said, "is if we were a new hotel, right out of the box, we could do it. But it's been done the other way for years. So we've let it go except for the rank and file."

Flowers added that it also didn't matter to him which entrance the employees came in. There was an employees' entrance in the basement, which most of the rank and file used, though management people typically came in the lobby entrances.

The discussion seemed to rub Hinton the wrong way. "I'm opposed to that," he spoke up. "I think it looks shitty to have the employees walk through the front door. I come from the school where the employees don't walk through that door. It pisses me off that I see employees waiting for the elevator in the morning. Why can't they take the goddam steps, like I do?"

Flowers didn't think Hinton's objections had much merit. "The thing is," he said, "if you make a policy and people have been here twenty years, it looks chickenshit to tell them they must do something differently just because it sounds like a good idea."

"Well, I don't think it's chickenshit," Hinton said. "It creates a privileged class."

"There is a privileged class," Flowers said. "If you're the manager of something, certain things come with that. You work toward that. I don't like making people do things when we're not solving a problem or anything. I just don't think it's a positive message."

Sablick glanced knowingly at Flowers and said, "Last thing. Do we want to have a warm-up golf outing prior to May 22?"

Flowers said, "I think it's absolutely necessary."

"Also, I hear spring cod and pollack are running," Sablick said. "Should I look into it?"

Flowers's eyes lit up. "Yes," he said. "Definitely do that."

3

J EFFREY Flowers was a relaxed, confident man. As the managing director, he worried about the overall goals of the hotel, and he reported directly to Ivana Trump, the president of the Plaza, though she had not yet become actively involved with the hotel. Flowers rarely met any of the hotel's guests, except for the truly important ones. When an irate guest banged his fist on the front desk and demanded to see the manager at once, it was Hud Hinton who got the call.

Both Flowers and Hinton lived right in the hotel. That was a New York custom, I was told. Hotel managers had found that to do their jobs right they needed to live in close proximity, and yet their pay was not so high that they could afford an apartment in midtown Manhattan. So most resided in their hotels. Hinton, along with his wife and two children, occupied a three-bedroom suite on the seventh floor, adjacent to Room 764. Flowers lived up in the magnificent eighteenth-floor penthouse, along with his wife and a young daughter and son (another son was at the Naval Academy).

Harry Black, who started out as a Northwest adventurer and had become the head of the United States Realty and Improvement Corporation when it built the Plaza, originally lived in the penthouse, which was then a seventeen-room apartment. As he moved into his late sixties, Black began to be overtaken by moods of lingering sadness, and one day in October 1929 he was discovered unconscious with his head underwater in one of the bathtubs of his suite. Doctors worked over him for nine hours and managed to save his life. The following July, however, when he was at his estate at Lloyd Harbor, Long Island, he put a bullet through his head, and this time there was no saving him.

The next occupant of the penthouse was John Barry Ryan of the Thomas Fortune Ryan family. After he left, the Gardiner School for Girls took up quarters, before being displaced by *Gourmet* magazine. In the middle 1960s, *Gourmet* moved and the penthouse was transformed into several offices and an apartment for the manager. Victor Posner, the wealthy Florida investor, occupied the apartment for a while in the mid-1970s, when he was chairman of the Sharon Steel Corporation. At that time, the place rented for $100,000 a year. It included four bedrooms, a wine vault, kitchen, breakfast room, card parlor, game room, dining room, living room, and various smaller chambers. Later on, Posner became the object of a complaint by the Securities and Exchange Commission. Among other alleged infractions, it was asserted that he and his son and daughter charged more than $1.7 million worth of personal housing, services, and travels to companies that he and his family controlled. Included in that amount was the suite at the Plaza, which the SEC said was used only occasionally for business purposes and more often purely for Posner's fun. That abruptly ended Posner's need for the top floor.

ABC leased the suite next, using it for its own executives and as a place to put up special guests and to throw parties. Barbara Walters conducted some of her televised interviews there. When Capital Cities Communications, a notoriously pinchpenny broadcast company, bought ABC in 1985, one of the first actions its management took was to relinquish the Plaza penthouse. At the time, ABC was paying $30,000 a month. Afterward the hotel rented out rooms in it to transient guests but found it difficult to keep it sufficiently full; the place was remote from the rest of the hotel, and the rooms had not been renovated in a long time and were somewhat shabby. Attempts were made to entice another corporation to rent it as ABC had. Beatrice Foods and various real estate brokers took a look at it, but nobody felt it was quite right. Finally the Plaza decided to renovate it for its managing director. It was not the most convenient place. For one thing, only one of the hotel's service elevators went to the penthouse. As a result, it was a hellish proposition to throw a party up there, which had been a serious drawback when the hotel had tried to rent it out.

Once you got to the floor, a long, winding hallway led to the entryway of the penthouse. Inside, another long hallway beckoned. Off it were three bedrooms. One was good-sized, with an attached bath and sauna; Flowers's daughter used it. The second was quite small—his son had that—but it connected to a pleasant wood-paneled room with a wet bar that the children used as a playroom. (ABC had equipped it with a pool table.) The master bedroom was spacious and had its own private bath. The hallway concluded in an oval foyer that led to a large living room with a marble fireplace and chandelier. There, among other things, was the Flowerses' baby grand piano. Adjacent to the living room was a sizable dining room with a long rectangular table. Then there was a small pantry, a comfortable kitchen, and a breakfast nook. A back hallway had a half bath off it, and a bank-vault-type door opened into what had been intended as a wine cellar. The Flowerses stashed a few bottles in it, but mostly they used it as a storage closet for kids' bicycles, unused lamps, and other miscellany of family life. They had had the lock removed to prevent the kids or their cat from being imprisoned in it. A narrow circular stairway led to an upstairs, where there was a low-ceilinged bedroom and a room that the Flowerses used as a den. There was also a square outdoor patio covered with green Astroturf. It would have been a splendid place for outdoor dining, except that the huge kitchen exhaust pipes on the roof of the hotel shot their fumes right over it.

Flowers had mixed feelings about living in the hotel. The good side of it was he never had to worry about commuter traffic, and he had an unbeatable view. On alternate weekends, though, he tried to get to a country house he owned in upstate New York. "The downside to living here is you're never out of the hotel," he told me. "You're always under scrutiny. Everyone knows if you're in or out, so there's a lack of privacy. Sometimes I go seven or eight days and never leave the building. That's a little strange." Another drawback to living in the place where he worked was that it was difficult for Flowers to shed his managerial persona during his off-duty hours, because his comings and goings were so visible to his guests and employees. Every so often, he would be heading off to the country for a weekend of fun and come down the elevators into the lobby in sport shirt and shorts, and he would hurry a bit, hoping no one he knew well would spot him.

I met Flowers in his office. He walked in, sat down behind his desk, and picked at his fingernails. "The nature of hotels is you're constantly dealing with a moving target," he said. "Circumstances change by the minute. So I try to keep my calendar fairly clear."

Flowers had taken the top job at the Plaza in the middle of 1984, and in the subsequent years he had been ever busy trying to restore some of the lost glory of the hotel and to keep the Plaza competitive in what is one of the best hotel cities in the world. Hotel people think that Hong Kong is probably the best city of all in which to operate, and they place Seoul, South Korea, second, but New York is not far behind. The city has a hundred thousand hotel rooms, but there are months during the spring and fall when barely one is available. "What happens in hotels is that as time goes on, problems develop," Flowers said. "You address a problem and you put a Band-Aid on it and it goes away. Then that problem goes someplace else and you put a Band-Aid on that. After a while, you have Band-Aids all over the place. That's about what it's been like here."

I asked Flowers to tell me about those who stayed at the hotel.

"The profile of the Plaza guest is upscale, discriminating. He understands what the product is and pays for it," he said. "That's the profile of any luxury-hotel customer. The typical customer is the senior-middle-management business type on an expense account. He comes from Monday through Thursday. He's here to meet with a banker or an architect or someone like that, or to sell a product or service. He's here on individual business. Then there's the CEO type, who's here for a speech or a meeting or a trade show.

The trade show may be at the Hilton, but he won't stay there. He's got to be at the Plaza. Then there's the small business meeting. Salomon Brothers is going to bring in some investors. They want a luncheon for thirty-five people and a deluxe suite. Then you're going to have an incentive group—the top Chevrolet dealers in the country. They're going to come in and go down and see *Cats* and eat some pasta at Mama Leone's. None of these people are paying their own way. Then there are high rollers on their own. They go to Europe on their own and come here on their own. And there's the celebrity market. There's a great deal of traffic between Los Angeles and New York. We always do a fair amount of junket business. Orion Pictures, for instance, may fly a bunch of people in for a screening.

"There's also quite a bit of overseas business traffic," Flowers continued. "That's a bit different. The overseas traveler stays a little longer. The European custom is different. They use the hotel a lot. Use the hotel dining room. The shops. Best of all, they're not looking for a discount. That's a great customer. We love those European customers.

"These are all the Monday-through-Thursday customers. They come seven months of the year—in the spring and the fall. The problem is, what about the other five months and Friday, Saturday, and Sunday? The second week of January, nobody's here. There's a marketing challenge to fill the hotel in the months when the chairman or whatever isn't here. He's not going to come in the middle of July. Hell no. He's out on his yacht or in the south of France. So we look for people like a couple who want to make a trip to New York for a special occasion. A couple with an anniversary, say. Thus we have a special weekend package for Friday, Saturday, and Sunday at fifty percent off. And we fill the hotel. We're getting a lot of the same profile—the guy with champagne taste—but he's paying his own way.

"We do continue to have a Sunday-night problem," Flowers said with a slight frown. "That guy who stayed Friday and Saturday night on his own nickel has to get back and get the kids ready for school or mow the grass. The high roller on an expense account doesn't travel on Sunday. He comes in on Monday. The individual traveler is known in the industry as an FIT, or free independent traveler. So, to solve Sunday, we try to get that individual traveler in for another reason. We use the group reason. Like we offer runners group discounts for the New York Marathon so they'll stay Sunday night. We'll make concessions to small conferences if they come in, say, February. We'll give them four-hundred-dollar rooms for a hundred and fifty. We offer this outside the seven peak months. We call this marketing mix. If we're going to get more business, we see it coming from the group market. That's where we're focusing our efforts. In the past, we haven't been that aggressive in the group market. We really have to be now. There are more hotel rooms in the city now—so when there's a valley, there's a deeper valley."

Flowers talked numbers. "This hotel, when everything's going right, should have an average occupancy of eighty percent. That's going some, because every month you run seventy percent, you have to have a month where you run ninety. So you need to have good inventory management. October, May, April—depending on when Easter falls—are the months where we have the potential to run ninety percent plus. Sunday night tends to be fifty percent or less, far below anything else. Saturday or Friday may be eighty percent. So you can see the pressure on Monday through Thursday."

Flowers's father was in the construction business and his mother was in real estate. "My father built a restaurant for a guy and wrote paper on it," he told me. "The restaurant went broke and Dad foreclosed on it and so we had a restaurant. I was in high school. We all sort of worked there. I'd go there on weekends and would cook and wait on tables. That was my first introduction to food and beverage. In college, I managed our fraternity house and got a little experience from that. In the Navy, I was in charge of food service on a major ship. I was also a licensed real estate broker and put myself through college selling real estate."

Flowers grew up in the state of Washington and graduated from Seattle University. He entered the service and became a naval officer. For a while, he was out on a ship, and then in 1966 he was stationed in Malaysia as the officer in charge of a rest and rehabilitation center for U.S. forces. There were nine R&R centers spaced throughout the Pacific. Flowers was assigned to Penang, a compact island resort in northern Malaysia, ninety miles south of the Thai border. It was a lovely area. They would send Pan American charter flights to these resort centers with soldiers bushed from Vietnam duty. They would come in their battle fatigues and stay there for five days. The first thing Flowers did was buy them a cold Tiger beer. As it happened, he struck a deal with the local beer supplier. He told him that these soldiers were big beer drinkers; give them some free beer, and they would become familiar with the brand and keep buying it. Besides offering them refreshment, Flowers would make hotel reservations and organize beach parties for the soldiers, as well as operate sight-seeing tours. The guys had a bawdy time, but, Flowers remembered, "I was there for a year and I never had to bail anybody out of jail."

The work got Flowers interested in the hotel business. "Sitting in Malaysia at night, I didn't have much to do, and so I wrote letters to the various hotel companies. I got a lot of form letters back, except one personal one from Westin. They were headquartered in Seattle. I interviewed there and got a job in 1969 at the Olympic Hotel in Seattle and worked in the mail room." He moved into sales and then into management, going to the Westin St. Francis in San Francisco, the Westin Ilikai in Honolulu, the Mayflower Hotel in Washington, D.C., the Philippine Plaza in Manila, and the Shangri-La Hotel in Hong Kong. Then he came to New York.

"I didn't know what I'd find at the Plaza," he said. "I still don't. Every morning when I get up, I don't know what I'm going to find."

4

PROBLEMS with a bathtub on the tenth floor. A call came in to the building department, down in the nether catacombs that were the subbasement. The dispatcher answered the phone. "Uh-huh, stopper doesn't work. . . . Right. . . . Ten forty-nine. . . . We'll send someone right up."

Tony Villafane was free and was given the assignment. He was one of four plumbers on duty. They were needed. Every day, there were three to five clogged toilets, a couple of improperly draining sinks, some broken pipes. Guests threw things down the pipes—combs, cups, rags. The plumbers had to root them out.

"Most of the calls are to report stoppages," Villafane told me on the way up to the room. "Dripping we don't get too much of anymore, because everything is new. Before we replaced them, we used to get a lot of leaking faucets. Most of the stoppages are too much hair. A lot of hair goes in the drain and eventually it clogs. Simple as that. Then people drop stuff in. They drop in small bottles. They drop in small towels. They drop in bobby pins. They'd drop in suitcases if they'd fit. I'm surprised they don't drop themselves in."

Nobody answered Villafane's knock at 1049, so he let himself in and headed straight for the bathroom. In manner, he seemed pretty diffident. The only problem, he discovered with a sigh of exasperation, was that the bathtub stopper had come off its chain. All that was needed was a new ring. Irritably, he dug into his pockets, but couldn't find one and had to return to the subbasement.

When we got there, he marched up to a counter where a small man sat—the supply center, a veritable hardware store, open only to the maintenance staff. On the shelves behind the counter I saw an explosion of faucets, pipes, mops, friction tape, caulk, Janitor in a Drum. Villafane requested a ring.

"Don't know if I got a ring, Tony," the small man said tersely, and he got up and walked down the rows of supplies. He stopped before one bin and fumbled around in it. "Well, I was wrong," he said, shaking his head in puzzled disbelief. "Got a ring after all."

Villafane took it and offered grumbled thanks, and we went back to await the next service elevator. "Elevators are awful here," he said. "I spend most of my life waiting to go up and go down. I've given most of the best years of my life to these elevators." Once he was back in the room, he fiddled with the ring for a few minutes, using a pair of pliers to tighten it, and pronounced the stopper fixed.

I remarked that it seemed like an awful lot of trouble to go to just to have a stopper attached to its chain.

Villafane shrugged, as if he had heard that line one too many times. "People want things perfect here," he said. "Some of these guests probably couldn't figure out how to get that stopper out unless there was a chain attached to it. I'm not knocking them, but they're sort of helpless, if you know what I mean."

On the way back downstairs, he said, "I like the retrieval work better. It's more exciting. Sometimes guests call and say they've dropped an earring or a ring in the sink. We have to open up the pipes. Usually we get it. About four weeks ago, I got an earring. Not long ago, I got a contact lens out of the sink pipe. The man was very happy about that one. I was pretty proud of myself. What these people drop in is unbelievable. You got any kids? Because that's what it's like. It's like watching kids."

•   •   •

JOHN Petrolino, the Plaza superintendent, liked to say that his building-operations department was the heartbeat of the hotel. He was the best person to seek out for anyone who had encountered something less than perfect. A miscellany of specialties fell under his control. His people repaired chandeliers. They oiled stoves. They kept track of the temperature. They fixed broken chairs. They silenced sputtering toilets. "Eventually," he told me, "everything that goes on in the hotel in some shape or form filters through building operations. I'm talking everything from a leaky faucet in a guest room to a fifty-thousand-dollar banquet. I'm not saying I'm glad it all filters through here. I'm just telling you that it does."

Petrolino was an amiable man in his early forties. He was firmly put together. His ovoid head was covered with curly white hair. For seven years, he had been the Plaza superintendent. Seventy people worked for him—electricians, engineers, plumbers, a laundry mechanic, a welder, three stove cleaners. "I've got a guy who, first thing in the morning, goes around to every kitchen and checks that the ice machines are working," he said. "We've got about thirty-five ice machines, so it's no soft job." He cleared his throat. "Every day, there are three or four rooms deliberately put out of service. Nobody can sleep in them. And then we do preventive maintenance. That's called 'maintaining the product.' We paint them, shampoo the carpets, tighten up drawers, fix the wallpaper —you name it. That's how you keep a hotel fit."

He blew his nose. "The thing that really gets to people is toilets," he said. "A clogged toilet is an immediate response. Immediate. Has to be. I've got a case I'm investigating right now. This guy said his wife noticed that the toilet water level was rising. He said a man came and looked at it and left black boot marks on the carpet and they had to get housekeeping to clean it up. The next day, he said his wife spotted the water rising again and so he went and threw a Kleenex in it and the toilet overflowed and soaked the carpet. Now, I don't want to say his wife threw a Kotex in it. But that happens more times than not."

Petrolino took a walk through the electrical shop, where a couple of toasters that were no longer properly toasting bread were disassembled on one of the workbenches. Several electrical grates from fireplaces were also awaiting attention. Hanging from the ceiling were thirteen exquisite chandeliers that stuck out in the drabness and disorder of the room. Petrolino gave the chandeliers a long, professional sniff. "These need more work," he said. "No way we put those babies back out in public view. More work. Definitely more work."

One of the electricians was tinkering with a vacuum cleaner that had the miseries. The top of his head was slick with perspiration. "We get at least twenty vacuum cleaners a day," he said. "The belts break. The cords break. Mostly it's misuse. The maids don't know how to put a bag in there or they work them too hard. We get lamps. Sometimes if a guest has a problem with an iron or a tape recorder, we'll fix it at no charge. You know Led Zeppelin, the rock band? They were here once and ruined a TV by letting candle wax drip down inside it. But mostly it's the same stuff over and over again."

Petrolino strolled over to the carpentry shop a little way down the corridor. "We repair chairs in here," he said. "We build new cabinets. We install hardware. We make displays for pastry chefs to present wedding cakes on. We make all the signs here." There was an "Exit" sign currently being worked on. Propped against the back wall was a tremendous wooden egg; at Easter, it got coated with chocolate and was put out in the lobby. Once things were built, they were carted up to the roof, where the hotel's paint shop was located. It was up there because of the fire hazard of the paints and oils.

The carpenters knelt on the floor. Music oozed from a radio. Tacked on the wall were insulting drawings of various members of the department. One of the carpenters confided that sketching was how they passed the slow hours. He took a moment to explain the nature of the work. "We get a lot of broken chairs. Somebody recently got drunk and couldn't get his key in the door and so he kicked in the door. Broke the whole damn frame. We had to fix it.

Every day something breaks. Guests try to remove headboards from the beds. The headboards are fastened to the wall and aren't to be removed. But they want to move the bed for one reason or another and they break the headboard. Guests come in and they want to redecorate the room and they're only here overnight. It's kind of absurd."

Petrolino elaborated. "One day we ended up with a headboard that was broken in three different places. I figure there must have been some awfully wild sex on that bed. Another time, a high chair came down broken in three pieces. Who sat in that? A gorilla? It's unbelievable what comes down here. How these people break the stuff, I don't know."

Across the corridor was the machine shop. Mostly it fixed kitchen equipment. Tony Roje, who was in charge of the shop, had a helmet on and was working with a blowtorch on something from a stove. "I got a piece of luggage just before," he said. "The guest lost the key, so I drilled the rivets out and opened it up. Most times that happens, the key is inside the suitcase. Stupid. We get bicycles here, too. People bring them and something goes wrong and they want me to fix them. I get a few wheelchairs from the handicapped. But most of my work is machines—stoves, dishwashers, washing machines. This place has seventy reach-in refrigerators and thirty-five walk-in freezers. So stuff is always breaking down."

Petrolino returned to his office and looked over the latest litany of grievances. Faucets. Drains. A lack of hot water. "We've got a small city here," he said. "In a small city, you've always got plumbing problems every day."

His biggest worry, he told me, was fire. "That has to be the worst," he said. "We've had some minor ones—grease fires in the kitchen—but that's about it. We've never had a big fire, thank God. I thank my lucky stars every day for that."

Some calls, understandably, got him fuming. A great many of the guest rooms contained fireplaces. Many years ago, they worked; now all of them have been plugged up. One day, a call came to building operations from a guest wondering where he could get some kindling wood. He was having difficulty keeping his fire blazing. Men were rushed to the room. It was filled with smoke. The man had just thrown in the telephone book.

Floods were also not unknown in the hotel. "What happens is a guest comes back from a party late at night and maybe has had too much to drink, and he turns on the tub and then lies down and falls asleep," Petrolino said. "That's a common occurrence. It happens about every couple of weeks. We have to mop up the place and then go and repair the ceiling below. There's nothing much you can do about that. We can't control partying and drinking, though sometimes I wish we could."

Petrolino fell silent. "Oh well," he said, shoving aside a stack of messages. "The calls never stop. The hotel's old. It's like an old lady. She looks good on the outside, because she puts on a lot of makeup. But on the inside, she's kind of messy."

5

*T*ALKING to a bright-eyed Midwestern businessman in his tenth-floor room, I was sternly instructed by him not to mention his name. He had brought his wife along, he explained, which was not exactly in keeping with company policy. "She gave me a hard time," he said. "She wanted to see New York. She wanted to see the Plaza. So what's she seeing? The insides of the stores on Fifth Avenue."

The man had the television on with the volume turned low. Some soap-opera people were sitting on a velvet couch, drinks in their hands, having a conversation that was tilting toward an argument. "Whenever I'm in a hotel room, I have to keep the TV on," the man said. "It makes me feel more like I'm at home. I'm in a lot of hotel rooms, believe me, and they can get to you—even nice ones like here. So I keep the TV going."

Excusing himself, he said he needed something to tide himself over until dinner, so he dialed room service and ordered soup and a pot of coffee. "Coffee here really sucks," he said, "but I love the cups and the little Plaza napkins. Knocks me out."

The food ordered, he took a seat, showing off perfect posture, and gave me a wooden look. He seemed a little embarrassed, but conversation worked to calm him. He said he had a wild story to tell about his last stay at the Plaza, a little over a year ago, as long as it was on deep background. "I was down at the Oak Bar having a drink after dinner, and I ran into these guys," he said. "There were four of them. They were businessmen from different parts of the country and they had reason to be in New York a few times a year. They always stayed at the Plaza. They said they coordinated one trip a year so they would be here at the same time and could play an all-night poker game. Good stakes. A good pot. Well, I always thought of myself as a halfway decent poker man. I used to play all the time in college. I mean, all the time. So I got suckered in. We went up to one of the guys' rooms. He had a portable table all set—chips, cards, a card shuffler. Unfortunately, there was plenty of booze, too."

Hitting a full house and then three eights, the man got a fairly good start, he told me, won a few pots, lost a few small ones. Then, slowed by booze, he bet badly. He drew dismal cards. He started to lose with ripping velocity. "After a couple of hours, I was down ten grand," he said. "But there was no getting out of there. Three hours later, when I couldn't sit up anymore, I was down thirty-five thousand."

The man talked nonstop and a little anxiously, as if he were desperate to share his story, not caring that he was telling it to a total stranger. The shame of his performance, he said, kept him from staying in touch with his poker partners. He gave them a phony company and number so they couldn't reach him. Afterward, he said, he felt like a beaten boxer—hit hard, with welts all over his face and lumps rising on his head. His trip wrecked, he just went through the motions at the next day's round of business meetings. Someone who knew him well asked if he was having trouble at home.

"My God, what a time that was," he said. "Awful. Just awful. I remember this fat, disgusting guy from Texas was the big winner. Smoked cigars and really held his liquor. He bet like a crazed man, but he always had the cards. Nobody could beat him. Back at the office, believe me, I kept my lips buttoned about the whole mess. Think of the stink."

"Why are you here?" I asked, a little tired of hearing about the pounding.

"Oh, the usual. Business meetings with the Eastern district.

You know the scene: slide shows, lunches, reports. Talk, talk, talk."

"Sounds less exciting than last time," I remarked.

"Listen, don't start that. I can do without that kind of excitement," he said. "I'm a pretty straight-arrow guy. No one likes to drop money like that, even if you've got a nice nest egg. I'll tell you the worst thing about it. Ever since I've gotten here, I've been afraid one of the others will be around. I know the odds are small, but you never know. And with my wife here, all I need is for one of those bastards to come strutting toward me and boom, 'Hey, we've been looking for you. How's about another poker game so you can make up for the drubbing?' I mean, I would die."

Now the man got up. Our conversation was over. He reached for his briefcase and tapped it. "Got some reports to review. Pays the bills, you know."

ALF a dozen people sat around the desk in Jeffrey Flowers's office. They were passing the time while waiting for the meeting to start. Every afternoon at four o'clock there was a so-called VIP meeting among various key department heads. The purpose was to run through the next day's significant arrivals and to determine how they should be welcomed. Presiding over the session was Harvey Robbins, a young man with an anxious-to-please personality whose title was guest-relations manager but whose basic function was to satisfy the needs of VIPs.

Fixed criteria had been established for VIP treatment. A VIP was someone classified by the sales team as important (even if it was a first visit) or someone who came all the time. People who might bring the hotel further business, such as meeting planners, automatically vaulted onto the VIP list. Meeting planners, in fact, could often stay for free and eat for free, depending on how many meetings they spoke for. A planner for the American Medical Association, which scheduled thousands of meetings a year, could pretty much stay anywhere and eat anything on the house. Chairmen and presidents of companies, as well as politicians, were also automatic VIPs. Guests celebrating their honeymoon or an anniversary made the grade. (A happy honeymoon couple will often return for subsequent anniversaries.) Movie stars and other celebrities got on the list—if the hotel knew they were coming, since many of them register under false names to avoid being swarmed by fans. The majority of VIPs, though, were repeat guests who were not even faint household names. There were guests who came every month. There were every-other-week guests. And there were guests who checked in on a weekly basis. "There's one middle-aged gentleman," a staffer told me, "and I don't know how he keeps his family together, but he's here every week. And not for a day. It's three, four nights."

Curiously, people who paid full freight were considered VIPs at the Plaza. With all the corporate rates, group packages, and special discounts, it was relatively rare for any guest to pay the room price that was listed in the rate pamphlet—the so-called rack rate. The Plaza was so thrilled when someone did consent to pay the full amount that it automatically inducted him into VIP-hood.

There was no greater VIP at the Plaza, however, than Harry Mullikin. Although he was unknown to much of the world, his status as the chief executive officer of the Westin Hotels Corporation accorded him super treatment at any of the hotels owned or run by Westin. When he was checking in, Jeffrey Flowers himself inspected his room beforehand and searched for any lurking crumb or bits of lint.

At VIP meetings, strategy was mapped out. The most important thing about VIP service was that the person's room was blocked out in advance and inspected for cleanliness by either an assistant housekeeper or an assistant manager. Additional amenities went in the rooms, including a Gucci gift box of soaps and white terry-cloth robes. Records were kept of repeat visitors so they would get a little something extra. A guest staying at the hotel for the fifth time, for example, always received a tray of candies or a small desk clock. Someone on his tenth trip got a Plaza history book and a card from the manager. The twentieth time merited a free weekend at the hotel.

At the VIP meeting, further amenities could be ordered for arriving guests, such as roses or other favored flowers. These were placed in the room within fifteen minutes of the guest's arrival, and Robbins knew about certain vital phrases in the language of flowers: someone of the Muslim faith wouldn't find white flowers, a symbol of mourning, in his room, and a Mexican visitor wouldn't get gardenias for the same reason. Or the treat might be a tin of cookies, Plaza ashtrays, wine or liquor, chocolate-covered strawberries, bottled waters of different kinds, or fruit. VIPs were preregistered, got priority luggage service, received a telephone call from Harvey Robbins or an assistant manager within a half hour of arrival to see if everything was all right, got ice service between four and five in the afternoon, received turn-down service between seven and eight in the evening rather than at four, and could check out as late as four in the afternoon for no extra charge.

All those things were automatic. The hotel management would accede to the most preposterous additional requests in order to make a big spender happy. Some could be real pains. King Hassan II of Morocco was well known among Plaza employees as a most valuable VIP. He had visited the hotel several times. On his most recent trip, he had occupied the sixth floor, wanting connecting rooms from 629 through 641. All of the rooms already happened to be connecting, except for one. The maintenance staff knocked a hole in the wall and installed a door. The cost was about $10,000, which the king paid for. He brought his own security men, who carried rifles and guns. He brought his own collection of mattresses (it was his custom to change mattresses every day). He was afforded a section of the main kitchen, where his personal chefs did the cooking and served him his meals in his room. Since alcoholic beverages are denied Muslims, they consumed gallons of orange juice, soft drinks, and coffee. A tremendous amount of incense was burned. Several times it set off smoke alarms, prompting the king's staff to ask the hotel if the alarms could be disabled. The hotel politely demurred. Months after the king had left, employees swore they could still smell the incense. One member of the hotel's staff was assigned to the king throughout his stay, and she moved into a room in the hotel. "She was an indentured servant," one of the hotel executives said of her assignment.

Why go to such bother? Money talks loudly in a hotel, and the king's wallet was shouting. He wound up spending something like $1 million in room charges and food and beverage orders. He was the biggest-spending guest the hotel had ever had. The employees had their own specific reason for liking the man. He tipped them with Rolex watches.

Everyone at the meeting was handed a list of the arriving VIPs, and Harvey Robbins rattled off the names. Twenty-three people appeared on the list, none a recognizable name to the world at large. The sheet revealed that a few of them had made special room requests. Two wanted to be sure they were getting king-sized beds. One man, presumably disliking heights, wanted a low floor. Another man wished an interior-facing room, a means of dodging street noises. As Robbins recited the names, Flowers or one of the others would occasionally interrupt to suggest an amenity.

For one woman, Flowers said, "Okay, she's here for a week. Let's give her some cookies to start out. Later on, maybe some fruit."

Another woman, staying nine days: "She should be getting some fruit."

"Any preference on the fruit?" Robbins asked.

"Make it a nice selection."

A man who was a meeting planner: "Definitely wine and cheese. Don't miss that one. That man has regularly brought us business."

Another guest coming for a week: "Cookies."

A honeymoon couple came up, and Robbins said they would be getting a complimentary bottle of champagne.

"Naturally," Flowers said.

AFTER the VIP meeting, Harvey Robbins and I returned to his office near the front desk. He had details to attend to. "It's crazy the things that matter to people," he told me. "Take room numbers. Some guests only want a particular room number, and I've got to juggle rooms to try to satisfy everyone." One guest—a man in the paper industry—felt that 33 was his lucky number. He conducted a lot of business in New York and had become convinced that staying in a lucky-numbered room had helped him immeasurably in his deals. Whenever he booked a room, 33 had to be part of its number.

Robbins's father had owned a couple of hotels near Gramercy Park. As a kid, Robbins would sometimes fill in at the front desk, soaking in the rhythms of hotel life. Later on, he worked for eight years at the Pan American Motor Inn in Queens, which was owned by an uncle. The motel did a lot of airport business, helped by the fact that it provided free round-trip transportation to both La-Guardia and Kennedy airports. Robbins rose to manager, but, in the long span of things, he couldn't shake a desire to work at the Plaza. "Growing up in New York," he said, "everyone always drove past the Plaza and wondered, 'Oh, what's it like at the Plaza?' " Three years before, he had responded to an ad in the *New York Times* for an assistant-manager position. On the day he was hired, he ran to the first pay phone and called all his friends.

"In a hotel, you meet the most amazing people," he said. "That's what I like about the work. A few months ago, I was escorting the prince of Kuwait out. He stayed a week and spent something like twelve to fifteen thousand dollars and didn't bat an eye. He slept all day, had breakfast at eight in the evening, and went out all night. He was here strictly for pleasure, though I understand he did buy a yacht."

Robbins gave me a rundown on his duties. "I make sure that any VIP who has a complaint, a problem, or a request gets taken care of and leaves the hotel happy. That's my goal, that everyone leave the hotel happy. One of the most important things for our VIPs is that a housekeeping supervisor does a double check on the room. If it's a really big wheel, I'll check it, too. After you've been cleaning for two hours, you lose objectivity. So a pair of fresh eyes can pick out that spot or that lint that's been missed. It can make the difference in how happy someone's stay was.

"If they use the laundry, I make sure the clean clothes get sent up on time. The laundry has a board with the VIPs posted on it, and their laundry gets special attention. They make sure it's not overstarched or understarched. Occasionally we get a shirt pressed and the cuff has an extra crease or there's an iron burn. So those clothes have to be checked an extra time. Normally we wash things in an hour, but if a VIP wants it in a half hour, we make sure it's picked up in thirty seconds and it gets washed in thirty minutes. We don't mean to say we neglect the other guests—it's just that we raise service to an extraordinary level for the VIPs. That's why they're designated VIPs."

Robbins took a phone call and made a few careful notes—flower arrangements for a couple of rooms. Restfulness again settled over the VIP desk. Robbins continued, "The biggest request we get is VIP families traveling together who want to be near each other. That sounds like a snap, but it's very hard to do when we're running close to full. Occasionally people want to cook for themselves. They want a toaster oven. Fire regulations won't permit it. We aren't even allowed to put an extension cord in a room because of fire regulations.

"Some of the Middle Eastern guests stay on the same biological clock when they travel. They buy their way through jet lag, I guess is one way to look at it. They eat lunch at four in the morning. They eat dinner at seven in the morning. So we have to have chefs on duty at odd hours to serve them."

Vivian Fiol, Robbins's predecessor in the job, who now was stationed on the concierge desk, once found it necessary to arrange a wedding. "This couple from California came in," she recalled. "They took a white stretch limousine all the way here. They had never been to New York before, but they loved the hotel and they decided to get married right here. I had to start from scratch. It was going to happen in two days. I had to get the ring. I had to get a minister to come to the hotel. Believe me, in this city that's not easy to do. A minister, whatever the faith, doesn't like to come to a hotel to perform a service. He wants you to go to the church. Finally I found a minister of interfaith. I had to run around with the groom until he found a suit he liked. I had to get the flowers. I got the decorations. I set up the mantel. I called room service and told them when to come in with the champagne. The only thing I didn't do—he did this—was order the dress for the lady. Then I had to get her ready. I fixed her hair. In this job, sometimes you have to be a hairdresser, too. I set up the altar. It turned out that I was a witness to the wedding. One of the drivers was the other witness. They were so happy. She loved the ring. I found out he was a restaurant owner. He had about seven restaurants in California, so he was all set financially. That evening, they said they wanted to take me somewhere. I said, 'It's your wedding night,' but they said, 'No, no, we want to celebrate with you.' So they took me driving around the city and I pointed out some spots of interest. Then they said they loved hamburgers; where could they go for a hamburger? So I took them to Jackson's Hole and we sat there and had hamburgers."

ROBBINS needed to have some VIP rooms inspected, so he dispatched one of the currently idle assistant lobby managers, a young woman, to do the work, and I went along.

A large luxury hotel will typically have a few superdeluxe suites for heads of state or celebrities or chief executives who insist on superior accommodations. Because the Plaza was originally designed for permanent guests, it had an abundance of suites, about ninety of them. Opinions differed on which were the best rooms. The number 23 room on each floor overlooked both Fifth Avenue and Central Park, and many people thought these rooms were the most appealing in the house. Room 737 was the one in which *Plaza Suite* was filmed, and some people requested it for that reason alone. In the movie, though, the room number was changed to 719, because that was the number in the play. The actual room 719 in the Plaza would not have done. It was a small single with a bath. Room 737 overlooked the ritzy Bergdorf Goodman department store and, like the other suites in the 37 line, had sliding doors between the parlor room and the bedroom. The line was a little larger than the others, and so the hotel recommended one of them for people planning on doing some entertaining during their stay.

For many years, it was a matter of perpetual regret to the management that no one suite stood out as the best in the house, for there was always some especially treasured visitor who wanted something unique and would pay a solid premium for it. Hence in 1987, after some planning, a Presidential Suite was finally constructed on the third floor. Prior to building it, the hotel consulted with the staff of the White House to make sure it suited the needs of a president. For instance, special phones that connected the outside world directly to the suite, without passing through the switchboard, were incorporated into the design. The suite was flexible and could be arranged in several configurations; at its most spacious, it consisted of a large sleeping chamber, Mr. and Mrs. baths, a dayroom, a staff room, a private dining room, and a living room. The rate was $3,000 a day.

The other special room in the hotel was the large suite on the second floor above the Fifty-ninth Street corner of the Edwardian Room. Frank Lloyd Wright lived in it for five years in the early 1900s while he was designing the Guggenheim Museum and some of his other New York projects. The hotel painstakingly restored the suite so that it was essentially as it had been back when Wright inhabited it, except it chose not to duplicate the red-and-purple interior he favored. It was the only suite in the hotel with hardwood floors and area rugs instead of wall-to-wall carpeting. What's more, a picture gallery on one wall displayed Wright's work, and the room had been named the Frank Lloyd Wright Suite. If you wanted to sleep there, you paid a little extra.

There was no debate at all about which were the worst rooms in the Plaza. They were the single-bed group. Back when the hotel opened, the Carnegies and the Mellons used to check in with their servants for stays of months or years. Thus there were a lot of big rooms for the high rollers, but also a lot of small rooms where the help did their dreaming. The hotel has had as many as seventy-five rooms that were only large enough to handle a single bed. Some of them measured about eight by ten feet, a walk-in closet at home for the richer guests. Renovation work had eliminated most of these. Twenty of the miniature rooms, however, couldn't be done away with because structural problems would arise, and they remained in the inventory.

I inspected one of them—Room 724—and found it difficult to think of it as a room at the Plaza. It was about eight feet by fifteen. In fact, it was higher than it was wide. There was the single bed, a small desk, a tiny armoire with the TV situated in such a way it would have been nearly impossible to watch it from the bed, and a small bathroom. The chandelier hanging from the ceiling seemed almost to mock the modesty of the room. Employees and guests derisively referred to the tiny rooms as "closets." They were mostly rented to special customers. For instance, the Plaza sometimes rented out a block of rooms at a cheap rate to visiting ballet troupes or, say, the Berlin Philharmonic. Government employees might at times be bedded there. Their rules limited them to an outlay of $100 a night for a hotel room. With the government discount that the Plaza extended, the small rooms could be had for $99, making them the only place in the house for someone from the Department of Defense. The bellmen told me they tried to avoid getting a call from these rooms, because the tips were invariably small.

SUITE 329 was the lobby assistant's first stop. Like most Plaza rooms, it was generous in size, lit by chandeliers and with a marble fireplace equipped with decorative red lights hidden behind the grate. The ceiling was a good twelve feet high, one of the great features of Plaza rooms. Even the king-sized bed looked small in the room. For the most part, the furniture was nondescript contemporary. A Westin executive had been assigned the suite. He was bringing a baby, so a crib needed to be installed in the room. Management had also ordered an F.A.O. Schwarz teddy bear. The woman unlocked the door and went through her routine. First her eyes dove downward, as she checked the carpet for stains. It was stainless. She took a look at the curtains and discovered a small smear on one of them; she thought it might be all right. She took a look inside the minibar, located in the bottom of the armoire that held the television. It was fully stocked (and fully priced) with miniatures of hard liquor—Dewar's at $5.25; Glenfiddich at $6; Armagnac at $7; Rémy Martin VSOP at $7; champagne splits at

$11.50; Miller Lite at $3.75; wine cooler at $4.50; Evian water at $2.75; Plaza cashews at $12.50; potato chips at $1.50; macadamia nuts at $8.

She moved around the room. The desk chair was too far away; she shoved it closer. She ran her finger over the wooden window ledge, turned it over, and reviewed it. Dustless. Then she opened the closet adjacent to the bathroom, checking to make sure there were two of the terry-cloth Plaza robes hung in there. She clicked on the television and confirmed that the remote control functioned. *General Hospital* was in full steam. She ran her gaze along the walls and then up onto the ceilings, sniffing out cracks. She plucked a piece of lint off the carpet, then made sure that there was a Gucci gift box on the dresser. She moved into the second bedroom. She found only one bathrobe in the closet and made a note to get a second one there on the double.

She swept into Suite 436, her next stop. Immediately the room was declared unfit. A strip of wood had fallen off the armoire. "The room is not all right for a VIP," the woman declared. "This room is not okay. A regular guest could get a room without a piece of wood molding. But not a VIP." She phoned the building department to report the armoire, then called the front desk to get another room to replace this one.

The next room was no good either. The armoire doors stuck. The guest might have difficulty getting them open to watch TV. "We give this one a big thumbs-down," she said.

Then another dud. The bathroom ceiling was badly peeling, and as an additional indignity there was a burned-out light bulb. "This one's a joke," the woman said.

Another room. Another peeling ceiling. "No way," the woman said. "Boy, what a day I'm having."

I WENT back downstairs, where a man from Florida was momentarily disgruntled. He spilled his story to Robbins. On Sunday, when he was trying to get some work done in his room, he had been bothered by some unreasonably noisy drum players on Fifth

Avenue. He called down to the assistant manager on duty, but the playing persisted. The next day, the drums resumed, louder than ever. He called once again, and the woman who took the complaint said briskly, "The laws in New York are different from the laws in Florida." The man responded, "Bullshit. Do you have a law degree?" He then phoned the police himself, and the drum playing ceased within fifteen minutes.

The man told Robbins, "Something's wrong when a guest in one of your best suites gets treated like that. That means the hotel system is breaking down. That's exactly what it means. The system isn't working."

"This isn't the end of it," Robbins assured him. "I'm going to follow it up and look into it. You'll get a report back on this."

After the man left, Robbins returned to putting VIPs into rooms. "Looks like we've got the regular group of people to be pampered," he said.

The phone trilled. A small crisis. A woman had gotten trapped in an elevator between floors. Robbins scooped up his walkie-talkie and headed for the bank of elevators. One of his responsibilities was to make sure that someone was talking to her through the elevator intercom so she didn't get claustrophobia. As it turned out, she was freed in ten minutes, before deep panic could set in. "That was a short one," Robbins said, "but we'll still give her and her husband the usual treatment. To make them feel better, they'll get a comp breakfast in the Edwardian Room and we'll send an amenity—some fruit or some cheese—on up to their room later. We always do that when people get stuck in the elevator. It helps them get over the awful experience."

$$7$$

B Y now, the lobby lizards had come in and arranged themselves in the chairs they would occupy for the next few hours. Some had brought time-passing diversions along with them—a paperback crossword-puzzle book, some crocheting, a miniature tic-tac-toe game. Others found activity altogether unnecessary. To the employees of the hotel, the lizards were familiar oddities. They were elderly individuals who liked to stop by around four o'clock in the afternoon, when the daily violin and piano music started up in the Palm Court, and just sit serenely in the Fifth Avenue lobby and soak in the solace. "Jules and Paul" were the attraction—Jules on the piano and Paul on the violin. The lizards never took a table in the restaurant. They didn't eat or drink anything. They didn't spend a cent. Some of them jabbed cigar butts into the hotel's gleaming ashtrays or dragged mud over the sparkling carpeting. What did they care?

All midtown hotels attract a certain number of lobby lizards, often bums and bag ladies who sometimes curl up on a couch and nod off, but the Plaza seemed to get more than most places because of the available entertainment. They were a group that security was especially aware of, though as long as they maintained proper demeanor, weren't too sartorially bizarre, and raised no ruckus, the guards would just leave them alone. It would have been needlessly callous, after all, to kick out someone who at least looks vaguely respectable. "As long as they're clean, we'll let them be," John McHugh told me. "Hey, it's lonely out there for a lot of people. Why shouldn't we let them hear the music?"

Only one of the lizards had lately presented problems that required attention. She was a woman in her late fifties who would settle herself into a seat and listen to the music for an hour or two. After a while, however, she would get testy. She would start talking rather loudly to people walking past. She would tell them, "You know, I used to stay at this hotel all the time. I can tell you stories about it you wouldn't believe for a minute." Then she would say to someone else, "I used to have dinner in the Palm Court every night. And I mean every night. Money meant nothing to me. Nothing." With every comment, her voice would rise several decibels. At last, one of the security men would approach her. As soon as she spotted him creeping up, she would abruptly stand up, as if scalded by hot water, and scream, "Nazi action! Nazi action!" The security man would hurriedly show her to the door, and she would stand on the outside steps for a little while, repeating "Nazi action" over and over again.

None of the eight chairs in the lobby ever stayed open for long around this time, so the lizards had to stake out their seating early if they were going to catch the full performance. It was not uncommon for one of them to zero in on a particular chair, like a bomber pilot sighting a target, and then hover around it until its occupant moved on to other activities. The person might be halfway out of the chair and the lizard would be already halfway in. At that point, the chair could be counted out of circulation for at least a couple of hours.

I crouched down near one firmly entrenched lizard, a slight, stoop-shouldered, radish-cheeked man. While he listened to the music, he was prying a nail out of one of his shoes with a small knife. He said that there was no reason to be a hard-liner with him, because he had a bum ticker that was going to give out any day. "I've maybe got one, two more freebie concerts left, and then I'm phssst," he said with a certain dour resignation. "So why not let me go with some nice music ringing in my ears? That's the way I figure it. You know, I put in forty-three years with the post office. They got plenty out of me—just about all there was—so it's my turn to take it slow. Jesus, I've seen enough letters for a lifetime, that's for sure."

Done with that peevish interlude, he went on to appraise the music. "This here's pretty damn good music. It's the only good music I know of you can get for free. It's disgusting how little there is in this world that's free." He smiled and toasted the musicians with a gesture of his shoe.

His eyes flashed. "You know, I got bit by a goose once. Happened on a golf course. I hit my tee shot too close to a flock of them, and when I went over to size up my next shot the bastard bit me. It's no big deal, though. It never changed my life. Did make me damn wary of geese, though. Perfectly contemptible creatures, if you ask me. Now, let's be quiet, or else we ain't gonna hear anything."

A couple of the lizards hooted their greetings to a wizened man who walked by accompanied by an elderly lady wearing a gigantic hat. "Hey, prince," one of them called. "Welcome."

It was the prince of Rumania. Or so he said. He came to the hotel a great many nights. He could never be a lizard, however, for he broke a cardinal rule of lizardhood. He took a table in the Palm Court and ate. And paid. He preferred to sit in a spot far in the back and right beside the piano. With most people, he offered one of his business cards, which bore some twelve different titles. Some days he would introduce himself as the prince of Rumania. Other days he was a Knight of Malta. He claimed that he had the power to bestow titles on others, but you had to pay for a demonstration. He didn't hand them out simply for merit.

The prince was very much in a rush. He brusquely nodded hello, said, "Can't talk to you now, boys," and moved with the woman toward his table.

A lizard with an olive complexion and hair like a gray-and-silver skullcap told me that he had made a lot of money over the years (he mentioned a spectrum of careers that included oil prospecting, real estate sales, and liquor wholesaling) but none of it had stuck to him. Right now, he said, he was stony broke. He laughed derisively at the thought and said, "Boy, would I love to have the bucks to spring for a suite at this joint. Just for a weekend. A Plaza suite for a weekend would be my idea of heaven."

He stared off for a second, then added, "So what, huh? Money's just money. I still got my friends here. I also belong to a video club where the rentals are only one fifty a night. Hell of a good rate."

He stroked his chin and said that during the day his favorite activity was to drop in on travel agencies and feign planning a four-week vacation. He would tell the agent that his mind wasn't quite made up about where he wished to go, and so he would sit there and glance through the shower of brochures that would be shown him. "I tell you, I learn a lot of geography this way," he said. "I've seen pictures of places I never knew existed. Did you ever hear of Corsica?"

The lizard was a good talker. His suit was carefully pressed, and his wide shoulders were accentuated by the padding his clothier had lavished on the garment. He had a long, curved nose and a solemn manner. He looked at the musicians fixedly and said, "You can't beat them. So sweet, that music. So sweet. I wonder how much they make."

He swept his wet hair back from his forehead with a pink comb that looked as if it belonged to a woman. He began to grind his teeth, and there was a soft, crackling sound as his jaws moved. Then he began to chew violently. After a few minutes, the jaws ceased moving. His face became blank and stiff as he returned to soaking in the music.

Across from him was an old woman with fluffy white hair who was wearing an extraordinary amount of garish makeup. She looked pensive. Stingy with words, she said she liked to come on alternate days to hear the music, but not more often, because she didn't want to grow complacent about it. "That's easy to have happen," she said thoughtfully. "Too much of a good thing—forget it. You got to watch your pleasures.

"The other thing is," she added, "too many people want to talk to you. They won't just sit there and listen and mind their business. They got to shoot their mouth. I hear about arthritis, bursitis,

hammertoes, slipped disks, clogged sinuses, hernias, cataracts—
every damned condition known to old men. Makes me sick."

She told me that she was always hushing one or another of the
lizards, but they didn't always obey her orders. Sometimes she was
in the mood to talk and would participate fully in the conversation.
If she did not wish to talk, she told people that a close relative had
just passed away and she was too broken up even to speak about it.
If that didn't discourage them, she would give out a low, strangling
sob. "That always works," she said.

A few seats away sat another lizard, a grizzled, sour-faced man
with a clarion voice. A panama hat was jammed on his head. A
newcomer to the ranks, he had a healthy, ginger-colored beard that
he said he combed for forty-five minutes every morning. It was
tiring, he admitted, but worthwhile. "Makes the beard look
smart," he said. "You got to look smart if you come to the Plaza,
am I right?" He laughed uproariously, a high-pitched laugh that
scooted up out of his belly.

I couldn't argue with that, and I laughed with him.

The man puckered his face and mentioned that he could tell
people's future by feeling the bumps on their heads. "C'mon," he
said, "bend over and let me take a feel."

I told him I wasn't all that keen to know the future, and he just
shrugged and said, "Suit yourself."

"You don't really take that stuff seriously, do you?" I asked.

"Nah," he said, "not at all. But people with bumpy heads get a
kick out of it, and so I do it. Why not?" With that, he laughed
loudly once again. By now, I had noticed he had a habit of laughing
nervously at practically everything he said.

"I also do impersonations," he said once he was done laughing.
"Wanna hear one?"

Before I could answer, he launched into a monologue. When he
finished, he explained it was supposed to be John Wayne, though
it sounded more like Dolly Parton to me.

As I got up to go, the man gave me a quizzical, faraway look
and laughed heartily again.

WEDNESDAY

1

*I*N the mild, calm morning, the building already hummed with energy, and there was a melodious chatter of guests moving through the echoing hallways toward breakfast. Outside, the sun was very strong. Thelma Jordan, carrying a bulky plastic tray and feeling slightly beat, got ready for a day of cleaning. All the maids on the various floors—bright-eyed women in starched uniforms—were gathering together their room-cleaning materials and getting started on their shift. Jordan glanced at her watch. Eight-thirty. She decided the best thing to do was not to think about how tired she was but just to move.

She was an alert, heavyset, melancholy woman in her forties, with thick dark hair and somewhat protuberant eyes. Like the other maids, she wore a light gray uniform with white trim and a spotless white apron. Briskly, she loaded up her plastic tray with soap, mouthwash, shampoo, ashtrays, pencils, and "Do Not Disturb" signs, then took the service elevator to the twelfth floor, her regular assignment, where her linen truck was parked in the pantry. A stream of men in greasy trousers—maintenance workers—shuffled in and out of the elevator, a few of them nodding hellos to Jordan. Most of the "back-of-the-house" people knew one another. When she reached the pantry, she had to fill her truck with sheets, towels, and washcloths. Then she got her bucket and some cleanser and grabbed a bunch of rags. "I always like to have extra rags," she said. "I don't know why. Makes me feel secure, I guess."

Her routine took little thought. She had followed it for almost ten years. Her monotonies included making thirty-five hundred beds a year, emptying seven thousand trash cans, replacing fourteen thousand towels. Still, she had few complaints. She enjoyed the predictability, the familiarity of the same regimen over and over. Every once in a while, she got to see a celebrity—most recently, Michael Spinks—though that took some planning. She worked the portion of the twelfth floor that overlooked Fifth Avenue, and most of the celebrities stayed in the park-view rooms. So she asked the maids who worked that side to let her know when famous people were on the floor so she could try to get a peek.

She rapped twice on the door of 1270. "Room attendant," she announced crisply. "Hello. Hello."

No answer. She unlocked the door with her passkey and went in. On the outside knob, she hung her sign: "Housekeeping Attendant on Duty." That way no guest would open up the door and be surprised to find someone rambling about in his room. Knowing the precautions, she brought along her plastic tray with the soap and mouthwash and set it down gently on a chair. "You always have to bring your basket with you into the room," she pointed out. "If you leave it out on the cart, some guest will pass by and clean you out. Guests are always taking stuff. Always. I've been in a room missing all four pillows. They take towels. They take bathroom glasses. They take ashtrays. They don't take telephone books, but they might try to get the Plaza cover off them. Yesterday someone swiped my 'Attendant on Duty' sign. Now you tell me what someone is going to do with that!"

The room was cool. It was also a mess. The place was strewn with garbage. An empty panty-hose wrapper was on the bed. Tissues littered the floor; clothes were scattered around. In the bathroom, wet towels lay in tangled heaps on the floor, and the garbage can was on its side, its ample contents spilled all over. Jordan's gaze wandered to the wall over the sink. Wads of toothpaste were stuck there, as if they had been shot out of a slingshot. As soon as she spotted the white heating pad lying on the unmade bed, she knew whose room it was. "She comes every year and always stays in this room," Jordan said. "She's in the fashion business, I think. And she always makes a mess. She brings her own pillows and her own heating pad. When I see the pad, I know she's back."

Dirt had been asserting itself boldly of late. "Every room is different," she said. "They all have a little mess. You sometimes get the big mess—usually when there are kids. Sometimes there's a man in the room and he uses one towel and doesn't make much of a mess. You can do that room really fast. Businessmen are always neat. The worst are the young people—the ones in their twenties. Pets also can be bad. The only pet I've had, though, was Lassie. I did Lassie's room. It was very neat, though. Very neat. What you'd expect of a star." (One of the other maids had told me that Perry Como was so tidy that he not only emptied but washed the ashtrays when he stayed at the hotel.)

The first thing Jordan did was go over and shove open one of the windows. A cool breeze blew in. "I like to get the air," she said. "It can be zero out and I'll put the window up. At home, my bedroom window is never closed."

She began with the linens. She stripped the white cotton sheets and pillowcases off the bed and rolled them up into a big ball, which she then took out and dropped into a laundry bag attached to the front of her cart. At the same time, she scooped up a bunch of fresh sheets.

Linen got washed three hundred times and then it was retired from service. Washcloths had lives of seventy-five washes, towels three hundred, bath mats and bath rugs a hundred and twenty. Once they were retired, the sheets and towels were ripped up and used for dustcloths. Before that happened, the laundry dyed them either pink or yellow, so that the supervisors could make sure the maids didn't tear apart a good sheet for dusting, as happened from time to time. Caught breaking the rules, the offending maid got a warning, and if she was spotted again she would be suspended for a couple of days.

Every three months, the mattress itself was turned over by a houseman. That was because guests tended to sit on the edges of the bed and the mattress would sag if it wasn't flipped over periodically.

"Okay, first thing we do now is make a fresh bed," Jordan said. "Once the bed is looking good, then we get on to the cleaning."

Jordan was one of sixty-five room attendants—their preferred title, even though guests almost always called them maids. There were also twenty housemen, who tackled the heavy vacuuming, moved furniture, cleaned windows, and scrubbed walls. Then there was a staff seamstress, a pair of upholsterers, a person who cared for the curtains and window shades, and two men who did nothing but clean all of the chandeliers. Hookmen went around and put cots and cribs into rooms and moved lamps and small items. The Plaza used feather pillows in all of its rooms, but some guests were allergic to them and requested foam. A hookman brought up the foam ones from the subbasement. He would also bring up out of storage blow dryers, electric shavers, and ironing boards and irons. Guests always wanted things from housekeeping. The hotel kept on hand about forty irons and ironing boards, dozens of socket adapters, sixty hair dryers, a few tables for small meetings, and a dozen heating pads.

The theory of the hotel was that each room attendant ought to be able to clean and tidy up fourteen rooms during a seven-hour shift, with a ten-minute coffee break in the morning and a half-hour lunch break. She was allotted twenty minutes to do an occupied room and twenty-eight minutes for a room that had just been vacated. The vacated rooms took longer because the maid was also supposed to root through all of the dresser drawers to make sure the guest hadn't forgotten something. Suites were a maid's favorite, because they counted as two rooms, even though there was only one bathroom and normally only one bed. The attendants got paid extra if they accomplished more; they also received additional money if they had to make up a cot in a room. Housekeeping, for the most part, was a nontipping profession. Every so often, a guest would leave some money on the dresser for the maid, but scant few did, and thus any work beyond the normal schedule was rewarded by more pay. Two or three times a week, Jordan tried to tidy up an extra room to earn a little cash.

Besides the conventional daytime maids, there was a separate evening platoon that, at four in the afternoon, folded up the bedspreads and turned down the beds, clicked on a bedside light, and left the guests foil-wrapped mints. Each night attendant was expected to do sixty turn-downs and sixty mints. One of the more curious house rules was that even if a room was occupied by a single person, the maid was to turn down both the right and left corners of the sheets, since the hotel couldn't be certain which side of the bed the person would choose to enter and it didn't ever want anyone to have to turn down his or her own sheet. Mint rules required that the wrapped candies be placed conspicuously on the table next to the bed. The Plaza used to put them right on the bed pillow, until one of its important guests went to sleep without taking adequate notice and woke up with chocolate smeared on his face. He was not amused.

Immersed in thought, Jordan positioned herself on the right side of the bed, spread the clean white cotton sheet out, and tucked the end underneath the mattress. She used a hospital corner to keep the fold in place, then smoothed the rest of the sheet across the bed. Plaza maids were taught to finish one side of the bed—all three sheets and blanket—before walking around to do the other side. That way, they cut down a bit on the walking, which could make a difference on the feet by the time they had gotten to their twelfth or thirteenth room of the day.

"Sometimes you follow the technique, and sometimes you don't," Jordan said. "Sometimes I just feel like running around, and so I say the heck with it."

Maids were not allowed to turn on the TV or radio, except briefly to check that they were working, so Jordan worked in silence. Occasionally she would hum to herself.

Jordan's strong arms laid a mustard-colored blanket over the two bottom sheets and added the top sheet. She pulled new pillowcases on the four pillows, fluffed them up, and arranged them neatly in a row. She then covered the bed with the spread. She carefully made a crease with her hand between the pillows. She didn't take the time to peer at the neat finished product. Not after all the beds she had made.

"Making the beds is the worst," she said. "It hurts your back and it hurts your feet. We have quite a few girls who have bad backs and bad feet. My heels bother me. The doctor says it's from walking all day on carpet. So I have to wear little cups on my shoes. The work is tiring, especially when you get older. Some of the maids skip coffee breaks and lunch to keep up. There's one girl who doesn't take any breaks and she's still late finishing. She can't keep up anymore."

The bathroom was next. Jordan took out the dirty towels and shook the shower curtain sharply a few times. "They're very particular about that," she said. "They want you to shake the hair off the curtain. Otherwise the guest may use the shower later and the hair will fall into the tub. Guests don't like that."

Jordan pulled on a pair of red rubber gloves, doused a cloth in hot water, and sponged off the toilet seat and the fixtures. She used a long white brush to clean the inside of the toilet bowl. The sink and the cabinet drew her attention next. She used a shorter brush to clean the sink and then wiped around the six bottles of pills that sat on the ledge. ("That's not a lot of pills. I've seen a lot more than that.") Kneeling down, she attacked the bathtub, which had an ugly ring of dirt. Inside of four minutes, it sparkled again. Then, back on her knees, she went after the floor with a wet cloth. Mops or sponges on a stick were taboo. The hotel claimed they didn't get into the corners, though they were a lot easier on the knees. "I'm so used to it by now," Jordan said, "that I don't even use a mop at home. I guess when I'm home I still have it in my mind that I'm cleaning at the Plaza."

On the wrist of her left hand she wore a copper bracelet. Eighteen years ago, the hand used to get numb inexplicably while she was working. A friend suggested she try a copper bracelet. The numbness never returned and so the bracelet stayed on.

She sprayed the floor with scrub-free cleanser and wiped it with quick, brisk strokes. The white tile gleamed again. All the bathroom needed was fresh towels. She went to her cart and picked up three large towels, three hand towels, three washcloths, and one bath mat. She peeked behind the bathroom door to make sure there was a shoehorn hanging on one of the hooks, and then she checked the basket of Caswell-Massey amenities. Regular rooms got a sewing kit, shampoo, body lotion, transparent soap, a small white soap, a large white soap, a shoe cloth, and a laundry card. A suite also got a hair conditioner, bath gel, a loofah mitt, and an emery board.

"It's funny, I don't see hardly any of the guests," Jordan said. "I don't see a quarter of them. I do their beds and I don't know who they are. I make it a point when I hear a door slam down the hall to hurry out there and see if I can catch a glimpse of the person. I like to know who stays in my rooms, but I don't get much chance to."

Grabbing a yellow cloth, Jordan dusted the marble-topped night tables and desk. She made sure that the requisite four ashtrays were there and that there was a notepad next to the telephone with a pencil (not any pencil; it had to be a six-inch, hexagonal pencil without an eraser). She sized up the room-service menu. When it was dirty, she was supposed to throw it out and replace it with a fresh one. "This looks a little ragged," she said, and ripped it in half. She got a new one from her cart and set it down. She opened the desk drawer and checked that there were three sheets of stationery and three envelopes. In the closet, she confirmed that there were laundry bags and a shoeshine kit. She flicked on the Zenith color television in the credenza to see that it worked. An ad for a health club blared on—sultry women in bikinis. "Jeez, will you look at that," Jordan said. She tried another channel—*Hollywood Squares*—and then switched off the set.

Next she unwound the long cord of her Sanitaire upright vacuum cleaner and plugged it into the bathroom socket. The room filled with its noisy whir. She stuck the nose of the vacuum under the bed, ran it around the desk and chairs and back and forth across the thick rug. The few pieces of dirt and lint were quickly sucked up, and she pulled out the cord. The room was quiet again.

"Now I'm going to put a rug on the bathroom floor and see that the lampshades are straight and turn off all the lights," she said. "When you leave, you're also supposed to keep the bathroom door half-closed."

After shutting the window, Jordan dialed a code on the push-button phone that told housekeeping and the front desk that 1270 was now clean. The last thing she did as she went out the door was insert the chain from the chain lock into its little storage hole.

JORDAN told me she had been born in Barbados and worked there as a maid starting when she was fifteen. She came to this country in 1971 and went to Boston to be a maid in a Sheraton before getting a job at the Plaza. "I came to New York on the last Saturday night of 1973. Some guys snatched my pocketbook that night. Nice welcome. I guess they knew I was a stranger. I'm married and have six kids. I live in Brooklyn. My husband is a watchmaker at Seiko Watch. This is what I've always done, what I've always known—cleaning up after people."

She opened the door to 1261. She took one look and said, "See that—we've got a Japanese man staying here." There was a dollar bill lying on the rumpled bed. "You always know if it's a Japanese person because they leave you a dollar on the bed every day. A very nice custom, if you ask me. Some of them leave fifty cents if they don't have as much, some leave two dollars if they're really well off. The Japanese are the only ones who always leave me something. But what are you going to do?"

As she stripped the bed, the minibar waiter entered to replenish the stock. Only a Coke was missing. The staff knew that many guests used the bar and then insisted that they'd never touched a thing. "They say someone else used it when the bottles are right there in the garbage," Jordan said. "Or they blame the maids. The maids get blamed for everything. Once a guest left a note for me saying that he had opened a bottle of gin but there was only water in it so don't charge him. I really had to laugh. That was a new one."

An occasional maid has had her sinister side. Back in the mid-

1960s, a maid named Marie Gidde was apprehended for looting rooms. After she had fallen under suspicion, a trap was set for her by the police. Jewels and money were planted in one of the rooms she regularly cleaned. A chemical powder had been sprayed on them that was invisible to the eye but glowed brilliant orange when doused with water. The bait worked. The goods disappeared. Gidde was ordered to wash her hands. They were stained orange. At her arraignment, it came out that Gidde was fairly diversified. She had done time for manslaughter and been arrested for prostitution.

Finished with the bed, Jordan headed for the bathroom and the heavy scrubbing.

"The guests are not the same as they used to be," she said. "It's the businessmen and the young ones. The young ones are the worst. Very messy. Very. That's not the way the Plaza guest used to be. It used to be easier to clean the rooms. They'd go out early so you could get in. The young ones sleep and sleep. You can't get them out of bed. I can't figure it. They come to New York and all they do is sleep."

One of the great paradoxes of the hotel and restaurant industry is that the employees are expected to provide a tremendous level of service and even to anticipate guest needs, and yet they can never afford to stay in a hotel or to eat in a restaurant of that quality. They have no idea what it feels like to receive that degree of service. Conscious of this, some hotels have started programs of honoring employees of the month by allowing them to stay in the hotel for a weekend, which helps, though it's unlikely they are ever treated like real guests. As it happened, Jordan had stayed in the hotel for four nights during a transit strike in the 1970s. But it wasn't at all like being a guest, if for no other reason than that there were three people assigned to each room.

"In the locker rooms, you sometimes hear the employees grumble about the guests," Jordan said. "They're resentful of the money they have and that they don't. I don't feel that way. The way I look at it, a lot of people with all this money, they're not happy. So the money makes no sense to me. I'm happy the way I am. Sometimes I see all this jewelry lying around, and it means nothing to me.

"I like this place," Jordan went on. "A good place to work. Some of the others complain there're too many rooms to clean. I do think the maids have the hardest job in the hotel. You go down to room service and when it's not busy the waiters are sitting around. The same thing with the bellhops. But the maids have to do those fourteen rooms every day. If you take a break, you fall behind. At the end of the day, sometimes I'm really tired. If you get an early start and the guests are pretty good and you don't have too many checkout rooms, then you're okay. Checkouts are hard. You have to search for missing things and you have to look through all the drawers and you have to look under the bed. You sometimes find shoes sitting there, forgotten by their owners."

2

ATER in the morning, I found myself sitting with Irene Correa in the housekeeping office in the sub-basement. She was working on her assignments. The office was a small, square, appropriately tidy room. As the head of housekeeping, Correa was a busy woman. She had to mount campaigns against insufficient towels, soiled linen, spotted rugs, and lumpy mattresses. Just then, she had gotten a report from Hinton that there was some gum on the carpet of the No. 5 elevator, and that provoked a sigh. Correa wore a light blue dress. She was an ample, friendly woman with warm eyes, a contemplative stare, and an outreaching smile. While she thumbed through linen reports, Correa told me that she was a native of Brazil and had worked as a telephone operator in Ouro Verde, a posh Brazilian hotel in Copacabana Beach. In 1963 some relatives scraped together money so she could come to the United States to learn English. "The reason I came was that a lot of the customers at the hotel in Brazil spoke English, and if you speak English, you earn more money in Brazil. So I was going to learn the language and return to Brazil. I learned at night school and by teaching myself. I decided not to read Brazilian newspapers and not to have Brazilian friends. That's a mistake a lot of people make. I did go back for three weeks, but I compared it with America and decided I didn't want to stay. I had seen something better." She applied for work at the Sheraton Motor Inn on Forty-second Street and was hired as a floor supervisor. She came to the Plaza housekeeping staff in 1976, left in 1980 for another opportunity, and then returned in the summer of 1987. "I really love the hotel business," she said. "I like to help the people."

Maids drifted in and out, and housekeeping stories, for a while, traversed the office. There were tales enough to tell. It was work that required resolute character, and it was not for the squeamish. "You clean up everything," Correa said. "It ranges from the cleanest type of work to the dirtiest type of work. Everything happens in a hotel."

Margaret Callender, eight years on the staff, said, "The holidays are when you get the wild rooms. There was one room that I got stuck with where the guest piled all of the garbage in the bathtub. Beer cans, vodka bottles, empty peanut cans, you name it. I guess he thought that was being neat. It was just more work for me. I never worked harder on a bathtub than I did that morning."

When the maids talked about guest behavior, they got very animated and waved their arms as they spoke. Irona Lewis, a heavy-set woman who had also cleaned rooms for eight years, had her arms working as she chimed in, "Some guests, they put ketchup on the walls, they break the mirrors, they break the lamps, they break the beds. The room's a goner. Sometimes it'd be better to just level the room and start over. You'd really be surprised at the messes some people make. They look at it that they spend the money, so they figure they can do what they do. And they do it."

"You want to know the worst thing I ever saw?" Margaret Callender said. "I've seen a room covered with condoms. I mean, just covered with condoms. The whole room. That really threw me for a loop. I didn't even want to see who it was who was staying there. He must have been mighty tired, that I'm sure of."

"Sometimes the guest is in the room and you knock on the door and they don't tell you they're there," Lewis put in. "So you open the door and there's the guest nude. You say, 'Oh, my God, I'm sorry,' and you leave. Sometimes they're in there making love and they don't even notice you. So you go in there and see the action.

"I worked with a robot once for four days," Lewis continued. "I walked into one of my rooms, and there was this robot there. A big fellow. It said, 'What's your name?' I told it, and it asked me how I was doing. I said I was doing fine. It was very friendly. It even asked me to dance. I didn't have the time for that, though."

"I had a guy once I'll never forget," said Mabel Mearise, who had been at the Plaza eighteen years. "When I came in, he was burning a hole in the rug. I don't know why. He couldn't answer me. But I do know I put a stop to that."

Housekeeping personnel learned quickly how many among even the ritziest class could be downright slovenly. Correa and her staff knew that a lot of the Plaza guests boozed. Indeed, some of them bordered on being certifiable alcoholics. Though the maids were not aggressively opposed to drink and drunkards, they were against the discourtesies that whiskey courage left behind in the rooms. This they didn't forgive guests for, even though they saw it every week. "You have people who get sick," one of the maids said. "Some people defecate in the room. They urinate in the room. These are dumb people. You just have to run up and clean up those areas. You get rooms where there was a wild party and the chandelier is broken and furniture is broken and the carpet has mustard all over it and the drapes are stained. I guess the worst nightmare a housekeeper wants to come across is a room where there was a really, really wild party. That's hard to clean. It's disheartening to see. It really is. I think of the hotel as my home, and I don't like to see people mess up my home."

One valued guest, a well-known performer who came to the hotel for an extended stay almost every year, was famous among the staff for his boozing. He got so roaring drunk that one of the restaurant managers, who had become a good friend of his, had to come up every evening he was at the Plaza to remove his contact lenses. Another of this performer's quirks was that he refused any housekeeping services during his stay. He might check in for a month or six weeks, but no maid was to enter his room until he departed. By that time, the place was filthy. Usually, after a week or so, anyone who walked by in the hallway could smell the stink from the room. Fumes seeped out from beneath the door. Decayed food, empty liquor bottles, filthy towels were everywhere. Several maids worked their fingers to the bone for a day to restore the room to habitable shape.

THE dirt that guests added to the rooms was but one of Correa's worries. What they removed was another. "Shrinkage" was a continual problem for housekeeping. Even though Plaza guests were normally a class of people well equipped to buy their own supplies, they could be relied on to swipe towels and ashtrays as remembrances of their Plaza stay. Even Elizabeth Taylor once confessed to having gone off with some of the hotel's possessions. After a lengthy stay to promote a movie, she did her packing with the help of her friend Montgomery Clift. When she later opened her luggage, she discovered that Clift had tossed in several Plaza towels, a bath nozzle, and one of the hotel's martini carafes. Unlike most guests, Taylor called the head housekeeper to apologize and sent along some flowers and candy.

In a given week, the hotel lost about 150 bath towels, 280 hand towels, 450 washcloths, and forty robes. The towels and washcloths were not for sale. The robes, however, were offered to guests for $80 apiece, but many guests who had the $80 just stuck them in their suitcases instead. Something like eighty ashtrays a week were swiped by guests, as well as ten alarm clocks and a couple of dozen hangers. Until recently, rooms were outfitted with conventional walnut hangers. In an effort to discourage theft, these were phased out and replaced with Beverly hangers, which boasted the same attractive walnut frame but had a hook about a third the conventional size. The closets had been fitted with thinner bars to accommodate the new hangers. Anyone who took a Beverly hanger would never be able to use it in his own closet. The skirt hangers, however, continued to have the larger hooks. They were regularly stolen.

An unwavering rule of the hotel was never to attempt to recover lost supplies or try to bill guests for the things they took. "How could we do that?" Correa said. "What will it generate and give us back? We'd seem like really petty people, really tacky. But no guest knows how many other guests are taking stuff, too. They don't know how ridiculous it gets."

When I wondered how ridiculous it got, Correa said, "We've even had blankets and lampshades disappear. About the only thing I've never heard of is a bed. That would throw me. The day somebody walks out with a bed, my eyebrows will be up. But I wouldn't rule it out. I've learned not to rule anything out." All the beds may be intact, but a long-unsolved Plaza mystery was who managed some years ago to take a piano from the ballroom.

Along with all the things the housekeepers found missing, they also discovered innumerable things left behind: dentures, furs, glasses, even entire suitcases full of clothes. With disturbing frequency, sexual paraphernalia turned up. The most common forgotten property was underwear, a few pair of which were found every day. Shoes were second, usually about a pair a week. All of these discoveries went into lost and found, a padlocked closet in Irene Correa's outer office. While I was visiting, Correa opened the door for me and I took a look at the latest collection. It was heaped on several orange metal shelves. There was an ITT desk phone, a briefcase, an umbrella, a Yellowbird hair dryer, an alarm clock, a vaporizer, a blue raincoat, a thick silver belt, Japanese slippers, one white high-heeled shoe, a chintzy bust of Elvis Presley, a toy sword, a pearl earring, a Minnie Mouse doll, one red sock, a picture frame, a toy Texaco oil truck, a red-striped necktie, some camera film, and a Ricky Van Shelton record album.

The goods were kept in lost and found for three months, after which they were distributed to the employees who discovered them or, if no one wanted them, hurled in the garbage. With items of clear value, such as jewelry or money (on several occasions, maids had found cash that was tucked beneath mattresses and forgotten), an effort was made to contact the guest and return the property. With everything else, housekeeping waited to hear from the guest. "It's against the rules to call a guest on these things," Correa said. "It's dangerous to do that. Maybe a guest will be here with someone else and the spouse doesn't know it. You know how it is at hotels.

So we must be discreet. You could call up a man's home about a negligee or something and the wife answers and it turns out it's not his wife's. That's playing with explosives. Sometimes I find a birth certificate or a passport and I want to call up the guest. But I can't. So we wait."

Thelma Jordan once found $495 in cash on the floor of a room, next to the bed. She turned it in, and it was kept in lost and found for six weeks. As the days passed, Jordan's hopes climbed. No one claimed it, and at last it was turned over to her. She gave $25 to each of the other maids on her floor and spent the rest on herself. She doesn't even remember on what. "Some silly thing or another," she said.

"I've gotten a bunch of other things," she said. "I've gotten men's shirts and shoes. They don't do me much good. If they look pretty good, I'll take them home and give them to the Salvation Army. Once I got a nice lady's hat. I kept that and wore it. Then there was that one bizarre thing. It was in 1256. I opened the door and I saw the sheet moving a little and I hear something going. I said to myself, 'What the hell is that?' I went over to the bed and something was moving in there. I pulled down the sheet and there was a vibrator. I turned it in, but nobody ever claimed it, and I didn't want it either."

<hr>

3

<hr>

N the Oak Room, the department heads lined up for coffee, and some of them picked out little pastries from a basket next to the coffee urns. Then they found seats at one or another of the empty dining tables. Every Wednesday, it was a weekly ritual for Hud Hinton to preside over a meeting of the department heads so that they could talk about the concerns of the hotel and share problems with each other.

For weeks there had been discussion among the managers about the Swedish royal visit. Would everything go smoothly? How would the king and queen find the place? By now, everyone in the hotel knew that King Carl XVI Gustaf and Queen Silvia were coming as part of a celebratory tour of the United States. The event being celebrated was the 350th anniversary of the arrival, in what is now Delaware, of the ships *Kalmar Nyckel* and *Fogel Grip*. The vessels had been dispatched by the kingdom of Sweden to establish New Sweden, the first permanent settlement of Swedes in North America. Congress had gone so far as to designate 1988 as the Year of New Sweden. This was the first visit to America by the king and queen in seven years (the last time, they had chosen to stay at the Pierre), and the Plaza, on the strength of its luster, hard work by a sales staff that kept on good terms with the Secret Service and the State Department, and a reputation for being a well-patrolled hotel, had managed to land them.

Though the booking had been made on December 16, 1986, most of the fine details had awaited recent weeks. Requests from the couple's staff were trickling in almost daily. Housekeeping was asked to provide a fabric-wrinkle remover for the king. Since none was on hand, Irene Correa had to go out and buy one. He also wanted an iron and ironing board, and four rooms from his entourage requested hair dryers. A portable bar was to be set up in the Presidential Suite, Room 323, where the king and queen were to stay, and there were to be fresh flowers in two foyers and in the king and queen's bedroom. The word was that neither was fond of strong-smelling flowers, and the queen did not much care for blue. They were not allergic to anything, an important point. The president of Costa Rica, for instance, was allergic to down feathers, and so his pillows had to be changed in advance. The hotel was going to present the queen with a copy of Kay Thompson's Eloise book for her children (two girls and a boy), and the king was getting a copy of the Plaza pictorial history. He was said to be a history buff. The chef had been informed about royal breakfast habits. Most of their lunches and dinners would be eaten at affairs outside the hotel, but the royal couple expected to have their breakfasts in their room. The king liked café au lait. The queen liked boiled eggs, not too hard.

Once everyone was seated, the meeting was called to order by Hinton and he turned to Joe Schneider, the head of the reservations department, for a report on the rooms forecast for the coming week and a review of the last month. Schneider said that the month had been slow so far, with occupancy down, but some upcoming significant events, including the royal visit and a few Japanese tour groups, were expected to improve the picture substantially. People from conference services, catering, and the comptroller's office offered their reports, most of which were upbeat.

Next, Malin Hammer gave a slow, spelling-it-out presentation on the royal visit. She was a sales manager, relatively new to the hotel, but as she was from Sweden, she had been given the task of attending to the visitors. She said that, in all, there would be 110 rooms taken. The king and queen themselves would arrive at ten

minutes of noon on Friday and leave at ten-fifty Sunday morning.
They would be accompanied by an aide-de-camp, a lady-in-waiting,
a hairdresser, and a chambermaid. There was one last-minute can-
cellation. The first lady to the court, who had been scheduled to
stay in the Presidential Suite with the royal couple, had broken her
arm and would not be coming. When someone asked Hammer what
it was that the first lady did, she replied that she "washed the
queen's dirty socks and stuff like that."

She went on to explain that there would be four groups: their
majesties, the king and queen; the royal party, which consisted of
those people closest to them; the entourage, mostly various businessmen who were following them on this twelve-city tour; and the
press. She said that the entourage and the press would come and go
via the Fifty-ninth Street entrance and travel in two buses, while
their majesties would use the Fifth Avenue entrance and have a
motorcade consisting of twelve Saabs. When there was movement
of the couple in or out of the hotel, one elevator was to be reserved
for their exclusive use.

The entourage would bring about four hundred pieces of luggage, and the king and queen would have about fifteen pieces. The
A and B and White and Gold suites were to be used to store luggage
and had to be guarded at all times. For transporting the baggage,
the bellmen would receive $1.40 a bag. It was good work, but
didn't stack up to the king of Morocco, who came with 1,269
suitcases, a number of them trunks that required three men to lift.

Much of the time, the couple would be out of the hotel at various
festivities scheduled around the city, Hammer said. They would be
going down to the South Street Seaport, which had been decorated
to look like Sweden. They had a luncheon Friday at the Waldorf-
Astoria hosted by the Swedish-American Chamber of Commerce.
The queen was then going to the Museum of Modern Art to see the
exhibition Design for Independent Living. After that, she would
go to see the Scandinavian Craft Today display at the American
Craft Museum, while the king took in a panel discussion at the
Waldorf on industrial investments and economic growth. They
would return briefly to the hotel before going to the Cooper-Hewitt

Museum to see an exhibit, The Triumph of Simplicity: 350 Years of Swedish Silver. Then they were invited to Gracie Mansion to have dinner with Mayor Koch. They wouldn't return to their room until ten-fifty. On Saturday, it was back to South Street Seaport for most of the day, followed by a concert at Carnegie Hall and then a dinner in the Plaza's Grand Ballroom. After checking out of the hotel on Sunday, they would attend services at St. Thomas's Church on West Fifty-third Street, go to a luncheon at the residence of the Swedish consul general, and then head for Kennedy Airport to catch a plane to Detroit.

Hammer went on to say that every member of the party was to receive a bottle of Swedish mineral water, and the hotel had arranged to get a facsimile from a Swedish journalist each morning at seven-thirty with a rundown of the latest Swedish news. Copies were to go to each room. As a further courtesy, the king and queen were being provided with a copy of *Svenska Dagbladet,* the Swedish newspaper, so they could read it with their breakfast. As Hammer put it, "That way, the king will know right away if the castle burns down."

When the fundamentals had been gone through, Hammer said she would be checking into the hotel so that she could minister to the group's needs throughout its stay. By Sunday evening, she said, she would "probably be a corpse."

"Okay," Hinton said. "Very good. Now make sure you get a copy of the résumé and share it with your staff. Also, this is a weekend deal, so if you're not going to be around make sure you have the appropriate people here. Make sure you know the arrival and departure patterns."

Janet Wright, the energetic publicity director for the hotel, had something to share, as she almost always did. She mentioned that the BBC would be doing some filming this week of the exterior of the hotel in conjunction with a documentary about hotels at which movies have been shot. "We have a couple of stills being shot in some suites for some foreign magazines," she said. "So we're getting foreign exposure." As a final treat, she had a trailer from the film *Big Business* to show the group. The comedy starred Bette Midler and Lily Tomlin. More important to those gathered here, it also starred the Plaza, since the pair checked into the hotel for several days and Plaza scenes were scattered throughout the film.

The lights were dimmed and everyone's attention was directed to a television screen set up in the corner. The beginning of the trailer showed a solid shot of the hotel's facade, and a surge of pride was summoned forth in the department heads. Everyone murmured approvingly. "Oh, super shot," one of them called out. "Place looks great," someone else said. Further on, Midler and Tomlin wreaked a certain amount of havoc in their room, committing some notable damage to furnishings and carpets, and there were a few winces and some laughs. When the several minutes of film were over, there was hearty applause.

"Very nice," Hinton said. "That looks like good exposure. Okay, let's get back to work."

4

A LEGGY French woman wanted to know if the white lace pajamas she had purchased had been delivered.

Manuel Mulero shook his head. The concierge desk, at the moment, was innocent of pajamas.

"Could you make a reservation for us tonight at La Grenouille? Nine-thirty. Four people," said a man whose smile was enhanced by perfect dental work.

"Absolutely," Mulero said.

A small, wrinkled man with an energetic stammer came up. "I'm looking for a place close by to get some copying done."

Mulero directed him to an establishment several blocks away.

"What is the best way to get down to Wall Street this time of day?"

"Best way?" Mulero said. "Cab."

"That's quicker than a subway?"

"Yes, yes. Cab."

After the man left, Mulero told me, "It always kills me when people say 'best way.' The best way is a nice stretch limo."

"Where is there a solarium where I can get a tan?" an older woman wondered.

Mulero suggested the Atrium Club, a health facility on Fifty-seventh Street that the Plaza is affiliated with and that extends privileges to guests. He handed her a pass that would gain her admission.

"Macy's? Can I walk there?" a young man wanted to know.

"It's a good walk if you're a walker. It's about a mile. A thirty-minute walk."

"I'll walk it."

"Could you tell me how long it would take to get to New Brunswick?" a young Englishman wearing a red sweater asked.

Mulero said, "New Brunswick? One hour. That's a guesstimate."

The young man brightened visibly. "Okay, could you organize a limousine to take me there? About twelve-thirty. And he'll have to wait two or three hours."

"Okay."

"I have another request. Do you have a slide projector I could get in my room for a couple of hours?"

"I'll check and call you."

"Do you have any Scotch tape?" a young Frenchman wanted to know.

Mulero did. The man took it and taped a cover on a small notebook.

A man from Saudi Arabia was in constant search of messages. He gave Mulero his whereabouts at all times. Now he was in the Palm Court. But there were no calls for him there. Now he was out of the Palm Court and on his way to his room. There were still no messages.

"Where would you go to get some bed linen?" a brown-hatted woman asked Mulero.

"Oh, Bloomingdale's. Bergdorf's. Fortunoff. One of those places."

"I see. Well, thank you."

Broad-shouldered, bald-headed Manuel Mulero was a celebrity at the Plaza, even though hardly anyone knew him outside the hotel. He was a tall man with a creased face and trusting eyes. As the chef concierge, he ran the ancillary services the hotel provided. He was like a favorite uncle, expected to fulfill every guest's whim and remove any obstacles that might get in any guest's way. Every day, he was surrounded by a profusion of requests, and he had no choice but to try to satisfy them. He wore a cutaway, the uniform of the profession. On the collar of it was clipped a pair of gold crossed keys, which signified that he was one of about 850 concierges registered with Les Clefs d'Or, the international brotherhood of concierges. Each year, he attended a national meeting of the U.S. members and another international session of the entire body. At these gatherings, the concierges traded war stories and helpful hints on how to keep smiles pasted on guests' faces.

Years of experience had introduced Mulero to the limits of the ridiculous—and the regions beyond. "Oh, the things people want," he said. "I had one guest who wanted to rent a helicopter to take his girlfriend on a tour of the city. So I called a helicopter service and asked for a charter. The fellow took it for an hour, and I believe it cost him eight hundred dollars. Then there was another guest whose mother-in-law fractured her hip outside and wanted me to get an ambulance plane to take her back to Mexico. Couldn't do it. Then he wanted to hire a regular jet and take the seats out. That didn't work, either. Finally I managed to get him a private plane. The cost there, I think, was about three thousand dollars.

"We get many requests to find items: candy, clothes, breads. Once a man from the Midwest wanted me to get him a pizza for his birthday that had 'Happy Birthday John' spelled out in pepperoni on it. I called a pizza place we know in the area and had it done. Another man wanted me to locate a fur coat, and so I set him up with a manufacturer in the fur district. A man from Saudi Arabia was here and he wanted me to track down a miniature working car for him to take home for his son. That was a challenge. I did find one at a toy store for about two thousand dollars. One of my associates once had to come up with twelve fresh whole chickens for a man to take with him back to Germany. That was an unusual request, I would say. It was hard, but she was able to dig up the chickens from a wholesale poultry place. Most things, I would say, we find—but not everything. Theater tickets for hit shows are sometimes impossible. People seem to think we have blocks of tickets that we draw on. We don't. We have to go through agents, like everyone else. Another thing, we get a lot of requests—especially from foreigners—for an escort service. We tell them straight away that we don't provide that. The Europeans are always amazed. They say it's always done at the European hotels. They end up going off on their own and manage to find what they want anyway."

Mulero had a genuine fondness for the people who came to stay in the hotel, and he was undoubtedly acquainted with more of them than anyone else who worked at the Plaza. He had habits, faces, names burned into his brain. "We make out sheets of requests by guests and keep them in a file for a year," he said. "When a guest returns, I can tell him what shows he saw last time and where he ate. You know, 'Last time, you went to the '21' Club and saw *Starlight Express*.' This helps, but one of the prerequisites for a concierge is to have a great memory."

Mulero's demeanor fluctuated between servility and rigidity. The rigidity was reserved for his staff, never demonstrated to a guest. In the company of some of his important clientele, he was meek. Those he had gotten to know especially well over years of service he was jocular with. If a guest found things not up to expectations, Mulero was always contrite and apologetic. Unhappy guests were bad for business, in a geometric way. Hotel surveys have indicated that a happy guest, on average, will tell three others about his stay, whereas a displeased guest will tell a dozen people. Mulero often adopted a sort of deadpan jauntiness. Sometimes he had one phone in each hand, telling people, "Bear with me one moment. Can you bear with me one moment?" Then, when he got back to someone, he said, "Okay, I'm so sorry. Now I'm all yours."

THE concierge desk, a small, slender counter, opened at seven in the morning and closed at one o'clock the following morning. It was a fairly bustling place. It was located near the Central Park South entrance; the front desk was to one side of it and the bellman station to the other. Its duties included answering the galactic variety of questions that guests had, passing on phone messages, making reservations, and offering advice. In all, six people worked at the desk. Mulero preferred to take the late shift, from three in the afternoon until eleven at night.

Three computer terminals were an indispensable part of the operation. Stored in the computer was a list of the occupants of all rooms. Taped to the counter was the Daily Function Sheet, telling what was going on in the hotel that day. Also taped to the desk was the day's weather and the next day's forecast: "52 degrees, 90 percent humidity. Mostly clouds, periodical showers. Clear, cool tonight. Sunny tomorrow." There was also a chart for converting Celsius and Fahrenheit temperatures. Scattered behind the desk, both on shelves and in various drawers, were information resources. These included things like Gray Line sight-seeing tour brochures, bus maps, limousine rates, subway maps, boat information, foreign-language city maps, and guides such as *New York in Your Pocket,* a directory of stores, museums, and theaters, *Zagat New York City Restaurant Guide,* and *Where to Find It, Buy It, Eat It in New York* by Gerry Frank. Frank, as it happened, was a regular guest. His full-time job was chief of staff for Senator Mark Hatfield. His book was his hobby. Two weekends a year, he came to New York to conduct research for a new edition, and he always stayed at the Plaza. He told me he had been coming to the hotel since he was fifteen and once got a kiss on the cheek from Hildegarde and refrained from washing his face for a month.

"Excuse me, sir, could you make sure we have extra towels and sheets sent to our room? We will be having a masseuse stopping by."

"Of course," Mulero said.

A man wanted a reservation tonight for eight at Romeo Salta, an Italian restaurant on Fifty-sixth Street.

A call came from a guest in his room. He was blind. Could someone be sent up to read to him from the Bible?

Contacts were the essence of Mulero's job. He found it difficult ever to have a real day off, because he felt obliged on so many of his nonworking days to drop in on restaurants and theater-ticket agencies and travel agents to pay his respects. "A concierge who decides that his days off are his own, well, he's not really a concierge,"

Mulero told me. He knew that, as a rule, it took two months to get in to have dinner at Lutèce, longer than at any other restaurant in the city. On occasion, though, he had gotten an important guest in on a few hours' notice. Contacts. "I happen to know the owner's wife," Mulero said, "and she controls the reservation book." Out of such magic does a huge reputation grow.

"For a concierge, the whole idea is contacts," Mulero said. "Without contacts, you're just another voice on the phone. Another useless voice. Most of the guests who come to me looking for a dinner reservation or for theater tickets have already tried on their own and failed. But they don't have the contacts. On my days off, I make it a point to go out and meet these people. I'll have them over here for a meal. The reason I deliberately work nights is that the contacts are there in the evenings. So I talk with them every chance I get."

Contacts, Mulero explained, can do a lot, but they can't accomplish everything. "We've been trying to talk to a lot of the restaurants about how when you need a table for a party of two, they will say they're sold out," he said. "They're not sold out. They just want four or more per table. The French restaurants are especially bad about this. So a party of two which wants to eat between eight and ten, the prime time, has severe restrictions. The restaurants want them at six or after ten. That's discrimination. Another problem used to be with the taxi drivers gouging the public. They would bring someone here from Kennedy Airport and charge sixty dollars. We complained about that and it's gotten a lot better."

His single biggest frustration—all the concierges in New York were disturbed about it—was his inability to find a dry cleaner to handle guest clothing on weekends, when the Plaza's own laundry was closed. "The commercial places close their presses at four o'clock on Saturday, and forget Sunday," Mulero said. "One day I took the Yellow Pages and I went through the whole list of dry cleaners, and the whole thing was a big nothing. None of them was available. Our guests find it hard to believe that in a city like New York they can't get their laundry done on the weekend. All my colleagues talk about this. So we've been looking for a place that will handle the problem. I think one of these days we'll solve it. But I don't know when and I don't know how."

Mulero's first job, when he was a teenager, was in a Brooklyn ice cream factory owned by his uncle. That was all right for a while, but Mulero didn't see it as a career. He got a job as an elevator operator at the New York Hilton. Next he went into the Navy, and after briefly returning to ice cream, he was hired as a rack clerk at the Hotel New York. In those days, there was a rack with slots in it that represented the whole hotel, and Mulero would fit the slips of check-ins into the proper slots. From there he had a succession of hotel jobs—the Hotel Manhattan, the Summit Hotel, the American in San Juan, Motel City, Howard Johnson's Motor Lodge, the Americana, the Midtown Motor Inn, the Regency, the Summit again, the Ramada Inn, the New York Hilton—working his way up to managerial positions. Finally, in 1980, he came to the Plaza as a concierge and found a permanent home. Concierges are reminders of permanence. "It's normal in the hotel business to transfer a lot," Mulero said. "When you become concierge, though, that's different. The good concierge should be a mainstay. Otherwise the hotel defeats the purpose of welcoming guests over and over. In Europe, a concierge is often at the same hotel for forty or fifty years. Guests expect to see the same face whether they come back after a year or after ten years."

THE concierge desk had gotten extremely congested, people two deep. Vivian Fiol, Nolacarol Murfee, and Alexander Bisbal—three of the senior members of the staff—were all occupied, fielding questions and throwing back answers. Mulero was on the phone, working on dinner reservations.

"Where are the house phones?"

"Around behind the elevators."

"I'm expecting a Federal Express package."

"I'll see if it has arrived."

"The South Street Seaport. How does one get there from here?"

"You take the N or the R train."

"Any messages for 1030?"

"None. Not one."

"Can you tell me where the garment district is?" a young couple wanted to know.

"Seventh Avenue in the twenties."

The husband said, "She's heard that there are places where you can get one or two dresses. Friends of hers have done that."

"Yes, there are," Nolacarol Murfee said. "If you walk along there, you'll see them."

"How do you get to Fifty-eighth and Sixth Avenue?" a thin young man wondered.

Vivian Fiol said, "You go out the door and turn left and walk to Sixth Avenue. You turn left, walk one block, and you're at Fifty-eighth."

"I think I can handle that."

"I think you can, too."

"Excuse me, where is the picture of Eloise?"

"Make a right, a left, and a right," Murfee said. "It's right across from the Palm Court."

"Okay, let's go."

A middle-aged woman came by, wanting to know if anyone might be interested in buying her paintings. She said she was an artist, and she had some color photographs of her work tucked under her arm. Murfee politely sent her to the purchasing department.

A call came from the eleventh floor. Was anyone available to come up and wash a man's back?

"I don't think so."

At times, concierge people feel as if they're doing therapy. "There's one young man who's claustrophobic," Vivian Fiol remembered. "Whenever he comes he has to have a suite and there have to be lots of windows. Even though he stays by himself, he's got to have all that space. I remember the first time he came here. He had on jeans and a T-shirt and was clutching a brown paper bag. I asked him how he was going to pay, and he said cash. He said he'd be staying awhile. Then he reached into the bag and pulled out three thousand dollars. Later I found out that his grandfather had left him an oil business. That happens."

There have always been eccentric characters who came to the hotel—people who had fallen into half-mad grooves of life and didn't work at all at trying to be normal. Some of them lived lives that were curious beyond words. Years ago, there was a man, one of the oddest ever to stay at the hotel, who came from Philadelphia and was extraordinarily fearful of germs. When he checked in, he rented not only one room but also the rooms to the left, to the right, across the corridor, above, and below. He then slept in each room in rotation. He believed that by the time he got back to the original room, the germs would have died out. His meals were served covered with a cloth. He was never seen without white gloves on. The chambermaid had to deliver fifty towels each morning. Letters were read to him over the phone. The Plaza staff, despite all the extras he demanded, were quite fond of him. He met the most important criterion of all—he tipped exceedingly well.

Evander Berry Wall (the "King of the Dudes," who used to be considered the best-dressed man in America—stiff shirts, tailcoats, Byron collars, silk hats) lived in the hotel in its early days and had to be kept well stocked with champagne because, besides drinking it, he reportedly rinsed his mouth with bubbly. He often boasted, "I have never had a drink of water." Anna Gould, one of the hotel's wealthiest tenants and the daughter of robber baron Jay Gould, stayed at the Plaza after the Second World War in a grand ninth-floor suite. She constantly suspected she was about to be poisoned. Therefore all her food was tasted before she ate it. Two bodyguards accompanied her everywhere. Each morning she was visited by her therapist. When Brigitte Bardot came to New York in 1965, she stayed in Gould's old suite.

"We get these special cases, but, all in all, the Europeans are the most demanding," Mulero said, scratching vaguely at his right elbow. "They're used to the concierges in Europe, who do everything but dress the guests. They don't understand it's different here. They walk in and expect me to go to Tiffany's and buy them something and bring it over. Or when a cab pulls up, they expect me to pay the fare. In Europe, the concierge has runners who go shopping for guests. We have to explain that we don't have them here."

A man came by and asked Alexander Bisbal if he knew where to go for dinner with a ten-year-old.

"Yes, I would try Rockefeller Center. There are restaurants there, and I think the skating is still on. That would be a nice thing for the child to watch."

A scruffy young man asked Mulero how he could get a license to be a tour operator in New York City.

Mulero stared meditatively at the man. "I would think you should get in touch with the New York Convention Bureau."

Next at the desk was a foreigner probing his teeth with a toothpick. "I'm wondering," he said, "is there a good place to go bowling nearby?"

"Bowling?" Mulero said. "Just one moment. Let me check."

5

ROBERT Bachofen, the food and beverage manager, came into Hud Hinton's office to say he was firing one of the waiters in the Oyster Bar. His offense was simple and unforgivable: stealing. The first whiff of trouble had come a couple of months ago, when it was discovered he had omitted a Perrier from a check. It was a well-known waiter trick. You deliberately neglect to include a dessert or a couple of drinks on a check and then jokingly explain to the customer your oversight. Since it was your mistake, you tell the customer not to worry, you won't bother to adjust the total. Delighted at saving $5 or $10, the guest will usually toss down an extra few dollars for the waiter. Meanwhile, the hotel has lost some revenue.

After one transgression, the hotel would have fired any newcomer to the staff. Because this particular man had clocked eighteen years of service, however, the hotel chose to overlook it on the chance that it was an honest error. But now a second report had come in reflecting further mischief. This time he had failed to mark down a soup and two portions of strawberries on a bill.

Hinton was a little bothered that an employee of such long standing would stoop to crime against the hotel. But facts were facts. "I guess it's pretty obvious what we're dealing with," he said to Bachofen. "There was no mistake here. The guy definitely goes."

"Okay," Bachofen said. "I'm going to give him the news."

A fairly persistent problem of all hotels, I had learned, was waiter theft. In fact, after hearing tales of bag boosters and guests making off with Plaza robes, and now waiters chiseling on checks, I had become convinced that, outside of sleeping, the main activity that went on at a hotel was stealing. The truth was, I was told by Hinton, that a hotel could quickly be pressed into bankruptcy by runaway theft.

The food and beverage people had the greatest opportunity to steal, since a vast amount of cash passed through their hands. Over the years, waiters had figured out a fair number of ways to rip off the hotel, all of them hard to detect. Often a waiter intent on stealing worked in concert with a cook. If a waiter could get the meals for a particular table out of the kitchen without presenting a check to the cook—the only evidence that a meal had been served —then he could give the party a phony check of his own. If the party paid by credit card, the waiter had no choice but to turn in the check. No money in that. If cash was presented, however, he could just pocket the bills and destroy the check. At some hotels, waiters went to the bother of having checks printed up that were exact duplicates of the real ones to make their scam as authentic as possible. It was well worth the effort. A party of four having dinner in the Edwardian Room might spend $300, more than a waiter's weekly salary.

Another method for easy money sidestepped phony checks altogether. When a customer paid cash—again, say, for a group of four —the waiter didn't bother presenting the check to the cashier, but kept the money and the check. His problem now, however, was to get rid of the check, because all checks that went through the kitchen had to be signed for by a waiter. What he did was wait until another party of four came along. Then, as skillfully as possible, he tried to suggest that the group order the same four entrees as had the previous party. If they did, then he palmed off the check on them. In practice, this wasn't as difficult to accomplish as it sounded. Waiters trying the scam for the first time were often amazed at how easily they pulled it off. "Oh, I must say that the filet mignon is extremely good today. The missus might like the shrimp. If anyone cares for steak, the sirloin is excellent. If you don't want red meat, the chicken is just exquisite." Even if a waiter managed to convince only three of the four to choose the same entrees, that usually was good enough. Very few people studied their checks closely enough that they would pick up one wrong entree. Experience taught a waiter which checks to pocket and which to pass on because they were too unusual. A party of four, for instance, that had two racks of lamb was not a pocket possibility. Not enough orders of rack of lamb occurred in a given day to make unloading that check likely.

Hotels are full of stories of thefts: the waiter who doubled his salary year after year and was once even named the employee of the month, the waiter who pocketed the cash from the same couple that dined every week at the same table and ordered the same entrees. News moved quickly when money was involved. One of the hotel's employees, now in management, told me about a fancy Mexican restaurant that was driven to the wall because of waiter theft. He used to work as a cashier at the place, which enjoyed a very good midtown location and attracted a rather faithful and well-heeled clientele. "The waiters were stealing like crazy," he said. "They used pretty much every imaginable trick. Some of them even used pens with disappearing ink to write orders with. They gave someone the check, pocketed the money, and then, when the ink vanished, reused the check. When they got tired of writing, they would present the check at the cash register. The place was always full, but no money was coming in. One Friday night, the manager came over to see me. The place was extremely busy. He asked how many checks had been presented, and I told him eighty. Then he asked the maître d' how many people had been seated, and he said two hundred. He was furious. Everybody but two guys was stealing. It was pretty absurd."

Bartenders got in the act, too. This same man mentioned a telltale sign of bartender theft. "If you ever go to a bar, particularly one at an airport, and see straws lined up on the bar, you can bet something is going on," he said. "Each round is measured by the bartender by a straw. With regular customers, he may have ten straws down there but he'll tell the guy he's only going to charge him for eight rounds. The happy customer will then tip more heavily. Here at the Plaza, we require the bartender to ring up every drink after every round."

Jeffrey Flowers once worked at a seafront hotel in Manila, and one month the food costs rose alarmingly. A canvass was made of the supply refrigerators, and a huge quantity of meat was discovered missing. For days, efforts were mounted to find out what had happened to it, to no avail. Finally, quite by accident, one of the assistant managers came across a concealed hole under a cutting table. Construction men had been fixing sewer pipes that snaked beneath the hotel and, in the course of their work, had burrowed under the kitchen, sawed a hole in the floor, and started filching steaks.

When Westin took over the management of the Plaza, it found rampant stealing in the Edwardian Room. Most of it resulted from checks being presented twice. The waiters were ringing up twenty breakfasts, when sixty or eighty had been eaten. Westin clamped down, fired many of the waiters, and began to keep a closer eye on the replacements. Some theft, though, continued. It was impossible to rid the hotel of all of it.

ONE way the Plaza tried to throttle theft was by engaging in spot undercover checks of its employees. Like most luxury hotels, it hired one or another of the outside investigative services that, for a fee, would study the quality and integrity of a hotel. This sort of work commonly was done—and to a large extent still is done—by lumpy ex-cops or private detectives, who would nurse a whiskey at the bar and wait to catch someone dipping a hand into the till. Some specialty firms, though, had recently seized much of the business. The Plaza had retained a few different outfits, but the most comprehensive report it got came from D. Richey Management, a Connecticut outfit founded ten years ago by two former chefs named Dave Richey and Todd Lapidus. They sank $2,000 into the concept and now had a business that attracted revenues of $4 million. It specialized in hotel inspections—it had some five hundred clients, and just about all the familiar hotels—though it also did snooping work for a few movie theaters, making certain ticket takers were on the up-and-up (they once found a man printing up fake tickets on his Apple computer) as well as checking to see that the seats weren't sticky from food residue.

D. Richey was extremely sneaky. Twice a year, two-person teams from the company checked into the Plaza unknown to any member of the staff or management. They adopted false names. They stayed for four days, and during the course of their stay they scoured the hotel, poking into everything, sampling every conceivable service. Richey and Lapidus went out themselves on some reviews. Detecting theft was not their main goal—though it was an inevitable by-product—but rather judging the overall quality of the hotel. They would look for cracks in the walls and lint on the carpets. They would check that the maid put the bedspread in the same place every day. "In a luxury hotel, consistency is very important," Richey told me when I spoke to him in Connecticut by phone. "Guests expect it." The team would note whether the turn-down maid left three mints on the nightstand rather than two. "That may not sound like much," Richey noted, "but putting down an extra mint could cost a hotel a thousand dollars a year." Two of the most important staff policies were eye contact and addressing guests by name, and so the inspectors would make note of any slipups in those areas. They would call the operator and leave a message for themselves. A little later, they would call back and change the message and wait to see if the operator gave them the corrected one. They would summon a bellman and ask him to fetch a pack of cigarettes and see how long it took and how courteously the errand was executed. They would send their shoes down to be shined. They would shove a candy wrapper under the bed and see if the maid cleaned it up. They would order room service and clock how long it took, as well as watch details such as whether the waiter removed the plastic cover from the glass. They would also take a picture of the cart and the meal. Then they would order the exact same thing the next day and take another photograph. They would compare the two pictures. In a luxury hotel, there should be no discernible difference. They would go so far as to get on their knees and see if the wheels of the room-service cart were clean. Grimy wheels were a common flaw in a less-than-perfect operation. D. Richey thought they should be sparkling.

What showed up all too frequently in the Richey reports was dishonest behavior on the part of one employee or another. They had caught sticky-fingered waiters, front-desk attendants who would collect $30 worth of phone charges from a bill and then erase them from the computer. They had discovered kickbacks in purchasing departments, though never at the Plaza. "We've learned that kickbacks can also happen with the concierge," Dave Richey explained. "The concierge may continually refer guests to his cousin's restaurant, even if the food is the pits, and then the cousin pays him a little something. We discovered one concierge at a well-known New York hotel who was getting a kickback from a barber, of all people. Every guest who needed a haircut was sent to this guy, and the concierge would get five bucks a pop."

Once they were finished, the Richey inspectors handed in a two-hundred-page report and about a dozen photographs, keeping the managers busy reading for days.

TODD Lapidus, in town for some checkups, had coffee with me in the Palm Court and filled me in on the Richey operation. Whenever he walked into a hotel, even when he wasn't working, he found it hard to shake his habits. He inspected every employee he came in contact with from the moment he entered the hotel. He deliberately asked a bellman to recommend a restful place to sit and have something to drink and grimaced when he suggested the Edwardian Room, which had closed until lunchtime. "He should have known that," Lapidus said. In the Palm Court, he was impressed that the waiter thoughtfully mentioned that he ought to move his briefcase closer to his chair, where it was less in danger of being stolen.

It was cool and quiet, with no sound but the clink of cutlery from a few other early diners. As we sat, Lapidus recalled some of the shortcomings that the Richey teams had found at hotels. "I'll tell you one of the classics. One of our agents, Steve Rubenfeld, had just finished an inspection of one of the great luxury hotels on the West Coast, and he was at the exit with the manager and he said, 'We're really concerned about the valet parking. I could literally take any car of yours and drive off.' The general manager shook his head and said, 'Oh, come on—when you say something like that, it makes me question all the other comments in your report.' 'Okay,' Steve said. 'Watch this.' He picked up one of the house phones and said, 'This is Mr. Chan. Could you bring around my Rolls.' You see, Steve had overheard Chan asking for the car the other day. Now Steve is a six-footer, very Jewish-looking. It's pretty hard for anyone with eyes to mistake him for oriental. Well, around came this beautiful Rolls-Royce. Steve went up to the car and handed the guy a dollar. 'Mr. Chan?' the man said. 'That's right,' Steve replied. And the man gave him the keys and he got in and drove the car around the block, making extra sure he didn't hit anything. Needless to say, the manager was flabbergasted. See, the hotel had procedures. You were supposed to present a claim check. But over time, procedures atrophy or they are only followed when the big man comes around."

Lapidus smiled wryly and then recounted another story about a bellman who tried too hard to please. "This was at a high-quality New Orleans hotel. I had this bellman, and when we got to the room, I asked him what there was to do around there. By asking that, we find out if he markets the facilities of the hotel or if he sends you down the street to the competition. The bellman replied, 'What do you mean?' 'Well,' I said, 'I'm looking to have some fun.' The bellman perked up and said, 'I can help you out.' Whereupon he reached into his pocket and pulled out four joints of marijuana and offered me one. 'Oh, no, I wouldn't want that,' I said. But he insisted I go ahead and take one, and he refused to take any money for the stuff. When I asked him his name in case I wanted more, he replied, 'Avis, like the rent-a-car company. We try harder.' I gave him a tip and brought the joint to the final interview with the hotel's general manager, which resulted in the end of that man's career at the hotel. The whole idea was to give free samples in the expectation of picking up subsequent sales. It was also a way to get bigger tips."

Lapidus said that hotels try very hard to invent new amenities and novel services. He brought up the Portman Hotel in San Francisco, which allowed complimentary car service to meetings and stores in Rolls-Royces, and he mentioned another hotel that furnished complimentary condoms to guests each morning. But he felt the timeless basics were what mattered the most. "If you ask me as a professional evaluator what the most important things are, it's that the reservation is there and correct, that I get from the curb to my room quickly, that the mattress is good and the sheets are clean, and that room service comes on time. Everything else is nice, but those are the important things. The reason guests return to a hotel is rarely something dramatic but usually some little subconscious thing that they can't even identify. It's a feeling. And it grows from simple things."

D. RICHEY had been stealthily checking up on the Plaza since 1982, and its impression of the hotel had changed rather markedly. "On our first visit to the Plaza, we weren't too thrilled," Richey had told me. "I frankly hated it. I couldn't understand why anyone went there. The employees were surly. The rooms were in bad shape. The food and beverage area was lousy. But I just saw Hud Hinton the other day and I told him what a marvelous job they've done in turning the place around. I'm not even sure how they've done it, but they've done it. Right now, I think the Plaza compares very well with other hotels in this class in New York."

As we sat in the Palm Court, Lapidus read me some notes from the most recent Richey report on the hotel, which was quite positive. "The inspectors seemed to like the Plaza a lot," he said as he scanned the pages. "Staying in so many hotels, we always like the hotels of distinction, the old grandes dames, because the cookie-cutter hotels are downright boring. They may be clean and all, but they're boring. Two years ago, I see, there was a problem at the Plaza with messages. Sometimes the message light wasn't turned on or there were incomplete messages. In our last survey, though, we put in six or seven messages and they were perfect. So they turned that baby around. There were a few inconsistencies in the turn-down service. We found that the bedspread was not always put in the same place. So that's something to watch for. With room service, the order takers were saying 'Anything else?' at the end of the order. That's not the preferable way. They should be marketing the menu by asking if the guest would like an appetizer or a dessert. That also gets the check up. We also wanted to make phone calls after we checked out, and the front desk was unresponsive. It's very expensive for a hotel to process late charges, but a good hotel should do it. I understand that's changed here. And the food got pretty good marks. Hotels take this bad rap, you know, about their food. The old saying is 'I don't sleep in restaurants and I don't eat in hotels.' But they don't deserve that here."

In the course of accumulating their reports, the Richey team members had to worry most of all about evading detection. If their cover was blown, their investigation became worthless. At times, when Lapidus feared he might be too familiar at a hotel, he would don glasses and paste on a wig. Even with physical disguises, remaining incognito could prove ticklish. During the course of their brief stay, the two agents were expected to order enough food and drink to kill most people. Necessarily, they had to leave some of it uneaten and undrunk. "Like in the movies, we have to do things such as pour drinks into planters and hurl chicken legs out of windows," Richey said. "If our people drank all the alcohol they have to order they'd pass out. I was doing a report myself at a Chicago hotel and came awfully close to getting caught. I had ordered a room-service meal that was a candlelight dinner for two. Unfortunately, I didn't realize it was served in four courses. The problem was, I was the only person in the room. So when the waiter knocked on the door to serve the first course, I had the shower running and told him my wife was still getting ready, just leave the tray. I even called to the bathroom, 'Honey, the food's here.'

When he came back the second time, I had to tell him, 'Oh, she's fixing herself up in there. I don't know what's going on with her.' Meanwhile, I was so full from eating the first course that just the sight of food made me incredibly sick. So I was flushing the food down the toilet while he was getting the next course. Well, by the time we should have been done with the entree, the toilet was now overflowing from all the stuff I had dumped into it, my wife was still nowhere in sight, and the waiter was breezing in with flaming baked Alaska. If he at all bought what I told him, he must have thought we were an unbelievably weird couple."

6

ONY Bonsanti, a wooden stepladder propped on his shoulder, moved speedily down the fourteenth-floor hallway. He was clutching a sawed-off cardboard box crammed with a miscellany of light bulbs. His eyes were trained upward. He saw what he was looking for, halted, and dug a bulb out of his box. His job—his only job—was replacing burned-out light bulbs.

"Bulbs all day long," he told me as he nimbly unscrewed the dead hallway light. "That's what I do. Nothing but bulbs. I'm a trained electrician, so whenever it's slow with bulbs, I'll do other things. But let me tell you, it's rarely slow with bulbs. This place is hard on lights."

Bonsanti dropped the expired bulb in his box for later disposal and twisted in a fresh one. "There," he said. "Light has been restored."

He picked up his stuff and headed to the next assignment. "Here's my routine," he said. "When I come in, I go down to the bulb storeroom in the subbasement and get my box and fill it up with bulbs. I go to the lobby and first floor and check the lights there. The lobby's the most important place. Every guest goes through there, so we can't ever have a bulb out. I really get chewed out if I don't have all the lobby bulbs glowing. Okay, after that, I refer to a list of bulbs that have been called in by the maids and the security people. I start at the top of the hotel and work down. I'm the only one here, so I have to plan things. I get all my work orders and I group the ones that don't call for a ladder and I do them. Then I'll do the ladder jobs. It's tiring carrying that ladder, so I don't want it on my shoulder any longer than I need it."

Room 1360. A hall light. "Hmm," Bonsanti said. "It's okay. It's supposed to be out. Someone screwed up." This didn't seem to faze him.

"How many bulbs do you replace in a day?" I asked.

"Ugh!" he exclaimed. "I've got thirty-five so far today, and more die as the day goes on. Thirty-five or forty is a normal day. During the busy season, I do fifty. That's when I really have to run. That's when the house is a hundred percent full and the lights are going out right and left."

Bonsanti was slight, with dark hair, watchful eyes, and a carefully coiffed beard. He was in his early thirties and quite extroverted.

Room 1256. Night-light. "It's dead, all right," Bonsanti said with conviction. In a few seconds, it was alive.

"Is there a technique?" I asked.

"You unscrew the bad one," he said, "and then you screw in a good one. That's about it. There's no magic to it."

He moved around the room, flipping switches on and off. "While I'm in a room, I always check all the other lights," he said. "Why not? That way I don't have to come back. There are usually bulbs out that people don't know about. I find them. I'm like a bulb detective."

As he left the room, he said, "I know every crack in the hotel. Because I see every crack. It's my job."

The dimensions of Bonsanti's job were better understood when one realized the Plaza had something like thirty thousand light bulbs. Each guest room alone contained about fifteen bulbs. In all, the hotel used about 150 different types of bulbs, from three-watt "Feeling Flame Lights" that went in the lobby chandeliers to the three-thousand-watt spotlights in the Grand Ballroom. When he walked through the hotel, Bonsanti was looking up with assessing eyes, hunting for dark bulbs.

Room 1068. Bed lamp. "I sometimes go into a room on one call and end up replacing three bulbs. See here. The desk lamp is out, too. Nobody caught it. I had to do it." After he fixed it, he inspected the bathroom, turning switches on. A light above the sink had expired. "Bulbs are going out on me like crazy," he said. "It's some battle today."

The sink light replaced, Bonsanti was ready to go. There was a dead bulb waiting on nine.

Between floors, Bonsanti told me how he got the light-bulb job. "I was born in Italy in the little town of Pomarico. I came to America with my mother when I was ten. I was in the Navy for four years, and then I worked as a gas heating and air conditioning mechanic. My cousin was in sales here at the Plaza and told me about the bulb opening. The benefits weren't that good at the old job. And the Plaza Hotel, as you know, is the Plaza Hotel. When I came here, there were three bulb men. One became an electrician and I worked with the other guy. A few years ago, the other guy quit, and I've been left alone, the whole weight of light on my shoulders. Partly it's my fault. I've been running around like a crazy man doing the job alone, so they think they don't need anybody else. I must admit, I've met a lot of stars. I do the spotlights for some of the functions at nights. I did the spots for Henny Youngman once. I did spots for Robert Klein. I did Red Buttons. You do meet the stars—that's an attraction of the job."

Room 805. A desk lamp. Bonsanti flicked it on. Nothing. He scrambled underneath the desk and found the plug out of the socket. "See that," he said. "Housekeeping unplugged it to plug in the vacuum and then they think the bulb is out. Happens constantly. Constantly." He shook his head from side to side and gave a small pout.

Bonsanti quickly checked the other lights, all of which were in order. "Okay," he said. "This room is physically fit."

He headed down the corridor. "I don't usually walk like this," he said to me. "I run. I have to keep up. You've got to fly through this hotel."

He rapped on the next door and a woman's voice, in an unpleasantly piercing tone, responded, "Who the hell is it?"

"Maintenance," Bonsanti said. "I'm here to replace a bulb."

The door whipped open, revealing a large-bodied woman. She had a swaying stance and gave every impression of having recently taken some relaxing refreshment.

"I've got a report of a bulb out," Bonsanti said.

"Well, let's put it back in," the woman said.

It was a closet lamp, a forty-watt job. Clothes on the floor blocked his way. "I've got to move this stuff," he said. "People just dump their stuff on the floor."

As he left, the woman said, "Let there be light."

"You get some of that," Bonsanti said as we headed down the stairwell. He talked in a barking voice, calling back over his shoulder.

"One problem for me," he continued, "is every management that comes in has a different theory on bulbs. Now we use forty-watt long-life bulbs. When I started here, they had seventeen-watt hallway lights. You could barely see what you were doing. The place was set up for bats. Now that kind of thinking was absolutely ridiculous. Seventeen watts! Fine, if you're a coal miner. My theory on bulbs is use the long-life guys. They make my job easier and you save money."

He whisked into Room 617. "Will you look at this!" he said. "I've got three out."

Bulbs flew out of his box and into sockets. The grumbling persisted. "The guests come in here and leave the lights on and it's ridiculous. They should help me. They should shut them off. It's an insult to the bulbs. You know, some days I change one of these GEs and two days later it's kaput again. Ridiculous."

Room 333. Foyer light out. Bonsanti gripped the bulb and turned. The bulb stayed put. He tried again. No luck. Again. Nothing. "It's too tight," he declared. "I'll have to get pliers and come back. What a pain."

As he left, he flicked off a burning bathroom light. "See, I don't like it when people leave the lights on," he said. "It really bugs me."

As he clambered down the stairs, Bonsanti said, "You know the worst part of the job? When I have to walk into a room that's air-conditioned and I've been in a hot area. That's tough."

I wondered whether there were other drawbacks to the work. Bonsanti thought on that for a millisecond and said, "Once I tried to put in one of those U-shaped bulbs and it blew up on me. Lots of times bulbs have blown up on me. That's what you call an occupational hazard.

"Sometimes I have to get on a ladder and climb forty feet high. I'm used to it, though. The only thing I find awkward is the Palm Court. That has the hardest bulbs in the place. There are four lights in the ceiling that shine down on the statue in there. To change one of them, you have to squeeze into this cramped crawl space. You can't see. You have to talk to someone on the floor to find out if you're aiming the bulb right. If you miss the statue, it looks terrible. By now, I figure I've changed every bulb in this hotel. I've been in every cubbyhole in the place. I've been in every room, every hallway, every closet, every bathroom. Those Palm Court bulbs are the worst. Don't let anyone tell you different."

It was time for Bonsanti's coffee break. He took the service elevator down to the basement and wandered into Café Eloise, the employee cafeteria. He poured himself some coffee, spooned in some sugar, and settled down at a table near the back.

One of the pay phones against the wall rang. Bonsanti scurried over to it. It was his wife calling. Every day she made a point of calling at three-ten, during his break. They hated to miss an opportunity to speak with each other.

After he got done talking to her, Bonsanti said, "When I go home, I get mad when my wife changes a bulb. I feel I have to do it. But she was brought up by a father who's an all-around handyman. So she sometimes beats me to it."

I asked him what he had learned about bulbs from spending so much time with them.

"I've learned that if you keep a bulb on all day long and turn it off and then on, the filament gives out. That about sums it up. There's not much to learn about light bulbs."

As it happened, Bonsanti was already thinking of a life beyond bulbs. He was a musician. "I'm a bulb man by day and a musician by night," he said. "I write my own songs and play guitar and sing. I go in for mostly popular-type songs, like the Police do. I've got a three-piece band. The drummer and I write the songs. I write the music and he handles the words. The name of the band is Standard Procedure. We used to go into rehearsal every day and if there was anything wrong we fixed it right then and there, before we went home. We said it was our standard procedure. So that's what we called ourselves. We rehearse now every Sunday and perform about once a week. I would love to sing for a living. It's hard to crack into music, though. Real tough. But I like my job. There's nothing to think about, so I can also concentrate on my music. Sometimes I think of a tune while I'm working and I go to the ballroom and try it out on the piano and then I write it down later. I'm really left alone at the hotel. I get to walk all over the building. I'm free."

7

I MET Robert Voigt by accident. He had dropped off some things in his room and was on his way to an appointment with a banker. He was a small, stoop-shouldered man with a weathered countenance. He was informally dressed and a little disheveled, and he looked out of place in the ornate lobby. He had eight pens poking out of his jacket pocket.

Relaxed, he was telling me that he was from Detroit, where he owned a metal-processing business, but he visited New York at least twice a year and remained for a couple of weeks at a time. He always stayed at the Plaza, except once when he arrived very late and the hotel was booked solid. They called a limousine and put him up for free at the Howard Hotel. "It was a nice room," he said, "but I'm sorry to say the breakfast was poor. I really like the breakfast here. I always get the same thing: a giant bowl of Cream of Wheat. I have to make sure to inform them that it must be an elephant-sized bowl, because sometimes they give me a small one." The only other difficulty he ever had at the Plaza was in 1979, when Jon Voight, the movie star, happened to be staying at the hotel at the same time, and, even though his name was different, Robert Voigt kept getting calls from women angling for parts in Jon Voight's movies. "Before I got a chance to say I wasn't the right person, the conversation would have gone on for twenty minutes," he said. "Then I'd tell them and they still kept talking. It got to be tiresome."

I asked him why he was in New York, and he gave a little snort and said he was here on business. "My current project is this," he said, and he handed me a leaflet. It was entitled "KINENERGY." Voigt waited while I read it. The leaflet explained that Kinenergy was "the revolutionary answer to radiation free energy and the total replacement for nuclear reactors which serve as the front end source for atomic energy plants. . . . The kinetic energy of the electrons contained in the atoms of heavy water (deuterium) are converted to heat energy by a newly invented process which is unique, radiation free, pollution free and completely safe."

"It's a replacement for current nuclear power plants," Voigt explained. "I'm the chief executive officer of the company that's developing and promoting it. I've been involved with it for six years. It's in the development stage. But there's no question that it works. There's an operating system in Germany. I have a German partner in this. It's a German project that I'm transferring to Columbus, Ohio, for security reasons."

Voigt said he was convinced that the process would in time put nuclear reactors out of business. Some money, of course, would be involved. The leaflet spelled that out: "The estimated cost to replace an existing front end nuclear power plant reactor with a Kinenergy system is $1 per watt; or $500 million for a 500 megawatt plant. On average, added to this cost is approximately $250 million to remove the existing hot reactor and to clean up the plant from all radiation."

"The atomic plants in the United States are in a lot of trouble," Voigt said. He frowned into space. "It's for political reasons and because of evacuation plans. People are afraid of the China Syndrome.

"Right now, we've got something that can solve the economic ills of the nation and can influence ten percent of the gross national product," he went on. "With this process, we can become a net exporter of power equipment."

Voigt mentioned that just one pint of the substance produced by the process could propel a six-thousand-pound car for 250,000 miles, which seemed awfully impressive and a little hard to imagine. "It's true," he said, as if sensing my skepticism. "This will replace gasoline. If you could load up once—even if you paid, say, five hundred dollars a pint—and then have enough fuel for your car for years, wouldn't you do it?"

I told him I supposed I would. Begging his pardon, I asked him when he thought this technology would be up and working.

"We're going on a crash basis right now," he said. "I compare it with the Manhattan Project. In eighteen months, we'll be able to install a unit in a Detroit-Edison plant. That plant is going to be shut down. They don't know we're going to buy it, but we are. We're going to make them an offer they can't refuse. And then we're going to grow from there. This nation is in plenty of trouble with deficit spending and all that. This is going to help get us out of the hole."

Meanwhile, Voigt could not handle this innovation without adequate financial help. He and his partner needed to augment their resources with additional dollars. What he had in mind was $2 billion. Thus the calls on bankers. Thus the trip to New York.

One way or the other, Voigt said, he would find the money. "I'm committed to the extent of buying a bank if I have to. But I expect to get the financing, probably mostly from Japanese sources."

He peered at his watch and said he had better go. "You don't like to keep bankers waiting," he said. "Not when you're asking them for money."

8

THE prostitutes always amazed me. They could usually be spotted right away, but they were never bashful about marching right into the lobby. The old pros who had worked the hotel for years had the sense to stay on the streets until they had solicited a guest so they could come in accompanied. That was the simplest way to avoid annoying run-ins with the security men.

There were at least a dozen prostitutes who operated along the Avenue of the Americas near the Plaza; often once it got dark out there would be a couple of them planted on each corner of Fifty-eighth Street. For street prostitutes, they were a fairly classy group, and even bothered to dress in cocktail dresses and high heels, since they tended to do most of their work in one of the good hotels and it didn't pay to stand out. Anyone who had been on the hotel security staff for any length of time and worked nights, however, knew most of the regulars. The guards held no particular animosity toward them, looking on most of them as good-natured individuals who had chosen an unfortunate calling. They were resigned to the fact that they could no more do away with them than they could rid the air outside the Plaza of New York's grime. They felt that hookers were as much a part of hotels as room service and wake-up calls. "These girls are often pretty nice girls," said John McHugh, the assistant security director. "I talk to them and kid around with them. They're like you and me. That's just the way they make a living."

The security men, as it happened, never referred to the girls as prostitutes or hookers. They were known simply as "fifty-fours." Fifty-four was the hotel's code for a "suspicious person."

Even though the security force was relaxed about the presence of fifty-fours, it wouldn't tolerate any of them working the lobby or the bars of the hotel. That would give the place a shabby and disreputable appearance, even though quite a few guests who stayed at the hotel were always in the market for a call girl. So the guards were always on the lookout for women who lingered over a drink in the Oak Bar and gave unescorted men the glad eye. The only way a security man would let a hooker in was if she was on the arm of a guest, which happened with fair regularity. Hotel employees could determine pretty reliably the relationship of a couple. If a man pushed through the revolving door with the woman trailing in his wake, it was a sure bet they were married. If the man allowed the woman to pass first, she was probably a hooker.

Though the security men were forgiving of first offenders, prostitutes who persisted in loitering in the lobby or bars of the hotel were asking for a confrontation. They would find themselves escorted upstairs to the security office, where their picture would be taken and they would be warned that they had better not appear in the hotel again. "There was one girl I took up," McHugh said, "and I got the Polaroid camera out and said, 'Okay, it's time to take pictures,' and she pulled her blouse off and said, 'Fine, let's go.' 'No, it's not those kind of pictures,' I said. There was another girl from Ohio. She must have just gotten off the bus. We took her upstairs and gave her a warning. We give them a form to sign that says they won't come back to the hotel. So this girl signs the form. I said, 'You know what this means? You can't come into the hotel to have a drink or to have dinner or to use the phone. Not for anything.' She said, sure, she understood. Would you believe it, she came into the hotel the very next night."

The hotel also didn't appreciate fifty-fours who turned up in the hotel too often, even if they were with guests. They became overly conspicuous. Another greenhorn to the streets, dressed in a give-away outfit of short skirt and fishnet stockings, was spotted one evening in the hotel heading for the elevators on the arm of a man. Security let her go, since she was accompanied. About forty-five minutes later, she was back, this time with another guest. Again she was noted but let be. Forty-five minutes later, she reappeared with still another prospect. This time, one of the security men trailed her out to the street.

When he caught up to her, he said, "You're new in New York, aren't you?"

"Yeah," she said, "and you're security, aren't you?"

"That's right. Now, what's going on? You've been in the hotel three times in less than three hours. Don't you know better?"

"Well, what's the problem?" she said. "That's where my friends were staying."

"Look," the security man said. "Let me give you a tip. If you meet someone from the Plaza, then the next customer who says he's staying at the Plaza, pass him by. Take someone from the Park Lane. Then get someone over at the Sherry Netherland. Then take someone from the Pierre. Mix them up and nobody will bother you. Otherwise you're not going to last long in this town."

The hooker thanked the security man, and from then on she staggered her appearances at the Plaza.

I spoke to one fifty-four. She was a cheap-speed blonde, loitering outside a deli on Sixth Avenue, combing the passersby. She wore a cool smile, and she kept her back poker-straight. Her voice was a bit raspy. You couldn't have asked for a better evening. It was unseasonably warm, and there wasn't a trace of a breeze.

"You really get a pretty nice crowd around here," said the blonde, who told me I could call her Heather. "This here is where you get the first-class people. Farther west, you get plenty of sleaze. Around here, most of the guys are out-of-town businessmen staying in one of the good hotels. I do them all—the Pierre, the St. Moritz, the Park Lane, the Plaza. The Plaza is probably my favorite, though the Pierre is awfully nice, too."

I asked her what she liked about the Plaza.

"I just find the guys who stay there treat you with class," she answered. "Sure, you get dismissed kind of abruptly sometimes, but I find most of the guys are polite. They ask how I'm doing. What I've been up to. 'Course, I'm never up to much but doing tricks. You do get some odd ones. I had this one guy in his sixties who had this collection of *Mad Magazine*s with him and he was showing me his favorite stuff in these *Mad*s. I didn't think it was all that great. I really like the rooms in the Plaza. They make me feel good. I always do one thing. I take the little shampoo bottle from the bathroom. I like to know I'm doing my hair with Plaza shampoo."

LAMENTABLY for the hotel management and its guests, hookers were increasingly doing more than hooking. They were robbing clients. A popular strategy was for the prostitutes to slip their sleeping partners knockout drugs to make it easier for them to fleece them. These women were known as "roll artists." One of their most popular offerings was scopolamine, which is used medicinally as eyedrops for people afflicted with cataracts. One drop in your drink will ensure unconsciousness for a good six hours. If you had a bad heart, it could also kill you.

The Japanese, I learned, were the most gullible patrons of the hookers. In Japan, prostitution was more acceptable. Thus Japanese visitors didn't realize they were dealing with an altogether different breed of women. "The Japanese guest thinks these girls are nice girls and they'll sleep with you and that's it," one of the security men told me. "Well, some will. But many of these girls are tough cookies. They'll rob you, too, and the orientals don't know that."

Some of the hookers were brazen enough to do their thievery without drugs to gain them an edge. In 1971, Franz Josef Strauss, the West German political leader, was returning to the hotel from the opening celebration of a German restaurant when, by his account, two prostitutes approached him looking to do a little business. When he spurned their invitation (as he later told police), one of them wrapped her arms around him and took his wallet from his pocket. It had $180 in it. Though the women were apprehended, they got off because, despite persistent requests by city authorities, Strauss refused to testify at the trial, pleading "pressing political business."

One morning not long ago, a fairly wealthy guest stormed down to Hud Hinton's office and angrily announced that he had been robbed of thousands of dollars' worth of jewelry, including a Rolex Presidential watch. The man had come unhinged and wanted to know exactly what the hotel was going to do about this outrage. "Someone on your staff stole it, and I'm going to hold you goddam accountable," the man shouted. Hinton, who had been through episodes exactly like this before, patiently asked the man whether he knew of anyone who had been up to his room. No one, the man insisted. Fine, Hinton said, he would talk to security and get right back to him. Security proceeded to play its videotapes from the previous evening. There was a lot of boring nothing on most of the tapes, but one of the reels from an elevator showed the man heading upstairs with a woman who, to even an unschooled eye, was quite clearly a prostitute. ("She sure as hell wasn't his wife," Hinton remembered.) While the two of them were in the elevator, she already had her hands probing in the man's pants. Hinton called the guest back to his office and played the tape for him. He squirmed as his face turned crimson. When the tape was done, he told Hinton, "Thank you very much." He got up and left the office and was never heard from again.

By Hinton's estimate, not two weeks went by that a guest didn't bring a prostitute to his room, get slipped something, and get rolled. During private moments, hotel managers admitted that if hookers dressed expensively enough that they couldn't easily be picked out as prostitutes and if they didn't rob their customers, then they would be welcome in hotels simply because so many guests desired their services.

A DARK, frizzy-haired woman, her face coated with makeup, was slowly cruising Sixth Avenue, expectant. She was a plain, buxom woman who had an unnaturally wide mouth with thin lips, a flaw perhaps of no great significance in her field. Her eyes were on the procession of pedestrians—the druggists, computer salesmen, honcho executives, heavyset women, real estate brokers, and rah-rah conventioneers—who streamed down the avenue. Whenever an unescorted man passed by, she fluttered her eyelashes in an exaggerated way. She got a few smiles and a few sneers, but no takers. Business had been a little slack, she told me through teeth clenching a cigarette, but she was confident it would pick up. It always did. "People coming to these fancy hotels are always going to need someone like me," she said with a world-weary smile. "You can bet on it."

Rates, I had been informed, were fairly standard in this neighborhood: twenty bucks for a hand job, $50 for fellatio, $100 to $200 for conventional intercourse. If the customer wanted the hooker to stay with him overnight, that was usually another $500 plus a room-service breakfast. Farther downtown around Times Square or in Greenwich Village, rates were often half these, but the class of hooker was also discount. Those men who put a value on high-priced talent and didn't go for street-corner pickups took their business to the escort services, which would deliver a bed partner right to your room. The women tended to be extremely well dressed and knew how to move through the lobby with the practiced air of an old-time guest. No matter what the price of the entertainment, some of the cost, no doubt, got tucked into expense accounts.

"I make it a habit to always ask for room service, even if it's going to be a short trick," the heavily made-up woman told me. "I like seeing those little trays come in. The waiters, I must say, are very polite at the Plaza."

I inquired how long she spent with a customer.

"A lot of times it's only about fifteen minutes, maybe a half hour," she said. "About a hundred bucks for fifteen minutes. I've gotten over a thousand a couple of times for an overnight."

"A thousand?" I said.

"Sure," she said. "Once I got a thousand to just talk with a guy at the Plaza and have a room-service order of shrimp cocktails and champagne with him. The guy loved shrimp cocktails and didn't

want to have his alone. He was telling me about how his boss was
jerking him around. He'd had to work the last three Sundays in a
row, and he was real pissed. Beats me why he wanted to tell this to
me."

"What sort of customers do you get?" I asked.

"All kinds," she replied. She was growing a little impatient,
because the weather was turning and now rain seemed likely.
"You'd be surprised at the variety. Big-business types. Salesmen
are always great. Lots and lots of foreigners. The Japanese are
wonderful. Excellent tippers, and very respectful. There's all this
Japan-bashing going on these days. Not from me. I love 'em."

Rain had begun to spit down, but then providentially stopped,
improving the woman's economic outlook for the night. "I'll tell
you about another real character," she went on. "He had this whole
routine. I had to draw a bubble bath for him and then call him
when it was ready, like I was his wife: 'Yoo-hoo, bath's ready,
dear.' While he was soaking in there, I was to order cognac from
room service. When it came, I had to bring it in to him on a tray.
Then I had to dial the weather number and get the report. Then I
had to dial this sports phone and tell him the latest sports scores.
Then I had to sit on the john and read to him from this book of
horror stories. All these creepy ghosts and blood and guts. The stuff
really seemed to scare the wits out of the guy. What can I say?
There's a lot of loneliness in those hotels."

A couple of good-looking but pudgy men were heading her way.
"Excuse me," she said. "I may see some work."

THURSDAY

1

T HE air smelled of soup boiling, potatoes frying. With a big spoon, a cook stirred the pot of mushroom soup, then stirred the clam chowder. Emanations of sage and garlic came at me.

The kitchen was like nothing I had ever seen—a sweltering hive of activity, deafening with the clanging of pots and pans. Cooks skipped to and fro, their faces dripping sweat. There were counters where a mob of waiters clamored with trays. Everyone seemed to be in a terrific hurry. The place served about two thousand meals a day.

The hotel actually had six kitchens—the main kitchen, a kitchen for each of the restaurants, and the banquet kitchen. To keep up with all the cooking and cleaning, close to a hundred people worked in all of them.

Reiner Greubal sagged into a seat in his tiny office. He studied a memo, signed a couple of papers, and then picked up a fistful of new recipes that had been recommended to him. As the executive chef, Greubal probably directed as many meals as any person alive. He was a wary, stone-faced man who wore one of those big white chef's caps that look like gargantuan mushrooms. His office was in the basement, adjacent to the main kitchen, and was predominantly walled with glass, so he could watch food being prepared at all times. "What you see here is the main kitchen," Greubal said. "It's primarily the preparation kitchen. Any food that arrives in the hotel in some form passes through the main kitchen. Take a vegetable. It comes through here and is cleaned and partly prepared; then it goes to one of the satellite kitchens to be used. It gets its final cooking there. The same thing happens with meats. We also have the cold kitchen, or pantry, where we prepare salads, dressings, fruits, and cold meats for all the other kitchens."

An assistant sauntered into the office and asked whether the menu had arrived for an upcoming banquet.

Greubal moved his shoulders expressively. "Haven't seen it yet," he said.

The chef normally got to the hotel at seven in the morning. He ate a plain roll or a bagel with a cup of tea in the little dining room next to his office. At two, he had a lunch that usually consisted of either pot roast or veal stew ("something with the sauce on it"), and he generally skipped dinner or munched some cold cuts. "If I ate what I liked," he said, "I'd roll down the stairs. Because we nibble too much. We have to."

Greubal was an active head chef, in the sense that he got his apron messy. "Occasionally—about thirty percent of the time—I'll cook things or try new things or tackle the delicate items. There's no new dish or recipe that I don't try out myself. I taste all the food for banquets. That's important. For VIP affairs, it's the same treatment, though you give more attention to details—the presentation of the food and the like. You might throw in a little bit more butter or cream in the cooking, too, but that's about it. The other thing is, for a VIP you always make the meal beforehand as a test and even take a picture of it so you can see how it looks. You don't wait and do it blindfolded. We're not here to gamble."

EACH morning at ten, a menu meeting was conducted in the chef's small dining room to discuss the meals for that day's functions. It went quickly—a few comments on each group and that was all.

The Women's Sports lunch. No wine to be served. "It's a fitness theme. So no booze." "Going to be a boring lunch."

UAL. "Give them VIP setups. The whole works."

Combustion Engineering. "The word is that they tend to take the danish with them, so we'd better put out extra danish. You know how those people are." "Just make sure we charge them for the extras."

After the meeting, I meandered through the main kitchen. It was a jumble of white-tiled walls, against which were gray-and-black ranges, dishwashers, and silver-polishing machines. The place was so enormous that there were directional signs on the walls to point the waiters to the stairs and elevators leading to the different banquet halls and dining rooms up above. Big ovens stood against the wall with yellow paper taped to them to show what was cooking inside. Château potatoes were in one. Veal was in another. Carrots and asparagus were in another. A man with wet, freshly combed hair hurriedly wheeled in a cart of cauliflower and dumped it into a bin to cool. Another man of indeterminate age was lugging a bag of rolls with a sense of authority. Someone else was sprinkling salt on the wet floor so workers wouldn't slip.

A great deal of specialization characterized the kitchen. Some cooks made only sauces. Others prepared soups. There was a meat butcher. There was a fish butcher. Some people made vegetables. There were pastry people and a baker. Several of the cooks also did ice carvings for banquets. They had done the ABC initials, an eagle, a lion, an old gramophone for RCA.

In one corner, I ran into Eric Bedoucha, the pastry chef. He was poking through the day's offerings. There were trays full of cookies. "We make half of the cookies and we buy half from La Côte Basque," he said. "Sometimes we go through a hundred and fifty pounds of cookies in a week. We don't have the time to make them all ourselves."

He looked at some cakes. "Here's the famous Opera Cake. For my taste, I love this the most. But it's very flat, and people don't go for it. They want big stuff."

Whenever he studied the newly made pastries, pretty as they might seem, the pastry chef would smolder. It seemed so silly, so unfair. Why did they have to be so big? "When I came here a little over a year ago," he said, "I tried to change the style and give people small pastries. I thought small was better. It looked better. But our clientele here are mostly tourists. They come off the street and are hungry. And there's a lot of Jewish clientele, and they want big stuff."

Bedoucha couldn't believe it, but a wild peal of protest rose from these shriveled spinsters and overweight tourists. They had rather fixed feelings about their food size. It had to be enormous. "So we now make a medium-sized pastry," Bedoucha said. "In a few months I'm thinking about making very small ones and letting them eat as much as they want. That just might work. Small is definitely classier."

He sighed. "It's so hard to do quality work in a big hotel. I worked in Chicago for two restaurants. It was two different worlds. It was amazing what I could do there. But here it's impossible. I try to do something special for an event—I do it myself—but it's so hard. We can't compete with the really good restaurants, because we can't devote the time. It discourages me when someone upstairs goes to eat in a good restaurant and says it was fabulous, they made this and they made that. Why can't I do it? I can't with this volume. Tomorrow for lunch we have seven hundred people. How can I do it?"

STEVE Soha, the meat butcher, was working on some short loins in a long, narrow room way in the back. "I do loins, strips, top rounds, rib eyes, legs of lamb, eye of veal, calves' liver, sweetbreads," he said. "I've been carving meat down here since 1971. I know meat."

I asked him if there was any technique to the cutting, and he said, "When you cut, you don't press. You move the knife in a sawing motion. The meat cuts better that way. Now we almost always have to get the bones out. The meat would taste better with the bone in it, because the bone has more flavor than the meat. But the people today don't want to cut around the bone. Twenty years ago, everything was with the bone. That's the way I like it."

Down the way, Frank Madera, the fish butcher, was carving up a tremendous swordfish with a large knife. "You want to know how we cut the portions?" he asked. "In the past, everybody got the same portions. Two years ago, we changed and wanted to make things different in the Oak Room. So we give the Oak Room about two ounces more of the fish. The same with the meat. Our normal portion is about eight ounces, except scallops are about six. For the Oak Room, we give them about ten ounces. The most popular fish in the Plaza are salmon, Boston sole, and red snapper. We serve about a thousand salmon steaks a week here. We serve that like crazy. We don't bring in any frozen fish, except shrimp. We order two hundred to three hundred pounds of it a day. We have to get it frozen."

Eric Riley, the soup and sauce man, was in a bright and cheerful mood. He stood over a ninety-gallon kettle of chicken stock. "The idea is to let it simmer," he said. "If it boils too fast, it changes color."

There were eight kettles of varying sizes. Soup was being made in each of them. "We've got four restaurants," he said, "so we make a half-dozen different soups a day."

He led me into a chilled room, where big pots of soup and sauce were stored. There was onion soup, chicken consommé, beef consommé, New England clam chowder, Manhattan clam chowder, lobster bisque, cream curry with mussels. There were also two big containers of tomato sauce and some mint sauce. "A small restaurant or hotel wouldn't do this," he said in a carefully modulated voice. "They would make it all new every day. But we couldn't keep up."

I RETURNED to the chef's office, where Greubal, one hand pressed against his temple, was reviewing some menus. "I make up the menus here for each of the restaurants," he explained. "Every three months, I try to change them a bit. Basically, I leave the popular things on them and I replace the less popular ones with new dishes. I'm in the process of going through the Edwardian Room and changing a few things. Smoked scallops are going. They're not doing too well. A menu is an extremely sensitive issue, because the guest really dictates what you sell. I arrived here in 1985 and I took a look at the Oak Room lunch menu. It had corned-beef hash on it. I said, 'What is this?' That's a breakfast item, and I didn't think it had any business being on a luncheon menu. So I immediately took it off. Well, that nearly set off a revolution. Guests went absolutely berserk, and they began to complain to the management. So I had to stick it back on. I can't figure it out, but that hash dish is one of our most popular luncheon choices. In the Palm Court, there was a chicken meat dish with mayonnaise. I nixed that and it was the same story. In this hotel, I've learned that there are some dishes that you just don't mess with."

He removed his cap and ran his fingers through his hair. "As a newcomer, you feel the Plaza Hotel should be a trend restaurant. Trend is nice. But once you're in this building for a while, you realize it's a very traditional place. People are very set in their ways. You have a lot of old-timers. Maybe not in age, but they want the same thing. Even in the size of portions. I'll give you an example. In any steak house on the West Coast, you serve ten-to-eleven-ounce steaks. And that's large. Here it used to be thirteen to fourteen ounces. I said that was ridiculous. I cut it back to ten or eleven. A guy came up to me and said, 'I like your cooking, but I don't like to have a breakfast steak for dinner.' So we're back to thirteen and fourteen ounces. I have a theory that people who entertain a lot don't have three meals. They skip lunch or have an early breakfast. I put myself in their shoes. They need a bigger meal."

Greubal had to take a phone call, and then he continued, "This is a lot different from running a restaurant. My philosophy is, if you want to learn how to cook you have to start in a restaurant. And you ought to go from a coffee shop or a diner all the way up to a quality restaurant, because all your decisions are based on history. You feel more comfortable in knowing the variety. That's necessary for a hotel chef, because you have that whole variety in a hotel—a coffee shop up to a gourmet restaurant. Here, of course, it's a little more uniform, since we have no coffee shop. By the way, a coffee shop doesn't mean you have to have second-quality food. It just means a different type of preparation. There's nothing wrong with a hamburger if it's seasoned properly."

I asked him how he estimated how many meals to prepare for.

Greubal said he did his planning according to the number of occupied rooms. Even though upward of 80 percent of the meals served in the restaurants were to local people who were not staying in the hotel, management had found that it could reliably predict the quantity of meals according to the number of guests. An occupied room, it found, generated an average of $97.50 per day in restaurant revenue. "We have quite good forecasting," Greubal said. "You know your room counts and there's a formula. As a rule, sixty percent of the rooms will have breakfast here. You should get at least thirty percent of your room count for lunch or dinner. I don't know why, but that's a formula that tends to work day in and day out. It's amazing."

I asked Greubal what ever went wrong, and he mentioned soups going sour and dishes burning, but he said those weren't what really worried him. "The biggest headache," he said, "is when you lose electric power. That's bad. We've also had the kitchen flood when some pipes broke. When there's heavy rain outside, water often leaks into the kitchen. These things you get used to."

"Is a meal for a function ever totally ruined?" I asked.

"If that happens, you can pack up your suitcase," he said. "That should never happen. You learn to prepare your food early enough and give yourself enough lead time so you can fix it if something goes wrong. If a soup goes sour or something is overseasoned, you do it over. If it's a little late, you serve another drink. My philosophy is you get the complaints that way, but it's better to serve the quality rather than not serve it right."

2

I TOOK a break and walked around the perimeter of the hotel. I stopped for a bit and admired the flags. On the five flagpoles outside the main entrance flapped the Australian flag, the Japanese flag, the American flag, the Plaza flag, and the Westin Hotels flag. On the roof of the hotel, as always, were two Plaza Hotel flags and an American flag.

The flag room was on the banquet level near the Blue and White Suite in, of all places, a small closet that was actually inside the men's room. The hotel owned 137 flags, give or take two or three. Every so often, an old one would finally wear out and be discarded or someone would donate a new one to the collection that he would like to see flown outside the Plaza. The room housed the flags of many of the world's countries—Bolivia, Chile, China, Cuba, Iraq, Mali, France, Haiti, Iceland, Libya, Ethiopia, Peru, Turkey, Trinidad, Norway—and a goodly number of state flags. There was also the presidential flag, the papal flag, the Red Cross flag, the Marymount flag (someone left it behind after a function), the United Nations flag, and the United Fund flag.

Even the hammer-and-sickle flag of the Soviet Union had fluttered on one of the poles in 1960, when Nikita Khrushchev had come by for a reception given by the Togo delegation to the United Nations. The attitude of other guests was simple and direct: they didn't like him. The Russian leader wasn't too proficient at keeping his cool, either. When he got riled because he had to wait for an elevator, he was roundly jeered by the crowd in the lobby. Khrushchev simply stuck out his tongue.

The flags were twelve feet by eighteen feet and were made out of nylon. They were changed every day by one of the lobby porters. An assistant lobby manager kept a flag log that showed which flags had been flown each day and why. The main reason was to welcome a guest of prominence from that country or state. If there was a bagpipers' convention, the hotel would make sure to put up the Scottish flag. When a French tour group was staying at the hotel, the French flag would be waving outside the doors. "We try to be promotional and respectful," one of the assistant managers said. "If there's nothing specific happening, the flags will be flown at random. Sometimes I'll fly the Austrian flag or the Polish flag just for kicks. We get complaints now and then. We've occasionally had someone put a flag up upside down. There's a chart in the flag room to show how they should look. But I've even had them fly the Westin flag upside down, if you can believe that. We also get complaints when we've got the flags out there and it starts to rain. Sometimes we forget. You're not supposed to fly flags in rain. We also won't fly a flag in anything over a fifteen-knot wind. That'll rip it to shreds. It's important having those flags out there, but like everything else, it can be a pain, too."

3

ALWAYS thought of the permanent residents as the shadowy figures of the hotel. They were hardly ever seen; they were given to staying drearily in their rooms for much, if not all, of each day. Although many of the employees seemed to know one fact or another about them, nobody knew all that much. Their pasts seemed shrouded in mystery. "Oh, they're pretty strange," one of the bellmen told me. "I generally stay away from them." A maid said, "The trouble with some of them is they don't think they're guests here. They think they own the place."

I spotted one eating in the Palm Court, humming to herself. She seemed to have a knowing aura about her, not so much haughty as well informed. Her eyes were a little shifty, and her breath came hard. I tried introducing myself, but she merely went on humming.

These women—all four in residence were elderly widows—were the hotel's most evident anachronism. The lodgers were a floating population, staying a day, a week, and then disappearing. But the permanent residents never left—and wouldn't, in all likelihood. They would dawdle here until they died.

Of course, they had no powerful reason to leave and a persuasive reason to stay. They were living in a classy hotel and paying a pittance. They had moved in many years ago, when World War II-vintage rent-control laws were enacted in New York that forbade landlords from hiking the rents of residents with long-term leases. There were many such tenants at one time, but their number had steadily diminished to the lingering four. Each of them paid less than $500 a month for suites that cost at least that much per day. One of them on the third floor occupied a suite that would rent for $750 a day and yet she paid just $465 a month. Their presence did not seem entirely fair to the hotel management. All of the permanent residents were believed to be quite well off. Employees had been convinced of that from their mail. One of them, I was told, got brokerage statements from sixteen or seventeen different firms. The hotel, nevertheless, had no choice but to grit its teeth and tolerantly collect the dismal payments.

Until recently, there was also one permanent resident in a class by herself. She was a middle-aged widow, quite comfortable financially, who preferred living in the hotel to buying a snappy apartment somewhere. She didn't inhabit a rent-controlled room, but rather received a 20 percent discount, the equivalent of what a regular corporate user got, for a medium-sized room. She had lived under this arrangement for many years. Her daily rate was $139, or $50,735 a year. After her room was renovated during the hotel-wide restoration, the management informed her that, like the other guests, she would have to pay an increase. She refused. After some back-and-forth bickering that led nowhere, the management contacted marshals and she was evicted. She moved to California and sued the hotel. The litigation was subsequently settled, and she has not returned to the Plaza.

A few decades ago, there used to be some couples among the permanents, though as time passed and husbands died, the permanents dwindled to a collection of widows. In fact, years ago, when they were more plentiful, they were referred to as "the thirty-nine widows of the Plaza."

Sadness is frequently a dominant emotion of widows, but the Plaza women always appeared to draw on a deep reservoir of spunk. One still heard tales of Mrs. Frank Stanley Freeman, whose father was one of the country's first radiator makers. Her husband, a

banker, died on their honeymoon in 1887 and she never bothered
to remarry. She lived in the hotel for more than thirty years, until
death claimed her at the age of 103. Though she gadded about,
enjoying conversations with many different men, she believed it
was a waste of time to talk to women. On her hundredth birthday,
she got a telegram from President Eisenhower. It seems she voted
for the first time—for Eisenhower—when she was ninety-nine.

One of the best-known of the widows was the lusty Clara Bell
Walsh. The descendant of a wealthy Kentucky horse family, she
moved into the hotel the day it opened, two years after her marriage
to Julius Walsh, Jr., who owned a streetcar line in St. Louis as well
as part of the Royal Typewriter Company. A great horse aficionado
herself, she traveled for years with a vanful of horses to endless race
meetings, collecting an impressive pile of trophies. Her husband
died in 1922 ("I have no near relatives surviving, thank God!" she
used to say), but she continued to live in her four-room suite on
the seventh floor, decorated with pink draperies and old English
hunting and racing prints, until she succumbed to a cerebral hem-
orrhage in 1957.

Soup was part of the spell the hotel held over Clara Walsh. She
thought the Plaza's chicken soup was the tastiest in the world.
Known for her tart tongue and her abundant charm, she was fond
of giving frequent parties. The only thing she drank was Kentucky
bourbon, straight. She was well acquainted with the show crowd,
and so she left her door open from five o'clock on each evening.
People like Jimmy Savo, Ed Wynn, Mae West, and Amos 'n' Andy
were apt to come by. In March 1957, three months before her
death, the hotel gave her a birthday bash and invited a couple of
hundred guests to the State Suite. Those who showed up included
Mary Martin, Richard Halliday, Dame Sybil Thorndike, and Ethel
Merman. Among other odd distinctions she enjoyed, Walsh was
one of two women permitted to have their hair cut in the barber
shop. Mary Martin was the other.

The remaining permanent residents, most of the employees
agreed, were in general a pretty crotchety set. Their partying days
were finished. Some workers—a few of the maids—managed to

strike up friendships with one or another of the permanents, but many of the staff members, even those used to suffering particularly insufferable guests, felt they would be happier if none of them existed.

Of the permanent tenants, Mrs. Courtland (not her real name) was considered the most obstreperous. She was so formidable that she gave pause to every employee who encountered her. When she appeared in the lobby or one of the restaurants, her stuttering steps drew anxious stares. She seemed to enjoy nothing so much as making trouble. She was, I was told by a few employees who had aroused her scorn, quite quarrelsome. Quarreling seemed to be her vocation. Her eyes were distrustful. Her mood was snippy. "She really figures this is her hotel," one of the maids informed me. "She will boss you every which way but sideways. You can't ever do enough for her. Clean this. Dust that. Move this. Get me that. I need another towel. There's a spot on the rug. Man, she'll have my tail going. I'm sweating by the time I get out of there."

Once she summoned housekeeping so her cigarette could be lit. She would want a chair painted antique gold rather than fancy gold. She would want something upholstered. She would want a table moved four inches to the left, please, and right now, if you didn't mind.

One afternoon, she decided to have lunch in the Palm Court. When she got to the lobby, there was a line of twenty people waiting to be seated. Ignoring them, she simply marched to the front and demanded to be seated first. When she was told that she would have to wait her turn, she threw a noisy fit and one of the assistant managers had to come by to calm her down. She was often quite rude to maids; she insisted on extraordinary cleaning performance, and would order a maid back to her room to remove a single piece of lint from the carpet. Don't ever try to interrupt her when she was talking, I was told, or her short fuse would get shorter.

For one thing, she had a lock on her door that the master key carried by the maids wouldn't fit. Thus her room could never be cleaned when she wasn't there. What was more, no maid was allowed to knock on her door to see if she could now do the room.

Instead, she had to go about attending to her other rooms until
Mrs. Courtland came trotting down the hall and gave her the
welcome news that she could now enter. A greenhorn who had
never had the special experience of cleaning Mrs. Courtland's room
would be in for a scathing denunciation if she went about making
her bed the normal Plaza way. Typically, Mrs. Courtland would
watch her do it, take a deep breath, let loose a torrent of fire, and
demand that the maid strip the bed and begin anew. Then she
would tell her that the sheets were not to be tucked into the
mattress, and the top sheet was to be turned over at the very top of
the bed, right next to the headboard. Nothing less would do. "She's
fussy and she wants to be nasty," one of the maids told me. "She
gets pleasure out of being that way. Don't ask me why. But she
gets something out of snapping at people."

The phone operators were always engaged in strained battles with
Mrs. Courtland. She would constantly ring them and request special attention. "I'll be in the Palm Court; put all calls through to
me there," she would say. Or, "I'm going out of the building for
an hour, so if a man calls for me, have him meet me at the corner
of Forty-eighth and Fifth." At one point, her regular room was
being renovated, and thus the hotel temporarily moved her to
another room. She didn't like it. She was given still another room.
It was better, she decided, but she wanted to test it for a few nights
before she relinquished the previous one. This went on and on. At
one point, she had three different rooms assigned to her. When
calls came in, the operators were instructed to try each of them
before taking a message. No one was sure where she was sleeping.

I tried to talk with Mrs. Courtland, but she greeted my overture
with great suspicion. "How did you know I lived here?" she wanted
to know. "Did the management tell you? Because they're not supposed to. That is not allowed." She said she would mull over my
request, but she could make no promises. When I phoned her room
again, she said, "Oh, no, I couldn't do that." And she hung up.

Another of the permanent residents was more agreeable. She had
had a stroke several years before, right after her husband had died.
As a result, she couldn't get about without help, though she could

talk perfectly well and her mind remained in good order. However, she needed to have a full-time attendant living with her, and, for whatever reasons, she chose not to leave her room. In the past, she had occasionally boarded a wheelchair and gone to see her doctor, but now even he came to her room. As far as the hotel staff knew, she hadn't been out of her room in years. For the most part, she lay in bed watching TV. Visitors were infrequent; the only regular was her lawyer. She had no children. When she needed any money, she called down to the manager and he had some sent up. For breakfast, she ordered something light from room service. For lunch and dinner, she dispatched her attendant to a nearby delicatessen to bring her something. She complained that the hotel food was too spicy for her taste buds. "She likes to talk to us when we clean her room," a maid said. "She talks about the hotel and the sort of life she led growing up. She's full of memories. She tells me all about going to school as a young girl and the fun she had skating in Central Park. I know she said that after she got married—I think her husband was on the stock exchange—they lived in an apartment. Then they moved into the Mayflower Hotel and then into the Plaza. She's been here a long, long time, but now all she sees is the walls of her room."

4

"RYING to fit people into beds is what this place is about," the man said. "It's answering the phone and trying to meet requests. It's about cribs and roll-aways and mostly about king-sized beds." The man's name was Joe Schneider. He was the director of reservations.

He hunkered before a computer terminal in his rather drab office, positioned in a corner of the hotel's second floor, near the executive offices. Through a sizable glass window he could watch the reservations staff. Seven steely-eyed agents sat like telephone operators, headsets wedged on their heads, their hands pecking away at computer keyboards, inputting names, dates, and special requests. Though many calls for a room at the Plaza went to travel agents or to an 800 number, about 60 percent rang in this room.

Schneider was a thin, pale man, with a bald pate and a somewhat bilious stare. He used to work in the car-rental business, for Hertz. Car reservations wouldn't seem likely to teach a man very much about hotel rooms. But then Schneider didn't take much personal interest in the people who stayed at the hotel, even though he was the one responsible for who got what bed. To him, the guests were digits in his computer.

It was impossible to satisfy everyone, for the preferences of guests were relentlessly alike. Everyone, Schneider said with a broad, slow smile, wanted a view of the park, though some of them backed off when they learned the price. It cost between $50 and $75 a day more for a room that allowed its occupants to peer down on Central Park than it did for a room overlooking Fifth Avenue, which cost $50 to $75 more than a room with no view at all. Most guests, however, shut their eyes to the price differentials and stuck with their requests.

"So many people want that park view," Schneider told me, nibbling on his nails and keeping one eye trained on the pulsating activity among the reservation agents. "But we get all types. Some people want quiet and to face into the interior courtyard. Some want to be away from elevators. Some are terrified of heights and so they insist on a low floor. Claustrophobic people want to be put on a low floor, though most want to be as high as possible for a better view. There are always special requests. Some people are allergic to foam pillows. Some want refrigerators for medicinal purposes. They want king-sized beds. Something like eighty percent of our guests request king-sized beds. Only a few people ever ask for twin beds. People ask about pets. A few people want pianos in their rooms. We turn them down because of the noise factor. Quite a few cribs are requested. We have about a dozen of them, and we have maybe eighty roll-away beds. During heavy periods, like Thanksgiving and Christmas, we make it a point to rent some more beds to satisfy the demand."

Schneider got up and went outside his office to confer with his assistant about a VIP request for a room. The date fell during an impossibly clogged week, and the reservation agents were conveying to callers of lesser standing their regrets that there were no more rooms available. Schneider's solution to this potentially sticky situation was to advise his assistant to accept the booking, for he felt certain that he could somehow juggle another arrival and squeeze the man in.

Schneider glanced at the upcoming bookings. Business at the hotel, he said, fluctuated dramatically according to the day of the week. Tuesday, Wednesday, and Saturday were the hotel's busiest days. Thursday and Sunday were the valley days, when the hotel would like to drag people in off the street and force them to take a room for the night.

Every Wednesday, a room-occupancy forecast was distributed by the reservations department to the hotel staff. It was their bible, telling them the expected occupancy for the next ten days as well as giving a ninety-day estimate. Those counts determined staffing and how much in the way of supplies to order. In a hotel, the most expensive cost was labor, and so having just enough manpower was critical to profitability.

"We've got quite a wide menu of rates," Schneider said. He picked up a rate schedule and perused it. He shook his head, pleased to see all those numbers. "If only we got the numbers that were on here," he said, and he shook his head again, a little less vigorously.

Schneider always viewed hotel rate schedules with suspicion, as any informed guest ought to. Schneider knew that relatively few guests, wherever they happened to be staying, paid "rack rate," the published full price for a room. Rack rate was pretty much a sham throughout the hotel industry. The main concern of guests was not whether they would get a discount, but how much of a discount. There was a corporate rate, which sounded impressive. Virtually anyone could get it; it was extremely rare for the hotel to ask a caller to offer any kind of proof that he was actually employed by a corporation.

Most weekday bookings were made forty-eight to seventy-two hours in advance, though the weekend tourist business was normally booked a week or two ahead of time. Reservations always followed a short cycle, making forecasting tough. Most people stayed for one or two nights. Foreigners lingered longer. Australians seemed to hang around the longest, typically putting up for five to ten nights.

Schneider said that there were also as many as ten "walk-ins" a day, people who simply turned up at the front desk looking for a room and had no reservation. Most times, they could be accommodated, even when the hotel was supposed to be booked solid. Like airlines, the hotel during congested periods would book more rooms than were available, expecting no-shows, which averaged about 5 percent of the reservations. On the other hand, five to ten people each day came to the conclusion that they were going to stay a night longer than they had originally planned. Some of the no-shows inevitably were pranksters or kooks. Every now and then, a person would call up posing as a celebrity and book a two-bedroom suite at $1,200 a night. One time a couple of teenagers reserved a room, and when they appeared to claim it they brought along twenty-five friends and more than a few cases of cheap beer. They were rather sharply counseled to try another hotel.

Once or twice a year, someone would show up who held a reservation and the hotel was full. (Despite common mythology, hotels don't routinely put aside a room in the event the president of the United States or Sting walks in off the street without any prior alert.) When that happened, the Plaza quickly found the guest a room at an equivalent hotel, paid for the transportation there, paid for the room for a night, and also picked up the cost of one telephone call. Sometimes, when New York was jam-packed, the hotel had to engage in frantic searching to dig up a room and wound up with a substitute that was of less than equivalent grandeur. On a couple of occasions, a guest bound for the Plaza found himself unhappily (and uncomfortably) sleeping in the Howard Johnson Motor Lodge.

LUNCHTIME was always the hotel's most convivial hour. The atmosphere was light, the drift to the various restaurants was casual, and talk was uninhibited. The patter ran from boyish and girlish gossip to business strategy and romantic whims.

In the commodious Palm Court, the waiters moved among the tables, falling into a small rhythm of their own. For a short while, I watched them work. There were several tables of heavy smokers in close proximity, and I played a little game. A hotel rule, I knew, required waiters never to allow an ashtray to contain more than two butts. Three presumably was too dastardly a sight even to imagine. So I watched the ashtrays fill and the waiters descend on them like locusts to see how well they stayed under the magic number. At one table, the ashtray never got beyond one. Filled. Emptied. Filled. Emptied. Two tables away, the drama was much greater. One butt. Two. Emptied. One butt. Two. A third halfway there, then an arm darting in just in time. The smoker reacted with a rather bewildered look.

Many of the guests were fussy, as well they ought to have been for what they had to pay for their meals.

The three guests at one table were women.

The oldest said, "These waiters take their sweet old time. I'd like my cake, wouldn't you?"

The second: "Oh, I suppose I would. You know help today. Just don't care. That's what Fay was saying."

Fay: "Let's watch it on the tip. That's the only way to be in this city. Skimp on the tip."

The oldest: "Good point, Fay. Why don't we keep it at ten percent."

I HAD coffee with Hope McCormack. A limber and lean-faced woman with a modest smile, she was a baby-sitter, but she was different from most baby-sitters in that almost all of her work took place in hotels. Just about every week, in fact, she could be found ensconced in one or another room at the Plaza, minding someone's child.

"I've been in and out of here for the last nine or ten years," she said. "I specialize in infants—from a month old to two years—and though I occasionally go to homes, I mostly do hotels—the Plaza, the Pierre, the Waldorf, the Carlyle, the Athénée. Those are my spots."

She worked for an outfit called the Baby Sitters Guild, which had cultivated a good rapport with the midtown hotels, and so it was often recommended by concierges to guests in search of sitters. Hotels don't like to have staff baby-sitters because of liability worries. McCormack was in her fifties. She considered her age one of her most important assets. "The agency doesn't have any twenty- or twenty-two-year-olds," she told me. "They can take care of the kids, all right. But they don't know how to maintain themselves in a hotel like this. And if young girls are in the lobby of a place like the Plaza, the men hanging around might want to date them. You know how it is. They shouldn't be working in hotels. Age is a very important consideration."

McCormack blinked blearily. She looked a bit tuckered out, and she confirmed that she had recently been through a rather trying experience. She had been hired by a fashion designer staying at the Wilson Hotel with a four-month-old. The designer was in town on business and was never around. "I worked for her for twelve straight days," McCormack said. "And some of these were eighteen- or nineteen-hour days. I'd get two or three hours of sleep. At the end, I thought I was going to have a nervous breakdown. I was shot. I adored her infant, but I was glad when those twelve days were over. These are the crazy things you get into."

McCormack sipped her coffee. She said that despite the occasional punishing schedules, her specialty made for marvelous times. New York's hotels had a grip on her. She loved their ambience, the smell of success about their guests. She was unashamedly happy about her work. "I very much prefer the hotels to homes," she said. "They have all the conveniences. They have these miniature refrigerators to keep the milk in. And they're near the park, so I can take the children there. I just feel good in them."

The Plaza was her particular favorite. "Every time there's a call here, the woman who runs the Guild gives it to me, because she knows how much I like it," she said. "When I was young, I used to come here on dates and go dancing. We used to go to the Oak Bar and everything, really do it up right. The old-fashioned rooms here are so lovely. I'm Norwegian, and so I love the old-world charm. In the evening, if the child gets restless upstairs, I'll take him down and walk him around the lobby. When the music is on in the Palm Court, we'll stand behind the palms and listen. Then we'll look in the windows of the stores. We'll window-shop. I can't stand the new hotels. For instance, I don't like the Palace at all. Too glitzy. It's not for me. I work there. But I don't like it."

An antique woman waddled past and bumped McCormack's chair. McCormack gave her a sharp, angry look, but the woman didn't notice and kept on waddling.

"I get mostly show people and business people," she said when I asked her for an account of her clientele. "I had an actress who had a baby two weeks old. She hadn't even lost her umbilical cord. The mother was finishing a film and I had to baby-sit. I had an Israeli child who spoke no English. I sort of used sign language. He really liked puzzles. In fact, when he was six he got a prize in school for putting together a puzzle of a thousand pieces. I had a Saudi Arabian child, too. I remember that when I ordered room service, the mother ran and put a towel over her head so the waiter wouldn't see her. I had a pair of five-year-old twins who had cystic fibrosis. Their parents had won some sort of contest and got an all-expense-paid trip to New York. They had a spare oxygen tank in the room for the kids. Fortunately, I only had to give them oxygen once. I'd say that was certainly my most difficult assignment.

"One of the hardest things is when people come from California and there's the time change," she continued. "You have to stay up late with the kids until they fall asleep. I find it takes at least two days before the kids adjust to the new hours."

Baby-sitting had proved to be gainful employment for Mc-Cormack. Her fee was $10 an hour for a baby less than six months old, $7.50 for older children. A four-hour minimum was required, and if she stayed after midnight she had to be paid $12.50 for transportation home. She was also to be provided with a meal. The prices at the hotel made her a trifle edgy. Parents always told her to go ahead and order whatever she liked from room service, but she was never cavalier. Her angular face broke into a slow smile. "I try to stay under twenty dollars for a meal. It's not as easy as it sounds. I usually have a bowl of soup or an omelette. Or I might order chicken for a two-year-old and I would share it. They don't eat everything, you know. The prices are really something else. I mean, it's six dollars for a pot of coffee."

McCormack came to baby-sitting late. Her first career was as a nightclub singer. "I traveled all over," she said. "It was wonderful. But I don't like to talk about it. It's a sore spot." When I pressed her to tell me more, she made a face and looked away, muttering something about how she didn't want to dredge up memories. She gave up singing to have a son. Her husband died young and she was forced to raise the child alone. "I regret it a little. I see now the mothers have two, three kids and they keep working. I stayed home from when he was born until he went to college."

Though she subsequently remarried, McCormack found herself adrift once her son was out of school. "I was looking for something to occupy my time," she said. "I'm full of energy. So I joined up with the agency ten years ago. I work six days a week. I can't get enough. I've taught kids how to walk. I've taught them how to eat, how to talk. The parents don't have the time. I do it. There's a four-month-old who I sit for regularly. I was just with her last night. She knows my voice. If someone else goes there, she cries all night."

When we were done, we stepped out into the lobby and were engulfed by a sea of businessmen. They surged forward, heading for the doors. McCormack said she had to hurry off. She was doing a stint for a seven-year-old and a nine-month-old at the Waldorf-Astoria.

$$6$$

"YOU really see a lot of messy clothes down here," said Leonard Labonia. Then he noticed a crescent-shaped gravy spot on his own shirt. He gave a cramped smile. "And I wasn't even including myself."

The laundry room, wedged deep into the far reaches of the sub-basement, was always hot and noisy. Its well-worn washing machines suggested years of laundering soiled linen and clothing. It was a vast place, cut up into several adjoining chambers. It was stiflingly hot—it must have been 120 degrees Fahrenheit—and somewhat dark. To get to it, you had to walk through what seemed to be miles of dark, labyrinthine passages that had the feel of the lower decks of an oil tanker. There was the heat and the crowded space and the odor of food and the humming noise. Aproned waiters and porters from the kitchens hurried through the passages transporting meat or bread or ice. One man had a huge slab of beef on his shoulder; sweat was pouring down his brow. If someone got in the porters' way, they would shout, "Look out, look out," and then dart past. It was no place to loiter or to stop and light a cigarette.

Leonard Labonia, the laundry manager, had plenty to occupy him. His department did so much washing that he sometimes felt as if he were annexed to one of the Washex washers, tossing in there with the detergent. Labonia, an extremely good-natured man, had a long, pudgy head and sported a bushy mustache. He once ran a commercial laundry in Atlantic City and then became a salesman for a laundry-equipment company based on Long Island. Among his many clients was the Plaza. ("Sold 'em an ironer once," he said.) Coincidentally, when the company he worked for found itself going to the cleaners and had to declare bankruptcy in 1987, the job of laundry manager opened up at the Plaza. Labonia applied and got it.

Outside his small office, big chattering machines stretched away into the distance; shapes of washers and dryers and steam tunnels loomed nearby. The laundry workers moved back and forth, their faces dripping sweat and their clothes drenched. Everyone was in a hurry. Sometimes the pandemonium was such that it seemed as if the workers had only three minutes to live. I began to understand that there had to be chaos behind the scenes in a hotel if there was to be order in the environment that the guests saw. Squads of workers waited impatiently for clothes to wash and dry, and then retrieved them. Fluttering fingers smoothed out towels and sent them through automatic ironers. There was more than $1 million worth of equipment in here, Labonia said, mopping at his face as he stood watching clothes tumble in one of the big washers.

Laundries are vital to a hotel. If linen can't be cleaned efficiently, rooms can't be gotten ready, and guests can't be accepted. "The laundry is one of the most important places in a hotel," Labonia said, wiping some hair from his forehead. "If you don't have a laundry, you can just forget it. No laundry, no hotel. I'm not kidding."

Ordinarily the laundry staff's morning started at six and the day ended at three-thirty in the afternoon. An extra person hung around until seven in the evening, in case any late pressing needed to be done. The laundry handled three kinds of work. There was the basic hotel laundry, which involved seventy thousand pounds of bed and table linens a week; the valet service, which took care of guest clothing; and the staff uniforms, a category that included the suits and dresses worn by anybody in the managerial ranks. That went for Lenny Labonia's suits, as well. "They always do a good job on them," he said with a big grin. "They'd better."

"Let me show you where it starts," Labonia told me, and he led me into a square room half a flight up from where the washers were whirring. There was a metal chute that emptied into one corner of the room; beneath it was an immense pile of dirty bedding. Along two walls of the room were chutes leading into the subbasement with numbers marked on them. A sour-faced laundry worker was bent over another giant pile of wash in the center of the room, containing all sorts of things; methodically, he picked through the mountain and hurled items into one or another of the numbered chutes.

"What we have in the hotel is a central chute that goes all the way to the eighteenth floor," Labonia explained. "The maids collect the sheets and pillowcases and then the houseman on the floor drops them down the chute. My man down here separates them by category and shoots them into the appropriate chute here. There are six categories: sheets, pillowcases, facecloths, hand towels and bath mats, bath towels, and rugs. I've got three chutes for sheets and, boy, I need them. They're my big category."

At times, he said, things arrived in the laundry that he didn't expect and wasn't particularly happy to see. Every so often, a maid for some reason tossed a vacuum cleaner down the chute. There were days when newspapers came fluttering down. Once a Snoopy dog came down that a woman guest had treasured since she was five. It had been tangled in the sheets. The woman just about did a jig when she got it back. Labonia found a calculator once, and another time a vibrator. On still another occasion, a can of Ajax cleanser came thundering down the chute. "It sounded like an atomic bomb when it hit," one of the laundrymen said. "Ka-boom! Scared the living daylights out of me."

Pleased with how the sorting was going, Labonia smiled and his eyes got big and round. He moved on to the room below.

After it was sorted, the laundry dropped into wheeled hampers. When the hampers were full, they got weighed on big scales set in the floor. Each one ought to weigh three hundred pounds. The washers each had a six-hundred-pound capacity, so two hampers filled them up. There were three of them, as well as one 125-pound washer and one thirty-five-pounder for employee uniforms and guest clothing.

I stepped out of the way so a man pushing a laundry hamper could get by. "Coming through, coming through," he shouted. "The wash must come through."

"All tablecloths, sheets, and pillowcases go straight from the washers to the ironers," Labonia said. "The smaller stuff goes to the dryers. I've got four hundred-pound dryers and one two-pound dryer. Uniforms go through a steam tunnel on a hanger, so I don't need to press them. Then we've got automatic folders. When they come out of them, my people put them on racks.

"Each floor has two racks," Labonia continued. "When an empty one comes down, I send up a full one. Here's the fifteenth floor. Here's number fourteen. They go up starting at eleven o'clock in the evening. Same time each day. That way the maids don't have to call me all day—where are some more sheets, some more rugs. It's all based on occupancy—what we call the 'par' allotment for each floor. If we're fifty-three percent full, I give them a rack that's fifty-three percent full. This is scientific stuff down here."

Labonia sailed into another room, where the dry-cleaning machine stood. He glanced at a clothesline of uniforms and suits. "Here's a security," he said. "Here's a manager. Here's an Edwardian Room. Here's public relations. We do them all. We'll do an employee's uniform every day if he wants. But he's got to get it to us. If a guy wants to be a bum, he can be a bum. If he gives it in, we clean it. I like a tidy employee. But what can I do? I can't rip the clothes off somebody's back so I can clean them. I mean, really! What can I do about a bum?"

Over time, Labonia had learned to expect pretty much anything in the laundry. Some fussy guests wanted all their lingerie returned on hangers. Occasionally he got ratty underwear with holes in it and then the guest complained the laundry had ruined it. Even if he knew better, Labonia took the position that the guest was always right. If he said his underwear was ruined, then the hotel agreed to pay for fresh shorts. Labonia would never forget the woman who sent down a metallic skirt with starburst pleats in it for pressing. "There must have been fifty pleats in it," he said. "We told her no way, because you have to block and iron every pleat individually. But she insisted. We had one guy work on it for two and a half hours. It was absolute murder. That's the sort of thing that makes this job so challenging."

Labonia dawdled in the dry-cleaning room for a few minutes watching sleeves being pressed. He was satisfied now and bounced up and down on the balls of his feet.

"Shirts are the bulk of the business on the laundry side for our guests," he said. "We do about two hundred a day. The charge is four dollars a shirt. It's no bargain. If we wash a pair of underpants, that's four dollars. A pair of socks is a dollar seventy-five. It's sixteen dollars to dry-clean a suit. Suits are the big item for dry cleaning. We do about fifteen or twenty a day. We have a shoe-shining machine, too. That's two fifty a pair. We get maybe ten or twenty pairs a day."

Labonia and his laundry staff were kept busy by dirty guest clothing, but not as busy as they would have liked to be. The laundry manager slumped in his chair and studied some statistics he had worked up. "We get about ten percent of the rooms," he said. "That's the way it is month in and month out—ten percent. We do what we can to get more. We put signs in the room. That's about all you can do. You can't advertise. It's the guest who is better off who uses the laundry. Probably the expense-account folk. Because we're expensive. It's my labor. These people are unionized and they make about ten dollars an hour. How can I wash shirts cheap with that? So we're never going to get everybody. That's just a fact of life the laundry lives with."

$$7$$

CREDIT problem had arisen with a man who had checked in several days ago. His room and food charges had climbed close to $2,800 and his credit card was now beyond its authorized limit. The front desk wanted some sort of certified check or cash. A couple of days before, the guest had left his passport with the front desk as security and under the condition that he would redeem it the following day by bringing his account up to date. But he had not been in touch despite several messages from the credit department. Finally, he had come down to straighten things out. The man was a little huffy when he was informed of the situation. He kept a hard, set expression on his face as he was invited into the back office, where he quickly handed over a check to cover his indebtedness.

The problem made me curious about credit, so I went to one of the cluster of cubicles behind the front desk and talked to John Walker, the front-office credit manager. He had thick brown hair and was going over the day's check-ins. He looked a little tired.

His job was to monitor guest accounts to make sure that the hotel had a suitable method of payment for every room. "We always have minor credit problems," he said, pursing his lips like a schoolmarm. "Major ones are pretty rare. Every night, when I go over the accounts, there are small things. The imprint of a credit card may not be clear and we can't read the number. So we have to have the guest come down and redo it. Or there might not be enough credit available on a card. When that happens, another card or cash will have to be offered to supplement the card."

Credit was always checked when a guest arrived at the front desk, unless it was extremely busy, in which case the people there would look into it an hour or so later, when their load lightened up. Decades ago, the hotel considered it impertinent to inquire how a guest was going to pay. It simply trusted that the bill would be satisfactorily handled. It did, though, take one small precaution. Bellmen, while waiting for a guest to finish signing in at the front desk, would pick up the luggage to feel how heavy it was. Light luggage was a signal that the guest was a "skipper," who was likely to take off and stiff the hotel. Thus whenever a bag felt empty, the bellman would hold it up in front of him to warn the front-desk person.

When there was a real credit problem, Walker's goal was to contain the spending. If the owed amount was less than $500, then Walker just instructed the guest to leave and the hotel absorbed the loss. It didn't consider such a sum sufficient to warrant further pursuit. If the debt was above $500, then the police were called. In the two years that Walker had had this job, he had summoned the police only once, when a bill reached $700 and the credit-card company notified the hotel that the card had been canceled for nonpayment.

There had been times, though, when unpaid debt had escalated well beyond the $500 barrier and no calls were made to the police. There was no point. The guests had already fled.

One time, a man checked in who asserted that he was a prince from Saudi Arabia. Walker attempted to confirm his standing with various embassies but was never able to validate the man's contention. Nevertheless, the supposed prince was allowed to stay at the hotel for about two months and ran up payments of nearly $15,000 on credit cards. Then the cards reached their limits. Walker called the attachés of the prince. They were slow to respond, so a security man was instructed to double-lock the room. The prince and his secretary stormed down to Walker's office and made a big show of heatedly protesting the treatment they were getting. Some associates came by and paid the outstanding debt, and the prince was allowed to continue his stay. That was a mistake. Several days later, the royal guest departed unannounced, stiffing the hotel for $1,500.

"I've always wondered why people like that would pay so much for so long," Walker said. "He paid us a lot more than he conned us out of. The comptroller here told me when I took this job that I would probably have the most problems with people who stay the longest and pay the most. That seems to be the pattern, he said. And he sure was right."

Credit managers learned telltale signs that were fairly reliable in alerting them to potential skippers. I made a stop at the office of Anna Chatzithomas, the hotel's overall credit manager, and she patiently filled me in on some of the tricks. Skippers, she said, always charged everything, so, unlike the typical guest, they ate just about all their meals in the hotel and put the bills on the room tab. "Your normal guest would have a dinner or a lunch, and definitely breakfast, in the hotel," she said. "The person who's not going to pay will eat everything here. And they'll use a lot of room service. And it starts the minute they check in. Always the minute they check in. They want to get all they can, so they race that clock. When you see meal after meal after meal being charged to a room, you know something's really fishy." Someone who checked in and right away started ordering the best bottles of whiskey from room service immediately became a skipper suspect. The type tended to drink a lot and usually made it a point to order some bottles to take along with him. "Skippers are apt to be very demanding," Chatzithomas added. "They'll often come in and throw names around: 'I know the manager. Oh, he's a very close friend.' The normal guest comes with money, not names."

Years ago, maids and bellmen were instructed to report certain giveaways to the credit department. If a maid noticed that a guest was stashing towels in his luggage every day, that boded ill for his paying his room charges. Rather than try to get the towels back, the maid would inform the credit manager. Shabby luggage and tattered clothing were other signs that bellmen and maids were asked to watch out for, though Chatzithomas said this wasn't done much anymore now that most people had credit cards, which were more reliable reflections of success than clothing.

One of the more bizarre credit cases happened a couple of years ago. The man registered under the name James Levin. His real name was James Pittman. A walk-in who had no reservation, he was given Room 1070 and in two weeks he ran up over $2,000 in charges. The credit department tried to contact him, but he didn't respond to the messages left for him. Security was sent to double-lock the door. That night, Richard Lebowitz was the assistant manager on duty and was delegated to deal with the situation. When Pittman came down to Lebowitz's office and asked why he couldn't get into his room, Lebowitz asked him how he planned to pay. He said by American Express. When Lebowitz checked the card, the response was "pick up"—meaning the card should be confiscated, which Lebowitz did. He told the man he couldn't get into his room until he came up with some money.

About an hour later, one of the Plaza security men who had inventoried the man's room was climbing the stairway when he saw someone coming down. He was carrying a metallic suitcase, the same sort that was in Pittman's room. He stopped the man and asked him why he was using the stairs. The man said the elevators were broken. The security man knew they weren't. He radioed for backup. When Pittman got down to the lobby, four other security men had gathered. This was early evening, and the lobby was fairly crowded. Pittman assumed a karate stance. He made a lunge to get through the revolving doors and broke the glass. Finally, the five men were able to restrain him and the police were called. It turned out he had gotten his suitcase by kicking down the door to his room, no mean feat. He was a first-degree black belt. Months later, Lebowitz got a call from the Los Angeles Police Department, and it turned out Pittman was wanted for murder as part of the so-called Billionaires Boys Club, a sinister group of rich kids who had turned to crime. Lebowitz was even flown out to testify when the case went to trial.

Most credit problems were tamer than that, and sometimes were unintentional results of a guest's steady run of bad luck. A few years ago, a young woman just out of college checked into the hotel. Her heartfelt intention was to become a writer. Within a matter of days, she bought a television, a typewriter, a drawing desk, and a computer. She stayed for a few months, pecking away at her writings, and the unpaid portion of her bill mounted up until it had exceeded $5,000. The returns from her writing did not arrive nearly as quickly as the room bills did. Security double-locked the door. It seized her computer, which helped bring the bill down. The other possessions were confiscated as well. "We even have her magazine articles that she couldn't sell, as well as the rejection notices," a security man told me. "The notices were mostly along the lines of 'Your writing is very promising but it's not right for us now.' All the stuff is still sitting in the storage room. The last I heard, the woman was living in Massachusetts. When she left here, she swore that she was going to pay us back. I guess we'll have to see."

8

BILL Reis's office was on the second floor and had an old black Burroughs adding machine as an ornament on a coffee table. If you hung around the office, you could almost feel the power of money, the interlocking of accounts. Reis was the man who kept the numbers. As the hotel's comptroller, he was an important figure. He had to add up all the revenues and the labyrinth of bills and see that the former were greater than the latter.

When I called on Reis in his office, I found a fit, alert-looking man. He leaned back in his chair, clasped his hands behind his head, and talked figures. When Westin bought the hotel in 1975, Reis said, it had been doing rather poorly. During much of the 1960s and into the mid-1970s, the hotel was losing money. In 1975, for instance, it lost $2 million, and it was $150,000 in the red in 1976 before edging back into the black in 1977.

Break-even at the hotel, Reis said, occurred at around 65 percent occupancy. An average occupancy of 80 percent was about the best a hotel could hope for. That essentially meant it was full during the week and had some vacancies on the weekends. (Resort hotels would follow the opposite pattern.) The average occupancy for hotels nationwide was a shade under 65 percent. In all of 1987, the Plaza averaged 70 percent, two percentage points above 1986. In 1987,

Reis said, revenues came to $70 million, and before-tax profit was
$2.5 million. With all its labor costs and the competition in the
New York market, the Plaza was not an especially profitable hotel.
The big expense in a hotel, Reis explained, was labor, and New
York had some of the toughest hotel unions in the country. That,
in part, explained why the typical hotel worker in New York was
older than those in probably any other city. I was surprised to learn
from Reis how much certain frills could add up to. Though the
Plaza was not especially known anymore for its entertainment, the
hotel spent $552,000 a year on musicians and singers. That in-
cluded Jules and Paul, the evening performers in the Palm Court;
Irving Fields, the longtime piano player who worked the keys
during lunchtime in the Palm Court; a trio who played ballroom-
dancing songs in the Edwardian Room; and the Oak Room evening
singer.

There was nothing too recondite about hotel finances. The Plaza's
money, Reis explained, came from four sources. Rooms provided
about 48 percent of it; food and beverages contributed 47.5 percent;
the laundry, valet service, telephone, and garage chipped in about
2.7; and rentals to shops and business tenants was 1.7 percent.
Some sources were better profit producers than others. The exorbi-
tantly priced minibars coughed up about $300,000 worth of reve-
nues a year, a third of which was profit. There were a few other
little things—such as revenues from movie companies that shot
footage on the premises—but they didn't add up to more than a
tenth of 1 percent.

Though the Plaza enjoyed higher-than-average food and beverage
revenue because of all the catering it did for social events, virtually
all the hotel's profits came from rooms. "Food and beverage is about
a break-even operation," Reis said. "The real money is made in
rooms. That's always the way it is in hotels."

Some additional revenue arrived from a few commercial tenants
who rented space on the seventeenth floor, a rather shabby expanse
that never had been properly finished. When you got off the elevator onto seventeen, you felt certain you had somehow been trans-
ported into another building. The tenants, mostly architectural and

design firms, were living on borrowed time, because management had determined to let their leases run out, after which Donald Trump intended to build exquisite suites up there that would be among the best in the hotel. He hoped to lease them on a long-term basis to the well-to-do.

Dribs and drabs of money trickled in from here and there. For example, the hotel rented out the glass display cases in the walls of the lobby, known as vitrines. There were about thirty of them, and the ones in the prime locations, most notably those around the Palm Court, went for $1,000 a month. The less prominent ones, such as those across from the ballroom elevators, fetched $300 a month. There was a waiting list to get a vitrine, since most of the occupants kept their windows for years. Because so many people wandered through the Plaza lobby, the displays were considered well worth their cost. My own favorite vitrine was the one near the ground-floor ladies' room, which was rented by a security store called the Counter Spy Shop. It marketed protective devices to edgy corporate executives. Much of the vitrine was filled by a mannequin garbed in a bulletproof jacket and a belt-buckle camera. He was wearing a long-range listening device and glasses for seeing in fog and in the dark. He clasped a Secret Communication Briefcase that detected "on-line eavesdropping" and contained an encryption scrambler useful for both voice and data. Elsewhere in the window was a B404 Tap Alert for your phone, a cigarette-lighter camera, a secret pen recorder that taped conversations discreetly for up to ten hours, a VL-34 Privacy Protector that swept your office clear of bugs, and a Night Vision Pocketscope that could be mounted on a gun. I tried to imagine what sort of company an executive wearing all that gear would work for, but I couldn't come up with any ideas. Reis didn't have any either.

9

N the Fifty-eighth Street side of the hotel, just before the entrance to the Oyster Bar, was Shapero's. It was undoubtedly the busiest of the Plaza shops. There was no pharmacy in the hotel—there hadn't been one in many years—but Shapero's, with its full supply of over-the-counter drugs, functioned in that capacity as well as it could. It was also the place where guests went for their morning paper or cigarettes. When I first stopped in there, my attention was engaged by the wide assortment of gifts: perfumes, stuffed animals, metal race cars, luggage, football mugs, postcards, even some Russian collector boxes that cost up to $500 apiece. I was also impressed by the wide selection of foreign newspapers. Each week, I was told, the store sold four or five copies of *Pravda*.

Shapero's had an odd history. It grew from ego. The chain was founded in about 1910 by a man named Nate Shapero. He traveled a lot and he liked the idea of having a drugstore bearing his name in the hotels he stayed in. And so he created a chain. Shapero died a number of years ago, and the stores were sold to an outfit in Detroit called Cunningham's Drug Stores. The chain hadn't been doing all that well in recent times, and many of its stores had been closed down. Shapero's had been in the Plaza for some fifteen years, though, and was hanging on.

I was standing by the counter when in came a lumpish, pallid woman in a dress that ended almost on the floor. She bought a tube of toothpaste, some deodorant, some bobby pins, and a package of breath mints. She took a quick look at some of the gift items, then went out.

A thewy man with a nervous neck twitch succeeded the woman at the cash register. He had selected some hairspray, shaving cream, a couple of magazines, and a box of candy. One of the magazines was *Penthouse,* which he had sandwiched between *Time* and *Vanity Fair.* "I think that'll be it," he told the woman at the cash register. "But, knowing me, I'm sure I'll be back tomorrow."

A tanned woman with tawny hair swept in. Two small children were tugging at her. "Candy, Mom, get us some candy," one of them was yelping. "Yeah, chocolate, Mom," the other chimed in. "Get us chocolate." The woman studied the racks of candy. She flipped back her hair, and one of her eyebrows went up dreamily. Finally she scooped up four or five bars of candy, grabbed a news-paper and a paperback mystery, picked up some nail enamel, asked for some film and two packages of Marlboro cigarettes, and was all set.

Jeff Harbison, a bucolic figure of a man who was the manager of Shapero's, was never surprised by what hotel guests chose to spend their money on. "Some of everything sells sooner or later," he said. "Cigarettes and newspapers, those are the big things. They would be followed by candy bars and magazines. I carry English chocolate and Swiss chocolate, but Snickers and M&M's sell the best. This is Middle America shopping for candy."

He went on, "About twenty percent of our business is health and beauty aids. People forget toothpaste, so we move a lot of that. No slur on the restaurants, but Pepto-Bismol is a big seller here."

Harbison rubbed his throat nervously. "The basic guest is a businessman. As a result, my T-shirt business has taken off. I added it about four years ago. Before that, we didn't think we'd stoop to that. But these people like to take New York T-shirts home with them. I had a Japanese guy in here this morning and he bought fifteen T-shirts. I had a Saudi come in here and buy a suitcase and then fill it up with perfume and stuffed animals and all sorts of gifts that he was going to give to a woman he had met while he was here. I was happy to help him out."

Harbison conducted me up toward the front of the store and pointed out several shelves full of merchandise. "We've got a whole collection here of Plaza items, maybe a dozen or so items with the hotel's name on them," he said. "They're very popular. The biggest seller is this 'I Slept at the Plaza' sleep shirt. It's fifteen dollars. The next-best one is the gold key chain, which is six ninety-five."

He showed me a three-minute oil-and-bead timer with the Plaza name on it. If you turned it upside down, the beads would tumble toward the bottom, the last one reaching there in about three minutes. The price was $11.85.

"What would you use it for?" I asked Harbison.

"Nothing," he said.

Harbison mentioned that the absolute best thing about his job was the opportunity to see celebrities. He said that Paul Newman had come in once and bought a small sewing kit. Jessica Hahn had stopped by to acquire some enemas. "I'm star-struck," Harbison said, "so I collect autographs, allegedly for my son." In recent times, he said he had gotten the signatures of Anthony Perkins, Michael Spinks, and Joe Candy.

One of the most conspicuous patrons of Shapero's was Perkins, probably most famous for his role as Norman Bates in *Psycho*. He was a highly predictable shopper. He would saunter into the store dressed in jogging clothes and stand and methodically read all the greeting cards displayed on the card rack by the door. Then he would drift over to the counter and purchase two rolls of SX70 Polaroid film. "I used to be at the register when he came in," Harbison said, shooting me a mischievous look, "and he'd always go through that same routine. Don't ask me why. When he came to the counter, I would always say, 'Yes, Mr. Perkins,' 'Of course, Mr. Perkins,' 'Thank you, Mr. Perkins.' Then one day he gave me a sly smile and said, 'You know, you don't have to call me Mr. Perkins. You can just call me Norman.'"

FRIDAY

1

DAN Sharp was hardly delighted with how the grave-yard shift was starting. Right away, he could see it was probably going to be a tormented night. It was just after midnight, heading into the hours of the insomniacs, and one of those prolonged nuisances that always seemed to develop after he reported for duty had manifested itself. This time the problem was a guest who had been discovered beating up his girlfriend. To further complicate matters, the man turned out to be a movie star of no small stature. He was in town for a couple of days to attend a dinner along with some other stars. His girlfriend, at the moment, was without an appetite.

As the night manager, Sharp would have to stay on top of the situation over the next eight hours. Such foolishness he didn't need, he told me. Glenn Goerke, one of the assistant managers, who was about to knock off for the day, filled him in on where things stood. As he listened, Sharp crinkled his brow and glanced down at his hands. He looked as if he had just been given some bad news about his finances. Goerke said that the incident had come to light when one of the bellmen was passing by a room and heard quite a com-motion and a woman's frantic screams. The bellman quickly noti-fied a security man, who sprinted to the room and rapped on the door. A great deal of yelling and crying was going on inside. The security man unlocked the door and discovered the couple flailing at each other. He had to pull them apart and told the man that he was removing the woman to safety. He made it clear that he was not joking. The woman was in a real panic, so she was escorted to a room on another floor, and instructions were given to the hotel operators not to put through any calls to her and not to give the room number to anyone. Once she calmed down, the woman placed a tearful call to her mother in California, telling her about the incident and mentioning that the man had her plane ticket and wallet in the couple's original room and so she had no way of returning home. Her mother arranged to have a prepaid ticket waiting at the airport so her daughter could catch a flight the next morning. Meanwhile, provisions were made with the assistant manager so that the woman would be supplied with adequate cash to pay for a cab to the airport. The hotel was giving her the other room for free.

How the fight had started was unclear to Sharp, but that didn't matter. His responsibility would be to keep the combatants separated. The woman didn't have the tiniest desire to see the movie star again, though she hoped the hotel could retrieve her possessions.

"Does she have bruises?" Sharp asked Goerke.

"She said her arm hurt her," he replied. "Her mother wanted a doctor called, but she didn't want one. We'll have to play wait-and-see on that."

"Okay," Sharp said, and he muttered something to himself, going into a big burn.

"I'm sure you'll be hearing from him," Goerke said. "He told me he won't give up her belongings unless he can speak to her. The guy's pissed."

"Great," Sharp mumbled.

"Have fun," the assistant manager said with a half-pitying glance, and he left for home.

Scarcely audibly, Sharp groaned, "Oh God, why is this happening to me? I've got so much paperwork to do. Couldn't he have beaten her up during the day?" He didn't care to think about it.

He had barely managed to get his complaint out, however, when the phone rang. It was the movie star. Sharp shifted in his seat. "I understand," he said. "No, I haven't had a chance to get through to her yet. . . . I understand. . . . Yes, I'll let you know as soon as I can. . . . Yes, that's right. I'll let you know. . . . Okay, fine. I'll call you."

Upon hanging up, Sharp said, "He's getting really obnoxious. What a night!"

Clearly he was in for a battle of wills.

FITS of desperate temper were not unknown at the hotel, and the goal of assistant managers was to keep incidents quiet. More often than not they succeeded, though sticky situations sometimes crept into the newspapers. One of the more appalling ones occurred in 1949, when Aleta Arlen, the ex-wife of the Wall Street banker Kurt Lowenthal, was having drinks at the hotel with Claudia Campbell, the heiress to the soup fortune, who had been a periodic date of Lowenthal's. After a while, the two women thought it would be interesting to drop in on Lowenthal and see what he was up to, especially since he was staying at the hotel. What he had been up to was getting married just hours before. Exactly what went on in his room when the women arrived is not entirely clear, but the turmoil was noisy enough that guests called down to the front desk to complain. According to reports by an assistant manager, the irate Campbell got so exercised over this bolt from the blue that she began swatting at Lowenthal. He responded by summarily giving her a black eye. Arlen presumably dodged all blows. The police had to be called to extinguish the brawl.

SINCE Sharp didn't have any bright ideas about how to rescue the woman's belongings, he decided to let things cool down somewhat before he pressed into action. For the time being, the hotel's isolation policy seemed adequate to ensure her safety. Right now, he had another task to complete. He needed to find a spare phone.

"We're running pretty close to full," he told me. "I've got fourteen expected arrivals and four rooms. Not all of those arrivals will show up, but more than four might. I've got one suite that's in perfect order except it doesn't have a phone. Thus if I can find a working phone in one of the out-of-order rooms and move it there, I'll have another bed I can rent. So I've got to play Ma Bell."

Scooping up a pager and a clutch of room keys, Sharp headed off for the elevators, and I went with him. He was not in the mood for chatter. He was totally preoccupied with finding a phone. It was twelve-fifty in the morning. The lobby was still bustling with people. Anonymous waves of blue suits, maroon dresses, and intent-looking faces swept past, going to and from rooms, seeking a final refreshment at the Oak Bar. Sharp threaded his way through the crowd and took the elevator to the fifth floor. Once he reached his destination—Room 572—he unlocked the door and cautiously entered. "Often when I come to check an out-of-order room, I find an employee there," he said. "When an employee stays late, we sometimes let him stay in an out-of-order room. That's why I don't just shoot in."

The room was empty, however. Upside-down chairs lay on the unmade bed. Papers were scattered on the floor. Drapery was missing. There was no phone, either. Sharp put his hands on his hips and tried to suppress his annoyance.

"Well, I struck out here," he said. "Let's go next door to 570."

It wasn't any tidier, but that didn't matter, because there was a phone. Sharp picked up the receiver and dialed the operator to check that it was working. It was, and so he disconnected it. It was pretty dusty, so Sharp carried it into the bathroom. With considerable meticulousness, he washed it off and dried it with a towel. He then took it up to Room 637, the otherwise available suite, and plugged it in. "I could get someone from the building department to do this," Sharp said, "but I like to do these things myself, because then I know they get done and they get done right. Okay, let's go back downstairs to see if we've got any nut cases."

Graveyard duty could get to you. Nobody particularly liked it, Sharp being no exception, but everyone had to cut his teeth on the shift for at least a year in order to qualify to move up to more pleasing hours. There was no end to the strangeness of life in the early hours. In order to understand it, you had to revise your ideas of what the hotel was. The contrast with the day shift could scarcely have been sharper. Then, for the most part, you dealt with well-behaved business travelers and occasional kings and queens. You had a full staff at your beckoning to handle all the little tribulations that came up. At night, you had a skeletal staff and you dealt with weirdos. It was a lonely time, when psychic wounds opened up.

Sharp was thankful that he was nearing the end of his tenure and would shortly be training his successor. A lean, sinewy man in his early twenties with short-cropped brown hair, Sharp had come to the Plaza in the fall of 1985. He had received his training at the University of Niagara Hotel School, and his only other hotel experience had been an internship at a Holiday Inn in Niagara, New York. The seasoning he got there was significantly limited by the fact that he worked during the dead of winter, when the hotel had an average occupancy rate of about 15 percent. You could go days without even bumping into a guest.

For the most part, the graveyard shift was unrelieved tedium. Paperwork was the consuming preoccupation. The quantity of it exceeded belief. "An awful, awful lot of my time is spent with computer printouts," Sharp said. "I've got to review the status of all the rooms and prepare the morning rooms report. There are a lot of little stupid things you've got to do. You also get plenty of strange people walking in at these hours. You see a quite different hotel."

When Sharp got back to his office behind the front desk, Josie Peterson, a fair-haired young woman who was one of the check-in attendants, came in and told him, "I just checked in this guest to a room that shows vacant and the door is double-locked. So I had to move the guest to another room."

Sharp picked up the phone. He called the double-locked room to see if it might be occupied. Nobody answered. Next he phoned security and advised them of the situation. "It's probably a problem with the lock," he said. "Boy, do I need that room. Is there any way you can get it fixed tonight?"

When he got off, he told Peterson, "Well, they're going to see what they can do. I could use the room."

A bellman entered the office. Addressing Sharp, he said, "The guest in 234 says she has tried to get the hotel operator for the last half hour. Then she called us. She wants a wake-up call at six-thirty."

"Okay," Sharp said.

He dialed the operator. "Maddy, Room 234 wants a wake-up call at six-thirty."

He hung up and a call came in. It was the movie star. He was hot. He wanted to be put through to his girlfriend. When Sharp explained that he couldn't do that, the movie star said he wanted to talk to her mother. Sharp said that he would save him the trouble and call her himself.

As he dialed, Sharp said, "He sounds real drunk. He says he's not mad or going to hurt her, but I think he's BS-ing me. He's had too, too many. No doubt about it. This man is plastered."

When the woman's mother answered, Sharp said, "This is Dan Sharp at the Plaza. I just had a conversation with Mr. ———, and he wanted to talk to your daughter. I didn't want to put him through to her without your permission. I feel she's been put through enough, and it's late here. He said he wanted to know what to do with her plane ticket and driver's license."

The mother told Sharp to call the daughter and ask her.

Sharp misdialed and woke up someone else. He profusely apologized. He tried again and got the girlfriend. She said she didn't want to talk to the movie star but would like security to attempt to retrieve her possessions.

"Okay, I'll tell them," Sharp said. He shook his head. "I could easily develop an incredible headache from this," he said. "If that guy thinks I'm ever going to one of his movies again, he's dead wrong."

2

I WALKED through the lobby, and suddenly the peace and mystery of midnight were over everything. Outside, in the darkness, light rain was spattering down. The early-morning hours were the mellowest for the hotel, aside from tantrums in some of the guest rooms. The nervous buzz that persisted during the daylight hours was gone. Everything was quiet and empty, except for a porter here and there with a scrub bucket shampooing a carpet or sweeping up a floor. This was the time when much of the cleaning of the hotel's public places was done. Vacuums intermittently whined as they rolled over lobby rugs. Nothing was open, except for room service.

I took the stairs down to the basement to look in on room service. Food apparently was not much in demand. Two waiters sat bored in cushioned chairs. Near them was a woman in front of a phone, ready to accept orders that didn't come. On weekends there were sometimes after-midnight calls, but rarely during the week. A bank of tables draped in blue tablecloths stood set up for breakfast delivery some hours from now. The room-service corridor contained a croissant and toast warmer, an egg poacher, an ice machine, a number of huge coffee urns, and row upon row of dishes, cups, and glasses.

One of the waiters, having nothing better to do, told me about the ghosts in the penthouse. Back before Jeffrey Flowers moved in, it had often been used for ritzy parties. A few years before, a big affair there had required the assistance of some of the room-service staff. The waiter picked up the story: "One of the guys was walking down the hallway when he saw a fellow in a white jacket duck into the billiards room. He thought it was one of the other waiters, so he followed him. As he watched, the guy sped out the other door into the foyer and vanished into thin air. Well, the poor guy turned white as a sheet. He took off down the hall and yelled at the others to get out of there; the place was haunted. They thought he had gone off the deep end. Anyway, the guests were coming in now, so the fellow settled down. Most of us wrote that off to a waiter taking a little of the stuff he was supposed to be serving. But then a really creepy thing happened. About a year later, one of the bartenders went up there to prepare his bar for a party. While he was waiting around, he figured he'd shoot some pool, and so he went to the billiards room and started a game. The first guest arrived, so he interrupted his play to get the man a drink. When the guest took his drink into the living room, the bartender went back to tidy up the billiards table. The balls were in completely different positions, and a few had even been shot into the pockets. And there was nobody else up there."

I said that sounded awfully strange.

"Yeah, you're not kidding," the waiter said. "But that's nothing compared with the guests we get. They're the strange ones."

THERE were different problems in the early-morning hours. More drunks, more guests with hookers, more guests with short fuses. Working the shift, you got to know people's secrets. You learned who liked to bring prostitutes to their rooms, and you knew who stayed longest at the bars and had to stumble back to their floors. For security purposes, the hotel locked the Fifth Avenue entrance beginning at two in the morning and all visitors had to enter on Fifty-ninth Street until six o'clock. Anyone who came in was re-quired to show his or her room key to a security man. Some guests, inevitably, didn't care to. A man might have had a bad business meeting or a long-delayed flight and he wasn't about to stand for the indignity of being questioned for his room key. The security man would do his best to coax it out of him. If he failed but got the feeling from the conversation that the man was actually staying there, he would let him go.

The early hours were the province of weirdos, misfits, and suicidals. There were moments that could be bad ones, lives transformed into miseries. Brian Andrews, the assistant manager of the Oak Room, who had worked the graveyard shift before Dan Sharp, came by to chat with Sharp now that the bar had closed. "Well, we had one drunk tonight," he said. "He went around to all of the waiters trying to order something, but we cut him off. I finally gave him a complimentary Perrier, but he just let it sit there while he stewed. Then a woman came up to me and said there was a man roaming around the ladies' room. Sure enough, there was. The funny thing is, he wasn't drunk or anything. He said he was just looking for his girlfriend. We got him out of there pretty fast."

"Well, I've got a guy beating up his girlfriend on my hands," Sharp said.

"Interesting," Andrews said.

Andrews had endured some rowdy nights of his own. He had been on duty the evening the Playboy Club had closed down and the Bunnies and some male colleagues had rented a couple of suites to hold a final-night party. As the drinking intensified, a decision was made by the males to stage a panty raid on the Bunnies. The Bunnies, in rather limited attire, tried to evade their pursuers by scampering through the lobby. Andrews called the police and the whole contingent was kicked out. He mentioned another time, when he got a call concerning a disturbed guest. He contacted a security man and the pair went up to her room. She was a woman of about thirty-five, not at all bad-looking, but definitely odd. One sign of her peculiarity was that there were five trays of orders from room service standing in the room, all untouched. She had a robe on and announced to Andrews and the security man that she had something she would very much like to show them. Whereupon she whipped open her robe and exposed her quite adequate breasts. The bug-eyed Andrews, envisioning the rapid decline of his hotel career, decided that they had better get out of there pretty quickly. Before they reached the exit, the woman darted into the bathroom, locked the door, and declared that she was going to kill herself. They tried to pacify her by pointing out some of the good points of life while the police were summoned. Once the cops arrived, the woman was extracted from the bathroom, strapped snugly into a wheelchair, and taken away to a hospital for a look at her head.

At times, inevitably, suicidal guests succeeded. Hotels, perhaps because people feel anonymous there, seem to be as popular as bridges as settings for suicides. Some hotels average two or three a year. Hud Hinton once worked at a hotel in Hawaii which had balconies outside the guest rooms, and each year several people would dive off to their deaths. It has always been a mystery to hotel managers why people choose to kill themselves in hotels, but they do. Many of them are even thoughtful enough to pay their bill in advance. It is particularly horrifying when the weapon involved is a gun or when the body has been decomposing for a few days. I heard about a man in a Detroit hotel who tried to kill himself by heaping his clothing in the middle of his room and setting it on fire to create suffocating smoke. A general rule of thumb, though, was that the more luxurious the hotel, the lower the suicide rate. The Plaza had found that it didn't get more than one every couple of years. The last death had been in 1986.

Harvey Robbins, who was then the night assistant manager, was unlucky enough to discover the body. The front-desk records showed that the room bill was a day overdue and so, following the prescribed procedure, Robbins called the guest. That was about ten o'clock in the evening. There was no answer. Thinking perhaps the person was deliberately dodging the hotel management, he made his way up to the room and knocked on the door. There was no response. Using his passkey, he unlocked the door. The inside bolt lock was on, however, and he couldn't get in. Robbins called security, and a man came up and drilled the lock. He pushed the door open, and as Robbins subsequently put it, "I didn't have to see any further. The odor was unbelievable. I just about barfed. The security man peered in and saw the body and practically gagged, too. This was real gross-out city. We called the police and they took over."

The woman—she looked to be in her early twenties—had knotted a sheet on the outside handle of the closet door and then flung it over the top of the door. It appeared that she had then clambered atop a chair, fashioned a noose from the sheet, fitted it around her neck, and jumped. With most people, the plan wouldn't have worked, because the top of the closet door was not high enough, but the woman was so short that she succeeded. She had been dead about twelve hours when she was found, and her body had turned black from head to toe. A note had been left behind, in which she wrote that she had a five-month-old son she wanted her mother to care for because life was entirely too overwhelming for her. She complained that she couldn't find work and still care for her child. Some days later, a man showed up at the hotel inquiring about her. Apparently he was a boyfriend and perhaps the father of the child. The hotel simply informed him of what had happened and gained no more insight into what had been the darkness of the woman's life.

As it happened, the suicide occurred in one of the cramped single-bed rooms up on the seventeenth floor. In the months following the death, some of the hotel employees developed their own theory of the tragedy. They whispered that the woman must surely have killed herself because the room she had was so depressingly small. They began to call it "the suicide room."

3

A T one-fifteen, outside a garage entrance on Fifty-eighth Street, a big Universal Sanitation truck spluttered to a stop, reversed gears, and then carefully backed in through the opening. The driver stepped out, smoothed his hair, and walked toward the rear of the truck. He had arrived to fetch the hotel's garbage.

Two stewards from the hotel had already lined up a dozen or so big bins of smelly trash as well as two bales of garbage that had gone through the compactor. They started wheeling the bins out to the edge of the truck. Cory Lappin, the driver of the truck, connected the first bin to a winch on the rear, which yanked it up and tilted it into its yawning opening. Out flew cardboard boxes, a half-eaten piece of chicken, shredded carrots, a white toothbrush, a broken Plaza hanger, a crushed Miller beer can, a Fanta orange bottle, that day's *New York Times,* an Edwardian Room menu, a stuffed mouse, and a pair of black panty hose that presumably had a run. Lappin flicked on the hopper and it began crushing the garbage. A loud, grinding noise echoed off the walls.

"On a normal night like tonight, it takes me about an hour to pick up all the garbage," Lappin told me. "On a Sunday night, forget about it. They don't have a pickup here on Saturday, so Sunday is a real mess. I'm here a couple of hours, easy. Sunday sucks, I'll tell you that much."

Another bin was hooked up to the winch and more garbage crashed into the truck. Lappin leaned back against the wall and watched with satisfaction as it disappeared from sight. He was a compact, bearded man with powerful arms, quick to talk to anyone willing to listen. ("You don't get a lot of people to talk to in garbage. That's the truth.")

"I do all the hotels around here," he said over the din. "I do the Hilton, the Carlyle, the Waldorf, the Windsor. I'm what you call a classy garbage collector. And I'll tell you this, the Plaza has the most garbage. My truck holds twenty tons of garbage, and I'd say two-thirds of it gets filled up here. There's more garbage here than at any other hotel I know of. The Waldorf is heavy, too, but this is the worst. I don't know how to explain it, but the people here throw away an awful lot of stuff. They're something. No pack rats at this joint."

Two more bins were brought forward by the stewards, and they wheeled the empty ones away. Lappin sank to his knees to pick up some of the overflow refuse that had fallen onto the pavement. He heaved it into the truck. "If I had to rate them, I'd say the Wellington is the worst hotel to pick up," Lappin said. "They have nobody helping you. Not a blessed soul. You've got to push carts from the basement up two ramps to get them to the truck. I leave that place just about dead. I'm aching like a son of a bitch. They figure you can do this work twenty-five years before you're shot. I got fifteen years in, and I tell you, when it's damp out my back and knees kill me. But I didn't stay in school and I've got a wife and kids, so what are you going to do? But the job's a pain in the ass."

"Do you ever find anything worthwhile in the garbage?" I asked.

"I find a lot of aluminum trays," he said. "I take them and sell them to a junk dealer. I got a couple of pots on the truck so far. They're all messed up, which is why they're in the garbage, but I can sell them for scrap. I used to work the Bronx route, and I'd find pistols. Just about every garbage bin you picked up had pistols in it. I just left them in the garbage. No way I was going to touch them and go through any questioning, if you get what I mean."

A bin had been shaken empty, so the steward rolled up another one and Lappin hooked it to the winch.

"I've never found anything really valuable," he continued. "I'm the unluckiest garbageman in the world. The other garbagemen, they find money, jewelry, all sorts of stuff. I never find anything. I had a friend who once found forty thousand dollars in a plain paper bag while he was dropping stuff off at the dump in New Jersey. It was all in this big fat roll—twenties and fifties. Why couldn't that have been me? You know what did happen to me? This is typical of my luck. I picked up the garbage outside a fruit market and the truck was full and I dumped it in New Jersey. Later on, the guy who owned the fruit stand contacted me and said he had left a paper bag on the edge of the garbage bin. There was thirty thousand dollars in it. Holy Christ, I thought. He wanted to know if I had dumped the truck yet, and I said I was afraid I had. He went out to the dump anyway looking for it, but forget it. That's like looking for a needle in a haystack. The money was history. Now, why couldn't I have seen that bag before I dumped it? But that's me. I tell you, if I didn't have bad luck, I'd have no luck at all."

$$4$$

ITTING bent over several ledgers and a spindle of bills, Richard Rodriquez looked like a schoolboy well behind on his homework. He was in a flurry of activity. Otherwise, desks in the accounting office, upstairs from the front desk, were empty and the room was still. Rodriquez was doing the night audit.

He poked through the pile, searching for mistakes made by those who worked during the day. "What we do here is balance the restaurant cashier books and set up the computer for the next day," he explained to me. "Basically, we clear out the day so it's ready for tomorrow. The front office balances the rooms. We just do restaurants. If checks are signed as complimentary, we have to verify the signatures and make sure it was a manager who signed them. All the credit-card receipts we check here. There are thousands of checks in a hotel like this. The Palm Court has the most —about five hundred checks today. It's the busiest restaurant. The Edwardian Room, being more expensive, has fewer checks, but the revenue is right up there. There were about two hundred and fifty checks today but a lot of money."

"How often do you find mistakes?" I asked.

"Not often," Rodriquez said lazily. "You find an American Express charged to a MasterCard or something like that. I've never found anything really fishy. The hardest night is New Year's Eve. The volume is incredible. The restaurants stay open late. Lots and lots of mistakes.''

I asked him how he liked working this shift.

He scratched his head and said, "The hours are somewhat tough. I'm usually very tired. But the atmosphere is quiet. We don't deal with guests and we're left to ourselves."

He stroked his chin. "I'll tell you one of the funny things about working these hours. One of the attractions of working at the Plaza is some of the exciting guests who stay here. I hear talk about this movie star being here or this politician. I understand the king of Sweden's coming in later. The employees really thrive off getting a glimpse of these people. But I never get to see any of them. I could just as well be working in some other hotel in some other city. And I'm too tired to be here during the day."

He said he was able to get only four hours of sleep a day. Sometimes his nerves could be stretched pretty tight. His wife, Amparo, also worked at the hotel, but she was in data processing on the day shift. They had a thirteen-month-old daughter. "I get home at eight in the morning," Rodriquez said, "and I go to bed until about one. Then my wife goes to work from two to ten, so I have to baby-sit."

He stifled a yawn. "I don't drink a lot of coffee or take any drugs," he said. "I just try not to think I'm tired. If I think about it, even for a minute, then I'm done for."

5

'VE got to get some chow or I'm going to faint," Dan Sharp announced to the desk attendants. "Let's go down."

"I'm not going to argue with that," one of the women said. "I'm all in favor of immediate food."

Three good-humored, outgoing women covered the front desk during the night shift and helped Sharp with the voluminous paperwork: Maria Furboch, Josie Peterson, and Atsede Elegba. They were all starved. It was two-forty, a little past the time that the front-office people normally took their meal break. Sharp rarely had anything else that might pass for a full meal, except what he ate at this ungodly hour, so a few minutes of delay taking a break went right to his stomach. A frozen look had come across his face.

Sharp set aside some printouts he had been tediously poring over. They reflected the charges of all the current guests, and he had to check that there were no errors before those charges were formally entered on the guest bills. "You always find a few mistakes," he said. "I just now found one rate running at twenty-one hundred dollars a day and it should have been two hundred and ten. I would say that might have annoyed the guest. So I'll correct that in the computer before it gets posted."

While Peterson kept watch over the desk, Sharp and the others filed down to the basement and picked their way to the kitchen. John McHugh, the assistant security officer, breezed by, on his rounds. "Nothing going on," he said. "Nothing at all." A man wearing a gas mask was spraying insecticide in the far corner. "Flies mostly," the man said. "They get a lot of flies down here. Got to be on top of it. When the flies see me coming, they know it's all over."

A night chef hung around until three, making meals especially for the early-hour workers. As Sharp and the others grabbed trays and fell into line behind some of the night cleaning men, the cook barked warnings and odd bits of advice:

"Watch your fingers there. Watch those fingers."

"Heed that steam. It can do some critical damage."

"Grab a knife and kill your wife."

The selections tonight were knockwurst, a veal patty, and eggplant. Sharp ran his eyes from one to the other and finally decided to take a chance on the patty.

Balancing trays, the group trooped back to the office, arranged plates wherever they could fit them, and dug in. There was nothing approaching formal dining on the graveyard shift. The four of them got along well, and there was a seamless jollity to their evenings. A portable radio was flicked on and soft rock music enlivened their meal.

They talked about the sort of characters who try to check in in the early morning. On one occasion, an older woman without a reservation showed up wearing platform shoes and a beehive hat with long springs protruding from it as if they were antennae. As she spoke to the attendant, the springs kept swatting the attendant in the face. She was accompanied by a man who was less weird but not exactly normal. They were given a room, stayed several nights, and paid their bill in full. Someone mentioned the man who kept calling all night and telling the attendants that Frank Sinatra, Jr., had just been killed in a car crash.

All of the attendants pretty much hated the hours, for they forced them to lead a rather reclusive life. Josie Peterson, however, saw the graveyard shift differently. Her ambition was to become an actress, and the only way she could appear for auditions was to have a night job. A lanky blond woman with a pealing laugh, she had come to New York from Montana with high expectations that were meeting stiff resistance.

"When I first moved to New York in June of 1986, I went out on auditions a lot," she told me. "It's dwindling now. I think I have a mediocre agent. I'm looking for a new one. I like classical theater the most. But I've auditioned for a lot of soap operas. I've yet to get on. I wasn't sure what I was getting into when I came here. You know, since I've been on the graveyard shift I've seen three assistant managers come and go. Nobody wants it. But I don't want to get off it."

Atsede Elegba, a talkative, chic young woman, put up with the work because she was fitting in classes at the New York City Technical College during the day. She was studying to become a pastry chef. "That's the only job in this business that's creative," she said. "And being pastry chef is something to be proud of."

There had been a prolonged period of peace at the front desk—no check-ins or checkouts—but now, at four-fifteen in the morning, two young men presented themselves and Peterson ducked out to handle them.

"Have you got a room?" one of the men asked expectantly. His face was filmed with sweat.

Peterson slowly looked the pair over. Neither of them seemed to be more than eighteen or nineteen. They were wearing badly wrinkled clothing and appeared, from their dopy motions and glassy-eyed looks, to have been drinking. They had no luggage. Peterson assumed that they had probably missed the last bus back to New Jersey and needed a place to stay.

"I'm sorry," she said with a sigh, "but we're full up." (There were in fact a few rooms left, but she knew that the teenagers were unlikely to be able to come up with enough to pay for a room.) "But you might want to try the Sheraton Centre."

The teenagers looked at her mistily and thanked her for the suggestion. They said they would do that and filed out.

Once they were done with their meals, Sharp and the others began ripping apart express checkout bills that had just arrived from the high-speed printer in the accounting office. They stuffed the bills into envelopes. Two bellmen waited for them, for it was their job to slip them under the room doors.

"This is the intellectually stimulating part of the job," Peterson said. "We all can't wait for it."

"C'mon," Sharp said. "Let's get the things out of here for these guys."

As they stuffed envelopes, they talked about kids.

"I can't stand kids," Furboch said.

Sharp said, "I think it's nice when they're other people's kids, so you can say good-bye to them."

"I once had a nightmare that I had children," Peterson said. "I had twelve of them. I didn't know where they came from. But I knew they were mine, because they all looked like me. And they were screaming and getting into the fridge."

"Wow," Furboch said. "Scary."

Finished with the express checkouts, Sharp reviewed the status of the rooms in order to prepare the morning rooms report that went to top management. Out of 313 guaranteed reservations, eight people hadn't shown up. "That's really low," Sharp said. "It's usually eight to ten percent. So we'll bill these people. We may not collect from all of them. But we'll charge them; you can bet on that." In actuality, two vacant rooms remained. Sharp, however, said that he would show the hotel as being full. It was a little game he played. "What I'll often do if we're supposed to show sold-out but we have one or two rooms left is I'll record them as being out of order so we'll be officially sold out," he said. "Then everyone will be happy, because management likes to see a sold-out night. In this job, you have to fudge it a little."

It was past five o'clock now, and a window washer started cleaning the revolving doors in the lobby, pulling a squeegee carefully down the glass. Then he moved to the store windows and attacked the grime there. A porter hung up the Friday event schedule on the wall across from the front desk:

Airline and Aircraft in the 1900s Lunch
The Bryce Currey Memorial Service Lunch

The Sugar Association
Volvo NA
Lord Affet & Co.
Cardiac Seminar
Leukemia Society of America Salute to the Corporate Stars
Compagnie Bancaire

As Sharp was putting the final touches on the rooms report, a call came in from a very anxious woman who needed to leave at six in the morning in order to catch a flight but had not had her shoes returned from the laundry. They were black pumps, a small size. Could she please have them immediately?

Sharp put down the receiver and gave an audible groan. The laundry was closed for another hour, so he would have to go down there himself and root around for the shoes. I went with him. "This is one of the annoying things that come up," he said on the way. "The laundry doesn't get something back and it's late and the guest is leaving early and so I get stuck with it."

When he arrived at the laundry, dark and silent, Sharp checked the shoe-shining area, but there were no shoes at all in evidence. He unlocked the laundry manager's office and poked about in there. "Where would I go if I were a pair of shoes?" Sharp asked himself. "The truth is I haven't any idea where I would go, though probably not back on that woman's feet."

No shoes presented themselves in the manager's office, so Sharp locked the door and searched the outer area.

"I know where shirts and trousers are," he said. "That's what I usually have to look for. Unfortunately, this is the first time I've had to look for shoes."

Sharp searched in the valet area. Nothing. "Where would they keep shoes?" he asked no one in particular. "I'm stumped."

Exasperated, Sharp gave up and headed back upstairs. He would be forced to tell the guest that the shoes would have to be sent to her. "These are the sorts of things that waste your time at night," he said. "It's not quite as glorious as the day. There's a lot more crap at night."

6

HE telephone room was squarish, with tables holding computer terminals and phones arranged around the perimeter. To get to the room, I had to take the elevator to the second floor, find the right service door, and ring a bell next to an unmarked entryway.

Maddy Vutrano, the telephone manager, and Mary Sullivan, the late-shift operator, were nursing mugs of coffee, alone with the phones. They were shaking their heads over a call that Vutrano had just picked up. A throaty voice said, "You're a conniver. You're a thief. Drop dead." And then he hung up.

"Those are the crackpots you get at these hours," Vutrano said wearily. "Why does someone need to say that? It just really makes no sense to me."

Vutrano was a hearty, good-natured woman with reddish shoulder-length hair. She had worked a stint as an operator for New York Telephone before coming to the Plaza. Her proudest moment had come when a man from Mexico was in the hotel and he called one night and said he was feeling ill. Vutrano said she would get a doctor, but he insisted that it wasn't that serious. He sounded bad, so Vutrano called the doctor anyway. When he arrived, the man was close to death, though quick medical attention saved him. In gratitude he sent Vutrano a gold coin, which she had always treasured.

A trilling sound, and Vutrano punched a button and said, "Hello, the Plaza, may I help you? . . . Okay, I'm ringing the room."

During these hours, not many calls came in, unless there was an abundance of foreigners in the hotel. With all the time differences, calls would then arrive almost continually. Sullivan, a tousled-looking woman, said that the shift had been slow, except for one obscene caller who had managed to get both Vutrano and Sullivan on the line. Heavy breathers were always phoning the hotel early in the morning, getting their kicks.

"We have no limitations on when we put someone through," Vutrano said. "If someone calls at three or four in the morning, we ring through to the room. Unless, that is, someone gives us instructions not to ring him. When we ring a guest room, it rings exactly six times and then comes back to the board as a 'don't answer.' I keep a traffic report of calls. Sometimes we get seven hundred to eight hundred calls an hour. We can handle up to about a thousand. Among other things, we take three hundred to five hundred messages a day for guests."

Another call came in. Sullivan took it and put it through, but there was no answer and no message. "I know who that is," Sullivan said. "She called before. It's this woman looking for her husband. She called and he wasn't in at two in the morning. Then she called back and wanted to know if there was a particular function here— I forget the name she gave me—but it wasn't on the list. So this guy is in hot water. I see this a lot. He just wasn't smart enough to put a 'do not disturb' on his calls. Then she would have assumed he was sleeping—and sleeping alone. I think there's going to be some fireworks when she gets hold of him."

"We get a lot of pranks," Vutrano said. "We've gotten calls from someone saying he's in the next building and there's someone dangling out of a window. We have to check it out, of course, but it's never true. We get bomb threats. We have to take those seriously. Usually they're fakes, though once security found a liquid bomb in one of the maid's pantries."

Back in 1973, in fact, a threat had come in from a man who claimed he was going to blow up the hotel if he didn't get $50,000.

He followed the threat up with a letter to James Lavenson, then the Plaza's president, that was signed "Black September," the name of the Arab terrorist group. Lavenson got in touch with the police, who advised him to follow the man's instructions. They furnished him with a bag full of cash, which he was supposed to deliver to the man at the Waldorf-Astoria. He was to get into a specific phone booth in the lobby and wait for a call. When it came, he was told that he would find further instructions beneath an ashtray at a fourth-floor elevator bank. He discovered a note there telling him to leave the money on the floor. He did. When the man arrived to retrieve it, the police descended on him. He turned out to be a twenty-three-year-old unemployed housepainter with no connection to the Arabs. He wanted the money to open a restaurant.

"Another time," Vutrano said, "we got a call from a guest who was putting his room-service tray out in the hall and he locked himself out. He said he was stark naked and wanted to know where was the best place to hide until someone opened the door for him. We suggested that he go behind one of the stairwell doors, because not too many people use the stairwell. At night, there are wackos who call the operators and say dirty things. They'll ask what color underpants they're wearing. Stuff like that. A lot of crazy people call a hotel."

It was six-fifteen. Sullivan checked some well-thumbed sheets she had in front of her and began making wake-up calls. As the late-shift operator, she had woken up many thousands of Plaza guests. The Plaza service included the time and the temperature. There were no windows in the room, so the operators had no firsthand clue to what it was like outside, but someone would call the weather bureau and post the latest weather on a board. Sullivan glanced at it: "Temp 41. Hum 76.1. Hi 50s. Partly cloudy & breezy." If someone asked if it was raining right then, the operator had to call down to the doorman and get a report. Guests always figured they had stepped aside to look out the window.

Sullivan dialed. "Hello, Mr. Grant. It's six-fifteen, forty-one degrees, and enjoy your day."

Vutrano got up and poured herself a cup of coffee, then fixed her hair. She said, "We had a tour group of Italians in here. There were four hundred and fifty of them. The day before they were leaving, the head of the group came in and said they all wanted wake-up calls at eight the next morning. I just about fainted. We had four people doing the calls. We started at about ten minutes to eight and didn't get done until about twelve minutes after. And getting their names right was absolute murder. My girls aren't known for their Italian. These are the things you get in this place.

"On a normal day, we get two hundred and fifty to three hundred wake-up calls, about half of them at seven in the morning. We have a time clock in the room that we can set to go off every fifteen minutes to remind us to make the wake-ups. We get wake-ups all day long. Noon. Five in the afternoon—we get about ten of those a day. They're for people who want to take a nap and be roused for dinner."

The operators knew from past experience with them that some people were extraordinarily hard to get up. Either they slept with earplugs or they were hard of hearing or they simply knew a slumber that air-raid sirens wouldn't penetrate. Thus the operators would put a red dot next to their names to remind them to be more persistent and to make an additional call or two to try to arouse them.

The normal procedure was that if there was no answer to a wake-up call, the operator would try the room again in five minutes. If there was still no answer and the guest was not one of those sound sleepers, then the room number was reported to security and a man was dispatched to see if everything was okay. In the movies, there would be a dead body sprawled on the floor, a pool of blood next to it, and maybe a dagger stuck in the wall. At the Plaza, more often than not, there was an empty room. The guest had awoken before the call and left.

When it did a check, security was required to call back the operator staff and report that the person was either "up and out" or "up and in." Usually they were up and out. Occasionally, security opened the door and the guest walked out of the shower naked. Because of the thunder of the water, he would not have heard the phone. Once a security man got no answer and the chain was on the door. He cut the chain and found a woman in the room passed out on the floor, thoroughly snookered. The carpet was coated with vomit. That was a job for housekeeping.

"Good morning, sir," Sullivan said now. "It's six-thirty. The temperature is forty-one degrees. Enjoy your day."

7

THE comings and goings at the front desk were spasmodic. There would be bursts of checkouts for a couple of minutes, and then nothing but a few loiterers. It was nearly ten now, and a precision operation was being put into motion. The security staff was preparing to sneak the abused woman from last night out of the hotel and get her into a cab to the airport. Arthur Hoyt, the security director, was commanding the drill.

First he called the movie star's room and told him that his girlfriend was still in New York—either at another hotel or at a friend's apartment, he wasn't sure which—and she had phoned to say that she wanted her wallet. The movie star said he wouldn't give up anything until he had spoken to her. All right, Hoyt said, he would call her and have her get in touch with him. Hoyt instructed him to wait by the phone; it shouldn't be too long.

All this was, in fact, a calculated dodge. Hoyt wanted to ensure that the man remained in his room while he escorted the woman out. He took the elevator to her room. She quickly opened the door after he identified himself as being from security.

She was a blonde, quite young, dressed in casual slacks and a striped blouse. Her hair was unkempt. Though she had calmed down, she apparently was still suffused with rage. "Boy, did I have nightmares last night," she said. "I had to leave the lights on to fall asleep. I tell you, I'm glad to be leaving."

"I'll bet you are," Hoyt said, and he handed her an envelope containing fifty dollars that the hotel had agreed to advance her for cab fare.

"I had no idea he had that kind of temper," she said. "It was pretty unbelievable. That's not what you see on the screen."

"No, I guess it isn't," Hoyt said.

"I'm not seeing that creep again. No way."

"I don't blame you," Hoyt said.

Hoyt's plan was to take her out the Fifth Avenue entrance. He had stationed several security men in the lobby and just outside the main entrance with instructions to keep an eye peeled for the movie star. If he was spotted, Hoyt would bring the woman out the other entrance. They moved briskly through the lobby, Hoyt glancing furtively from side to side, but there was no sign of trouble.

As Hoyt was ushering the woman through the revolving doors onto Fifth Avenue, however, a security guard frantically waved him back. At the bottom of the stairs stood the movie star. Either he had not swallowed Hoyt's story or else he had gotten suspicious when so much time had elapsed without a phone call from the woman. Nervously tapping his foot, his eyes trained on the doors, he had not given up.

"Go back in, go back in," Hoyt hissed to the woman. "He's out there." But it was too late. She had been seen. Hurriedly, Hoyt went ahead and put her into a cab, but before he could get the door closed, the movie star was leaning in, trying to coax her into staying. A look of vexation came across the woman's face. She became snappish. "Leave me alone," she said firmly. "Just leave me alone. I'm going."

Hoyt told the man that she didn't want to speak to him; he had better let her be. The man stopped his harangue. Hoyt slammed the door shut and the cab took off. Rather than return to the hotel, however, the movie star climbed into his limousine, which had been idling out front, and took off as well.

"I know where he's going," Hoyt said. "He's going to follow her to the airport. But it's not our problem anymore. We can only worry about it until they're off the premises. But I'll tell you what I think. I bet they'll make up. It looks to me just like a classic lovers' spat."

8

HE king and queen were due soon, and while waiting for them I walked in on Arturo Buendia. He was talking animatedly on the phone. "Mmmm-hmmm," he said. "No, I don't think we need any."

Just outside the door was a tray on which were samples of several different patterns of china; the hotel was contemplating buying new plates for the restaurants. Behind his desk was a glass picture of a steamboat. It said, "Southern Comfort. The Grand Old Drink of the South."

As the head of purchasing for the hotel, Buendia got a lot of phone calls from suppliers wishing to sell the Plaza some merchandise. Most of the calls were nothing but a nuisance, because they pertained to items Buendia already had plenty of. When these calls arrived, Buendia adopted a kind of lachrymose air.

A gracious, rawboned man in his fifties, Buendia did a lot of shopping. Food was the principal thing he bought. "We buy roughly eight million dollars' worth of food a year," he said. "The way it breaks down is about two point one million worth of fish, one point seven million of meat, one point five million of groceries, nine hundred thousand of produce, eight hundred thousand of dairy products, five hundred thousand of bread, and three hundred thousand of poultry. Even little things can add up. For instance, we buy one million two hundred and twenty thousand turn-down mints a year from Astor Mints at a cost of seven hundred and fifty-six thousand four hundred dollars. A lot of mints. I hope the guests enjoy them."

Liquor, of course, was another heavy item for the purchasing department. The Plaza was very much a drinking hotel. All told, Buendia bought close to $2 million worth of liquor, wine, beer, and soda a year.

He told me about an oddity of purchasing at a hotel. When he ordered a new item—a change in the china, a fresh set of silverware, different-colored towels—he said he always had to factor in enough quantity for the majority of the employees. Past experience had taught him that in time, they would steal enough for their own use. "If you go to the homes of ninety percent of the employees here, you'll find the hotel's china, the hotel's silverware, the hotel's linen," he said. "It's just a fact of hotel life."

Buendia and the hotel management tolerated modest amounts of pilferage. They allowed employees to take care of their kitchens and their bathrooooms and their bedrooms. They didn't have all that much choice, since it would cost too much to try to prevent the stealing. What could they do? Search people every time they left the hotel? But when the theft reached major proportions, then their tolerance ran out. There was a rather flagrant case a few years ago. One of the regular guests of the hotel was dining at a restaurant on Long Island and found it awfully curious that the silverware at his table had the Plaza stamp on it. He glanced around and noticed that all of the silverware in the restaurant was Plaza silverware. Not long afterward, he was booking a banquet at the Plaza and mentioned the discovery to the banquet manager, who phoned the police. The restaurant owner confessed that he had bought the silverware from a low-level management employee of the hotel. The man had worked at the hotel for years and was trusted. He had apparently been swiping goods in considerable quantity and selling them. Though the man was not prosecuted, that was the end of his Plaza career.

. . .

AFTER I left Buendia, I went downstairs to take a look at the wine cellar. It was stuck way back in the subbasement, not far from the laundry. Two large steel doors guarded it, and next to the doors there was a buzzer to ring. A small man in a blue smock opened up. He was quick, fluid, dark-haired. His manner was quiet and he seemed not to have had a drink in a very long time. He was one of three attendants who worked full-time in the cellar, checking on the stock, filling requisitions. All day long, day after day, the three of them sat with the bottles. Drinking on the job, though, was strictly against the rules.

It was quite a daunting place, with more wine and booze than I had ever seen before—steel shelves packed full of Dewar's, Johnnie Walker, Haig & Haig, Gordon's, Seagrams. The hard stuff was in one long room and the wine—about two hundred different labels —was in an adjacent chamber. Everything went by numbers. No. 671—Gordon's Gin. No. 569—Rémy Martin. No. 836—Glenlivet. No. 851—Cutty Sark. Purchasing standards prohibited any Blue Nun or Ripple. According to Buendia, the hotel used an outside consultant to review its wine lists periodically and make sure that the latest favorites among the well-to-do were represented. Minimum standards existed, as well, for the liquors. They had to be name brands, such as Ballantine's, Dewar's White Label, J&B, and Johnnie Walker Red for scotches and Gordon's, Smirnoff, and Gilbey's for vodkas.

The most expensive wine in the cellar was Château Lafite Rothschild 1966. The hotel got it for $226.77 a bottle but sold it for $780. Apparently you make your money where you can. "We've got just two bottles in stock right now," the little man said. "I'd say we sell maybe one or two a month. I'll bet it's damn good, though I wouldn't really know."

Every morning, the wine cellar issued a supply of liquor to each of the outlets in the hotel. So many bottles went to the Oak Bar, so many to the banquet department, so many to room service, so many to the Oyster Bar. Rarely during the course of a day did people venture directly to the wine cellar to retrieve a bottle. They drew on their allotment. Besides, the cellar kept to strict hours—

eight-thirty in the morning until four-thirty in the afternoon. If someone needed some wine before or after those hours, then the beverage manager or his assistant had to phone the security department, which assigned a man to go down there with him. Security alone had the key. The precautions made sense. The cellar was a valuable place. When the supply was particularly large, there was more than $1 million worth of liquor and wine stored there. Right now, however, it was down to about $275,000.

Champagne was kept in a cold room of its own. Another cold room contained beer, and a third soda. There was also a narrow chamber in which I noticed a couple of boxes crammed with empty liquor bottles. I asked what they were doing there. "They're waiting to be broken," the man told me. It was a safeguard against bartender theft, he explained. When liquor bottles were empty, they were brought down to the wine cellar and exchanged for the same quantity of full bottles. The attendants then broke the empties to make sure the bartenders didn't keep them around and play tricks with them. They could, for instance, bring in some cheap liquor of their own and transfer it into empty bottles and then keep the money from the drinks. It happened.

The bottles were broken by a machine, a black, narrow-necked contraption that shattered them into hundreds of pieces and then fed them into a trash bin. "I'd say we break a couple of hundred bottles a day," the attendant said. "Makes a hell of a racket."

I figured I had seen enough, so I thanked the man and went to the door.

"Stay sober," he said. "It's the best way."

9

ECAUSE the king and queen of Sweden would soon be arriving, Harvey Robbins wanted to get his rooms set up early. He invited me to stick around and watch him work until the royal couple arrived. "Let's get this show on the road," he exclaimed. "Let's make some guests happy."

As he did every morning, Robbins was reviewing the rooms assigned to arriving VIPs to see if their prior occupants had checked out and if housekeeping had cleaned them. If there was a delay, Robbins would find an alternative room. He accomplished all this on a computer terminal that sat on his desk. As he went down his VIP sheet, he stopped at one name. "Here's a wedding couple," he said. "We'll be nice to them—if it's really their wedding night. Sometimes people say it's their wedding night and it isn't. You can tell by the nature of their arrival and how they treat each other. I've seen a lot of fakes. They lie so they get treated a little better and to pick up some free champagne."

Returning to the screen, Robbins said, "Okay, here we go. Here we go. Let's get this show rolling. Ross goes to Room 921. You're in there. Whew. Whew. Room 934 we'll give to Roman. Okay, you're in there. Now we're going to 935. Guido's going to get that. You're in there."

When he was done with his assignments, Robbins had to make

sure he had ordered enough flowers to decorate the rooms of the day's quota of VIPs. "This is going to be a heavy flower day," he said to himself. "A totally heavy flower day." Flowers were ordered from Rialto Florist on Lexington Avenue and Fifty-eighth Street. "It's the only twenty-four-hour, seven-day-a-week florist in New York," Robbins said. "And they make very nice displays. They make a fortune off me."

A young couple dressed in jeans approached Robbins and asked him if they could look at a deluxe suite and a single room. Robbins, saying he was too busy to show them himself, offered them keys to two unoccupied rooms they could look at. They walked briskly off and, about a half hour later, returned.

Handing over the keys, the man asked, "Now what are the prices on those?"

Robbins said, "The deluxe suite is nine hundred dollars and the single for two people is two hundred and eighty dollars."

The wife sputtered, "Is there a different category of suite? You said that was a deluxe."

"Yes," Robbins said. "There's a junior, medium, and deluxe. A medium is seven hundred dollars and a junior is five hundred."

"Do they connect to two bedrooms?" the woman asked.

"No," Robbins said. "Only the deluxe and some of the mediums. In fact, only two of the mediums."

Slightly fazed, the man said, "Okay, I'll let you know."

As they pushed through the revolving doors, Robbins said, "Those people are never coming here. I can tell by now. A lot of people are afraid to say that's too much money for them. So they start asking a lot of questions. About fifty percent of the people who look at a room don't ever take it. And I can usually tell which ones will and which ones won't. Everyone wants to see rooms at the Plaza. And they come up with every imaginable excuse. It's for some company. My grandmother's coming next July Fourth. Can I see a deluxe suite? My rich cousin twice removed is jetting in from Bulgaria. May I see a nice room? They never say, 'Can I see a room for myself for curiosity?' I'd let them. But they've always got these stories."

Robbins returned to his screen and began blocking out rooms for a group of Japanese visitors from an environmental agency. He was meticulous about whom he put where, and he explained why: "The Japanese have very special protocol. The highest-ranking official has to be on a higher floor than the others, and then the next-ranking guy has to be above the ones below him. That can be rough to do, but this is working out great. I've got the top guy in 1501, the next one in 808, and the next one in 703, and the next one in 605. Beautiful! Japan is the only country we've encountered that is like that, although some of the Germans are fussy. Mercedes-Benz, in fact, is the most rigid company on protocol. They are incredible. The highest guy in the company has to have the highest floor as well as the largest room. A lower guy can't be in a bigger room on a lower floor. They would go nuts if the top man went into one of his men's rooms and it was two or three inches larger. So I've got to know the dimensions, everything. The Mercedes-Benz people, I'm sure, bring rulers with them."

Robbins looked up. A couple stood before him.

The man cleared his throat and said, "We're getting married in August and we've been told that the place to stay is in your bridal suite. So we'd like to look at it."

"We don't have a bridal suite per se," Robbins said. "But we have some lovely rooms to show you."

"Something overlooking the park?" the man asked.

"Okay," Robbins said. "I've got a key for you for a lovely room on the ninth floor. You can see the whole city."

The couple headed for the elevators. They looked to be in their late forties and probably had been married years ago, though maybe not to each other.

When they returned, the woman said, "Oh, just beautiful."

"The room's great if the price is right," the man said.

Robbins said, "That room is four hundred and twenty-five dollars."

"Wait a minute," the man said. "What about in August?"

"It's the same price all year round," Robbins replied.

"In August, New York is dead," the man said. "There's got to be a discount."

"Nope," Robbins said. "I'm sorry, it's never discounted."

The man glanced at a plaque on Robbins's desk. "Look, you're an assistant manager. Do I have to call the manager to find out about the discount?"

Robbins said, "Our regular rooms are discounted fifty percent on Friday, Saturday, and Sunday, but not the park-view rooms."

"All right," the man said. "Let us look at one of those regular rooms. We're not that fussy."

"Here's a deluxe room," Robbins said, shoving over a key. "It's normally three hundred and eighty dollars. So fifty percent off makes it a hundred and ninety."

The couple went up and looked at it and were back at Robbins's desk in about ten minutes.

"Lovely," the man said. "We'll have our travel agent get in touch. I'm sure he has the number."

Robbins gave their backs a sneer. "They'll never stay here. I heard him say to her, 'It's just across the street.' They're checking out the Pierre. They're going to all the hotels. Mark my words, they'll end up taking a room overlooking the park at the Park Lane for two hundred and sixty dollars. It won't be anywhere near as nice a room as they would get here. But they'll get that view and they'll get that price."

Lou Corrozola, an assistant manager, poked his head in and asked Robbins if he could take one of his flower displays. "What's up?" Robbins asked.

"A man in 911 is not happy," Corrozola said. "He says if this is a renovation, he can't imagine what the rooms used to look like. He's just extremely disappointed. We've already adjusted his rate from eleven hundred and forty to nine forty."

"You think flowers will make him happy?" Robbins said.

"It'll help," Corrozola said.

"Okay, take a bunch."

"Can I take one for the mantel? It's a two-bedroom."

"Take 'em away," Robbins said.

I was surprised to hear that a rate had been lowered because of disappointment and asked Robbins if that was customary procedure.

"If a guest doesn't like his room, we will automatically adjust the rate by up to twenty-five percent," he said.

"Just like that?"

"Yes."

"But what if they're bluffing to save some money?" I asked.

"We don't take the chance," Robbins said.

Now Robbins started yelling at room service. A cheese tray that was to be delivered to a room had not been sent up and the shop that made cheese trays was closed. "If I don't get it I'll be very, very pissed," Robbins shouted. "I want the cheese tray. I don't want excuses. Excuses I get plenty of."

THE arrival of the king and queen was getting near. When royalty checked into a hotel, tradition insisted that the management do more than double-check that there was a reservation at the front desk and the Presidential Suite didn't still have dirty towels on the bathroom floor from the previous occupant. Hotel custom dictated that the front steps of the hotel be covered with a red carpet, that somebody be waiting with flowers, and that the manager be standing in the lobby with a smile and an extended hand. The staff of the Plaza were not nervous. They, of course, had seen all this time and again. Nevertheless, they were intent on making a good impression, and some last-minute dashes had to be made.

The Secret Service (there were agents from both the United States and from the Swedish Secret Service swarming around the hotel) had already completed preparations. Agents had physically inspected the Presidential Suite, and earlier today a bomb-squad dog had sniffed inquisitively around the premises, finding nothing of any interest. The dogs (the squad used to go with German shepherds, but Labrador retrievers had more recently proved to boast superior noses) were trained to recognize thirty-two different scents of chemicals commonly used in bombs, and they were felt to be more reliable than any mechanical detector. The suite, of course, had also been swept for listening devices. As an added precaution, Secret Service men had taken the rooms directly above and below

the suite, to guard against interlopers burrowing through the floor
or ceiling. Fresh flowers had been placed in the suite, along with a
bottle of Dom Pérignon champagne that had been ordered by Donald Trump and was accompanied by a signed card from him greeting the royal couple.

A call came in to Robbins's office. The word was that the king
and queen had left the South Street Seaport early and would arrive
at the hotel in five to seven minutes. Robbins slammed the phone
down with a bang and shouted, "Five to seven minutes. Let's get
out there."

Robbins and several lobby assistants moved like jackrabbits toward the Fifth Avenue doors. "I hope they're done cleaning the red
carpet," one of the assistants said. "They were still at it five minutes
ago."

When Robbins got outside, a porter, his face flushed from work,
was busily vacuuming the carpet. The carpet used to be literally
rolled out once the dignitary it was meant for arrived; the Plaza
now nailed it in place in advance. Robbins peered critically at the
rug. "Five to seven minutes," he yelled at the man. "Speed it up."

The porter began vacuuming at something approaching Mach
speed.

As Robbins soaked in the scene, something disturbing suddenly
dawned on him. Although the carpet ran from the revolving doors
all the way to the bottom of the steps, it didn't extend out to the
curb, where the king and queen would be disembarking from their
car. "Hey, where's the other piece of carpet?" Robbins said. "It's
supposed to go to the curb."

No one seemed to know where it was. Robbins sighed deeply
and looked at the sky. Turning on his heels, he dashed off to
housekeeping. Within minutes, he reappeared with a roll of red
carpet slung over his shoulder. Kneeling down, he unfurled it and
spread it out on the sidewalk, patting it down to smooth it.
"You've got to do things yourself around here to get them done,"
he said.

The additional piece was coated with lint, so Robbins had the
porter hastily vacuum it, and it quickly entered a new dimension

of cleanliness. It looked spotless and luxurious, ready to receive the steps of royal feet.

Jeffrey Flowers and Hud Hinton walked into the lobby and solemnly arranged themselves just before the revolving doors. This was not their favorite post, and they both looked a little anxious. Flowers examined his suit scrupulously and adjusted the rose in his lapel. They would greet the royal couple there in the lobby. From the Secret Service's standpoint, the highest risk time for the king and queen was from the moment they left the car until they got inside the hotel, so the welcome was to take place inside.

A photographer showed up. He had been hired by the hotel to take publicity shots of the welcome. He trotted over to Flowers and asked him what he should shoot. "Just focus in on the greeting of the king and queen," Flowers told him. "They're not going to stay here long."

Quite a wind had kicked up and was swirling around the revolving doors. "Jesus, it's windy as hell out there," Flowers said to Hinton. "We don't want them hurt."

Hinton looked vague.

A crowd of about thirty people had trooped into the lobby, anticipating the arrival. They were very dressy, for the most part, though there were a couple of giggling young women in shorts and one sour-faced man in jeans. A second, larger crowd milled aimlessly around the front steps of the hotel—a shifting, leaning, chattering group of people. Every time a car pulled up, necks craned for a look.

Finally, a long black limousine slid to a stop. It was the royal guests.

All eyes fastened on the couple as they were helped out of the car. They smiled and nodded at the crowd. They were a pleasingly handsome pair. The king had a wide, leathery face and dark, short-cropped hair. He was fiercely handsome. The queen had shoulder-length blond hair, good eyes, and a nice face. She gave a warm smile.

First to greet them was Malin Hammer, the sales manager, who curtsied and presented the queen with a dozen long-stemmed roses.

Then the couple made their way up the stairs and through the revolving doors, where Flowers and Hinton waited.

There were not a great many things to say to the king and queen of Sweden upon their arrival at a hotel. A brief and cordial word would do. "We're happy to have you with us," Flowers said with hand outthrust.

"Happy to have you with us, king," Hinton said with great solicitude.

"Thank you," the king said in a strong, resonant voice.

"Thank you," the queen said.

There was a burst of flashes from the photographer's camera followed by polite applause from the crowd. The greeting was over. Enveloped by Secret Service men, the king and queen walked in stately fashion to the elevators and were whisked to the Presidential Suite.

As they vanished in the blur of dark suits, Hinton looked slightly discomfited. He said to Flowers, "I held his hand too long. I was waiting for the photographer and he didn't snap. Did you notice the king looking at me as if he was wondering what is wrong with this guy?"

"Ah, it was a cinch." Flowers said. "Ho-hum, another king."

SATURDAY

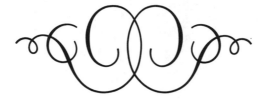

1

HORTLY after nine, as I was walking past the rows of house phones toward the front desk, two determined-looking women came barreling around the corner, bearing down on me. Uncommitted to any appointments, I decided to follow them. They were on the far side of middle age, with the requisite short, puffed hairdos, and had inexpensive cameras dangling around their necks.

"Okay, let's start here, Selma," one of the women said to her companion. They had pulled up before the Palm Court. Selma struck a pose there, one hand on her hip, one hand arched behind her head, while her companion got positioned to take her picture.

Her companion made a disgusted face. "No, no," she said. "I don't like that pose. It makes you look too cheap."

Selma removed her hand from behind her head and put it on her other hip. She arched her back a little, and that did the trick. Her friend snapped the picture, and then they traded roles.

"Over here next," Selma said, and they roved over to the chairs in the lobby, where several more pictures were taken, one of them with Selma seated and her head thrown back in a laugh. People paraded past in the background, framing the shots.

They repeated the process before the giant vase of flowers in the lobby, then moved off in a rush toward the Oyster Bar. "Oh, Selma, these are going to be too much," the other woman said. "Wait till the neighbors get a load of these. I'm not a bragging person, but I'm a proud person."

"Yes, that you are," Selma said.

Her friend clucked through her teeth. "Shirley will definitely die," she said.

"And that'll be a blessing," Selma said.

ASIDE from the ongoing hubbub around the check-in desk in the early morning, the Plaza was very calm. Hardly anyone was seeking help at the concierge desk, and it was still too soon for people to be coming by to eat at the restaurants. This wouldn't last. Starting at about ten on Saturday mornings, the lobby got so crowded with legions of gawking tourists that it resembled a metropolitan train terminal during the peak hours. The place became an encampment of tourists—people who would never stay or eat at the hotel. The heavy foot traffic made it hard for those who performed essential services—the bellmen, the concierges, the assistant managers—to pass and do their jobs.

There was an entirely different feel to the hotel on the weekends. Those days attracted a less savvy type of traveler. He tended to check in earlier, before nine in the morning, and he wanted to check out as late as possible, wringing the maximum time out of his dollar. There was a need for more rooms with double beds, as families crammed themselves into the smallest possible space. Far fewer men and women in business attire passed through the place. Clothes were more casual and characterized by a general absence of good taste. Suburbanites in New York for a day of shopping or to take in a play or movie strolled leisurely through the hotel, satisfying their craving to see what it was like. A pale-skinned woman pushing a stroller now moved past the concierge desk, two doe-eyed children trailing behind her. "Can you imagine?" she said to the children. "I hear you need to make a reservation about a year in advance and it's probably a thousand dollars a night for just a small room looking into an alley." The children exhibited no signs of

being impressed. Then the older one, who looked about six, bit his
lip and blurted out, "I'm hungry, Mom. I'm really hungry." Before
the woman could respond, they had faded into the throng. Another
woman, holding a small boy on her hip, filed past, looking as
wonderingly as the previous mother had. Children were always part
of the weekend scene.

Two teenage girls, both of them with teeth encased in copious
metal, sidled up to the concierge desk. One of them cleared her
throat and said, "Excuse me, could you tell me where the Eloise
Room is?"

"I'm sorry," one of the attendants said, "we no longer have that.
But there's a picture of Eloise around the corner by the Palm
Court."

"Oh, okay, thanks," the girl said, containing her disappointment. "But the room would have been much better."

"No room?" the other girl said. "What's wrong with this place?"

"It's hard to believe," the attendant said to me. "We haven't had
an Eloise Room for years, and yet people keep asking about it. I
get an inquiry like that almost every week. Some people even ask
how old Eloise is today and what she's doing for a living. I mean,
they really believe in that story."

For all the pitched anticipation of the arrival of the king and
queen, now that they were checked into the hotel the staff didn't
expect all that much work related to their stay. Most of the time,
after all, they were out and about on their preordained adventures.
In spare moments, they fitted in occasional frivolity. The night
before, they had been out until the early hours dancing at Nell's,
one of the popular downtown dance clubs. Like most celebrated
guests, they became nearly invisible once they were in the hotel,
not bothering to drop by at the Oak Bar for a drink or to wander
around the lobby shops for toothpaste or a scarf. The hotel staff's
main concern was that elevators be reserved for them when they
came and went and that any request for service be granted top
priority. Other than that, the only worry was that nothing embarrassing should happen on the premises that the king and queen
would hear about or—worse still—actually witness.

Little things, though, kept cropping up from the Swedish entourage. Unknown to the hotel when the bookings were made, the king and queen preferred to sleep in separate bedrooms. That had created a slight stir. The bedroom that the queen took was adjacent to the room where her chambermaid would sleep. However, there was no door between the two rooms. Hence the building department had to have some men go up and erect a screen at record speed to give the queen the privacy she was accustomed to. Malin Hammer had already been off to the jeweler with her majesty's chambermaid's watch. She thought it needed a new battery. A Secret Service man had contacted Harvey Robbins this morning to inform him that the mantel flowers in the Presidential Suite struck him as droopy and probably ought to be replaced with fresh ones. Though not ordinarily governed by the Secret Service in such matters, Robbins dutifully brought new ones up on a trolley; they were inspected by the guard at the door before being let in. The guard, I noticed, had been installed with a chair right outside the entrance, and since the king and queen spent most of their stay outside the hotel, he said he had found time to turn a great many pages in the book he was reading: *The Collected Stories of W. Somerset Maugham.*

The latest request was now in the hands of Elizabeth Allen, a sales manager who was pulling out strands of her hair down by the front desk. The assistant to the king wanted to take some gifts home for friends but, being busy with assorted duties, didn't have the time to shop for them, so he wanted the hotel to take care of the errands. Allen stared at the list that had been phoned in: "Light sweaters for jogging, ten yellow towels (Cannon or Fieldcrest), Canon 35mm automatic camera with flash, walking shoes (same as ones he has in his room), and a Spalding Executive right-hand sand wedge."

"I can't believe this," Allen said. "I'm sitting here getting ready for a Japanese group that's about to arrive like any second and I get this call. This is nuts. I can't do this. I have no one around who can do this. Who is this man? What are these presents? What does he mean, shoes like he has? Who knows what kind of shoes he has? Am I supposed to be watching everyone's feet?"

"Calm down, Elizabeth," one of the front-desk attendants said. "This is always the way it goes with this kind of people. They farm out everything. They don't even do their own sneezing."

"This is so stupid," Allen said.

Bill Dougherty, the assistant manager on duty, said, "How do we know what he wants to spend? This stuff could cost a thousand dollars, easy. Does he know the prices? Does he know what a good sand wedge costs?"

"I don't know what he wants to spend," Allen said. "I just wish he would spend it himself."

The staff talked a bit about dispatching a lobby assistant manager to do the shopping, but views diverged.

"That's nuts," Allen said. "The person would have to go to a half-dozen different stores. And you know what the crowds are like on Saturday. It'll take forever."

"Okay, here's what we'll do," Dougherty said. "I'll have one of the lobby assistant managers call and find out his budget. Then we'll see if we can call the stores and order the stuff over the phone and have them deliver it here. And somebody's got to go up to his room and look at his walking shoes so we know what he's talking about."

"All right," Allen said. "Let's try it. But this is really asking a lot."

2

JEFFREY Flowers and Hud Hinton had the weekend off, though, like doctors, they could be reached if anything of great importance came up. Each week, a rotation schedule was in effect to determine who ran the place on the weekends. One of the senior department heads was put in charge. That person moved into a room in the hotel for the two nights, was entitled to eat free in any of the restaurants, and in return had to tackle any operational problems that occurred.

This weekend, the rotation had turned up Howard Hardiman, who was normally working numbers in the accounting department. The assignment required someone fleet of foot. Before the weekend was out, he had to complete a fourteen-page report critiquing the hotel's operations. He was supposed to check in at the front desk, just as a regular guest would, and comment on the efficiency and friendliness of the agent who handled him. He was supposed to use a bellman and comment on his efficiency and friendliness. He was to do a perimeter check of the building and note the condition and activity levels. Besides remarking on his own accommodations, Hardiman was supposed to pick an unoccupied guest room at random and inspect it. For each meal, he was to eat at a different restaurant in the hotel and appraise the food and service. On one of the mornings, he was to order room service to check up on it. He was to send something to the laundry and see if it came back spotless, leave a message with the operator, and call housekeeping for either an iron, hair dryer, or additional night service and record the timeliness of service. He was to visit three guest corridors and remark on the cleanliness, lighting, and stairways. He was to drop in on the various departments and see how they were performing. Finally, before exhaustion claimed him, he was to offer a brief synopsis of the weekend and make any suggestions that he felt would improve hotel service.

"My main priority is to make sure everything is in place," Hardiman told me. He had just eaten breakfast and looked refreshed. "I'll check with all the departments to make sure they don't have any problems. So far, nothing's come up. This morning, I ate at the Edwardian Room. It was very good. Service was very quick. I didn't even have time to look at my paper and the food was there. That was a pleasant surprise. We sometimes have service problems there."

Hardiman was a lean man. His face was angular, and he had wide-set eyebrows and a neat mustache. He was placid and easy to get to know. "You get this duty about twice a year," he said. "By now, I've had it four or five times. Usually it's pretty routine, but you have your occasional crises. On one of my previous stints, there was a family from London staying here who reported their daughter missing. That was a mess. She had gone with her sister to the Palladium. Her sister came back, but she didn't. Needless to say, I was pretty concerned. I had to inform the police and everything and try to calm some very upset parents. They were off the wall. This was not something I do much of in accounting. Well, the next day at noon she finally showed up on her own. She was grounded for the rest of the trip and probably even after they got back to London."

With things relatively quiet, Hardiman said he was just going to cruise around and try to fulfill some of his weekend requirements. "Mostly I'll be praying nothing awful happens," he said. "I'm really not interested in dealing with trouble."

3

THE banquet staff was terribly busy. A phalanx of workers was spread throughout the cavernous Grand Ballroom, in the midst of the final preparations for the reception and dinner tonight for the king and queen. In the anteroom to the ballroom, four people were sitting at long tables folding napkins and wrapping a galax leaf around each one. Long-stemmed yellow flowers in slender glass vases were being prepared as centerpieces for the tables. Inside the ballroom, tables were being arranged and white linen tablecloths were being put on them. A piano had been wheeled out on the stage and electricians were hooking up speakers.

Near the kitchen were stacked cases of Absolut vodka, the only brand that would be served this evening, as well as Nordic wild lingonberry juice and Ramlosa mineral water. Some men were unpacking the bottles and moving them into the kitchen. A couple of porters were sweeping the kitchen floor. It always seemed as if a big banquet just came together of its own accord, but it normally took weeks of planning and many hours of setting up. The Plaza staff had begun transforming the ballroom at seven in the morning and didn't expect to be finished until at least five. Any sort of hitch could add several hours to the task, cutting things close.

Socrates Alexander, the silver-haired director of catering, and Paul Nicaj, the assistant director of banquet waiters, were wandering around to see how things were going. "The dinner is pretty simple," Alexander told me, "but the executive chef will give the king and queen's table a special touch. We'll have a lot of supervision tonight. You don't take this kind of affair lightly."

Alexander had the duty of arranging some of the most expensive functions in New York. Saturday, for instance, was a popular wedding day at the Plaza. Fifty or sixty weddings a year were held in the hotel, among them the weddings of Steve Ross, the head of Warner Communications, and of Marilyn Vos Savant and Dr. Robert Jarvik, the inventor of the artificial heart. Richard Nixon had held the wedding reception for his daughter Julie and David Eisenhower at the Plaza. The hotel, though, was far from fussy, which made for a curious mix of clientele. Back in the late 1960s, the Plaza was the setting for the wedding receptions of the son of reputed crime figure Vincent Napoli and the son of Carlo Gambino, the alleged head of a Mafia family. Some law-enforcement officials even made a few cracks about those events, contending that the Plaza had departed from its normal procedures in not requiring the reputed criminals to sign contracts or furnish seating lists. The hotel retorted that lots of guests were treated the same way. No doubt the catering people then were well enough informed to know that the mob never gave out seating lists.

Saturday was also the day a fair number of birthday parties or anniversary bashes were held in one or another of the function rooms. The Grand Ballroom was usually booked by one dinner dance or ball of some sort. Every year, there was a roster of annual balls that repeated: Le Ball Blanc, the Tiffany Ball, the Alcohol Council of New York Ball, the Society of Mayflower Descendants, the Junior League, the Annual Debutante Assemblies, the Petrauska Ball, the Chrysanthemum Ball. Fashion shows were held for Bill Blass, Carolina Herrera, and Escada. Fund-raising functions were commonplace: Brandeis, UJA, ADL, AJC, Yeshiva University, the Weizman Institute of Science. The Plaza hosted Brooke Astor's book party, John Loeb's anniversary banquet, the *National Review*'s twenty-fifth anniversary, and Truman Capote's amply publicized Black and White Ball.

Nothing in recent years quite matched that ball. Ever since he was a small boy, Capote had always wanted to throw the biggest and grandest party, and he finally did it on the chilly evening of November 18, 1968, choosing the Plaza because, like many others, he felt it had the only beautiful ballroom left in New York. Everyone had to wear black or white, and masks were also mandatory. He picked Katharine Graham, whose family owned the *Washington Post,* as the guest of honor. Five hundred people showed up and had a memorable time. The Museum of the City of New York read enough special significance into the event to install some of the masks from the party in its collection.

A young brown-haired woman was walking around the ballroom checking tablecloths. She seemed satisfied with the first few, and then her mood changed abruptly. "Ugh, this one is not even," she huffed. "We're going to have to go around and check every table. I knew this was going to happen. Every table had better be checked."

The arrangers of the dinner had specified pillowcase-type covers for the dining chairs. They were intended to keep the chairs from sweating, but they looked chintzy. "I think they're absolutely silly," Paul Nicaj said. "But we're stuck with them." Nicaj remarked that a total of nine hundred people were attending the dinner. "We're going to have ninety waiters, the entire department, working it. Our formula is one waiter per ten guests, and we've got ninety tables. The guys will be moving fast."

I noticed a couple of workers were rehearsing their golf swings with imaginary clubs. One of them was, at the same time, practicing what he would say should he happen to bump into the king or queen. "Your majesties," he intoned, "it's a pleasure to serve you. How about I get you a drink? Will it be Blue Nun or is a beer fine? By the way, if you ever need anything done at the old castle—clogged toilet, leaky faucet—just give me a jingle."

As I left, I passed through the adjoining Baroque Room, where I encountered a panel of four doctors giving a presentation titled "Cardiac Imaging and Intervention Update." Someone had recently finished presenting "The Role of Ultrafast Computed Tomography in the Evaluation of Coronary Artery Heart Disease."

I sat down for a few minutes and looked through the packet of material that was available to the audience. There was a paper entitled "Intravascular Stents for Angioplasty." Another was "Balloon-Expandable Intracoronary Stents in the Adult Dog."

A blond woman clutching a microphone began going around to attendees to take questions. About forty people were in the audience, some of them looking eagerly to their right, where lunch tables had been set up for them. There was a man walking around filling up water pitchers.

Question: "I'd like to hear more on thallium and complications."

Answer: "I'm glad you asked that. We've had one patient who was infarcted . . ."

The talk was arcane, incomprehensible. I tiptoed out.

4

ROM the back of the Palm Court came a commotion of sounds: low, steadily rising dissension vibrating the air. Some guests had had too much and were not doing well at concealing their inebriation.

They were a middle-aged man and a somewhat younger woman. He had shaggy gray hair, a rufous beard, and a hawk nose. He was wearing a sports coat, dark slacks, and white sneakers. The woman was pale, with delicate features, and her long brown hair was piled up on top of her head and fastened with bobby pins. She had on jeans and a baggy blouse. Their present request was for more champagne, but the waiter, realizing that the couple had far surpassed their limit, demurred. Neighboring diners, having put up with their boorish behavior, would have agreed. The hostess came over and offered to serve them some complimentary cookies and milk. The man didn't take kindly to that. He barked a few unpleasant remarks.

"You know, I'm a handicapped person," the woman said snippily. "You're prejudiced against the handicapped. I'm going to sue."

"I didn't notice you were handicapped," the hostess said.

"Oh, really?" the woman said, and she reached under her chair and held up a cane. "What the hell do you think this is for? To hit people with?"

"Don't make me answer that," the hostess said, and she turned on her heel and returned to her station.

Jumping up from his chair, the man stomped after her to renew his attempt to be served. His face glowered. In a paroxysm of anger, he began shouting: "Listen, lady, this is not about us. This is about the hotel. We'll have what we want. Why don't you just leave, lady, and I'll be very happy. Very happy. Now, for the last time, that will be two more splits of champagne. Send them over." He raised two fingers to reaffirm the order and went back to his seat. He bent over to the woman, and she laughed at something he whispered in her ear.

By now, Hud Hinton, Howard Hardiman, and Arthur Hoyt had arrived on the scene. While Hinton and Hardiman waited by the entrance, Hoyt went over and shook the man's hand, exchanged some pleasantries. His voice was wooden and a little uncertain. Yet he seemed to calm the man down. The tone of the conversation, at any rate, suddenly became more cordial. The man mentioned that he was a good friend of Donald Trump's, and Hoyt said that was wonderful. Returning to Hinton's side, he reported, "I think they'll go quietly."

He had barely gotten that prediction out when the man, wobbling slightly, mounted the little stage in the center of the Palm Court, sat down at the piano, and began playing an entirely unrecognizable tune. The air filled with the faint and random music. Soon the man began to hum along with the music, his body swaying from side to side. The woman began to click her fingers. Two rather aged women sipping tea near the stage craned their necks and looked wonderingly at the performer, presumably disappointed with the quality of the morning's entertainment.

The problem was now becoming worrisome. Hinton and Hoyt had been alerted that the king and queen would be leaving the hotel shortly. They would be walking by the Palm Court, and it would be unfortunate if, in passing the restaurant, they noticed a drunken guest playing the piano.

"Oh, Jesus," Hinton said. "Maybe we should get Secret Service and have them yank his ass out of here."

"No, no," Hoyt insisted. "Let me handle this. I know drunks."

"Arthur's so diplomatic about these things," Hinton said. "Not me. I lose my cool. I just want to throw out people like that."

Some guests lingered, transfixed, to see what happened next.

Hoyt sauntered over to the piano and bent over. "Hey, you're really playing well," he told the man.

"Well, thank you," the man responded.

"But we've got one problem," Hoyt said. "I understand you're a friend of Donald Trump's."

"That's right," the man said, and he began to chew at his lower lip.

"Well, this is a union shop, and you can get in trouble for playing and Mr. Trump will get in trouble."

The man drew back rigidly. He gave a searching look. "Gee, I didn't know that," he said. "I don't want that to happen."

With that, he meekly left the stage and sat down once again at his table. He said something to the woman, who nodded slowly.

Hinton went over to Hoyt and said, "Get the check to them right away and let's try to get them out of here."

At that moment, the king and queen came walking past the Palm Court. Hoyt and Hinton each took in a breath. The man and woman stayed put. The situation did not tilt in the direction of chaos.

Hinton said, "Okay, we're fine. That worked out just fine."

A few minutes later, the couple rose and decided to leave. As they moved past Hoyt and Hinton, the man said, pointing to the hostess, "By the way, fire that lady over there."

"Okay," Hoyt said, "we'll do that."

The woman said, "And you have to be fired, too. Right away."

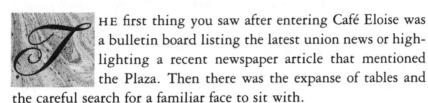

HE first thing you saw after entering Café Eloise was a bulletin board listing the latest union news or highlighting a recent newspaper article that mentioned the Plaza. Then there was the expanse of tables and the careful search for a familiar face to sit with.

While I had the time, I went to grab some lunch at the employee cafeteria, down in the hotel's basement, where leftovers could be gotten at a fraction of the food's cost in one of the upstairs dining rooms. Before Café Eloise was built, there used to be a different cafeteria for the employees, which was referred to as the Nurses' Hall because the private nurses and maids for the wealthy people who stayed at the Plaza usually ate down there. But there was no more need for anything like that.

Two cooks were assigned to full-time cafeteria duty, and they managed to come up with three hot specials each day. Employees were pretty much always lambasting the selection and quality of the food in the cafeteria, though they kept on eating there. The complaints occasionally had some impact. I noticed a flyer that reported that some "new and exciting" changes would be taking place in coming months. Among them were that "two or three mixed salad items will be rotated daily (i.e., pickled peppers, pickled cucumbers, coleslaw, Waldorf salad, etc.)"; "the quality of cold cuts used in sandwiches has been upgraded and all sandwiches will be labeled"; "theme days will take place once a month and all entrees served will reflect the theme"; "holiday meals (i.e., Thanksgiving and Christmas) will be served at no charge, including second helpings, and a selection of fruits and nuts will be provided."

Near the cafeteria were the employee lockers. On their breaks the workers would often pick up a book or paper there to read while they ate. Some years ago, lunch breaks for employees were restricted to a half hour, but now most of them got a full hour.

The cafeteria was a good-sized rectangular room, with rows of beige Formica-topped tables and fluorescent orange plastic chairs. I took a look at the menu, and the prices were pretty amazing. Scrambled eggs were 50 cents, cereal was 40 cents, sandwiches $1, cake or pie 45 cents, a full meal $1.50, a banana 25 cents, a hot dog 60 cents, and a cup of coffee 10 cents. If you ate too often down there, though, it became clear to you why the prices were as low as they were.

Right now, the place was so crowded with people coming and going with trays full of food that you could hardly move without banging into somebody else's tray. A couple of cops were eating at one of the tables, which reminded me of a story I had heard about a deputy police inspector who was demoted and transferred to the Bronx for accepting free meals at the cafeteria. Rather than report to the Bronx, the inspector took early retirement.

Traffic in the cafeteria was spasmodic. During many hours of the day and night—all three meals were served there—hardly a soul was in the place. But at lunchtime the room was jammed, for there were virtually no other cheap places nearby for the employees to patronize. Once that period of turmoil was over, the place returned to its sleepy state, picking up again at the dinner hour, when many members of the late shift ate there before commencing their duties. There were also the loiterers from the day shift, employees who had no particular place to go and were in no rush to go home. There was one man I saw a number of times, working on coffee for a good hour or two after his day was complete, who said straight out that the less he saw of his wife and kids the better, so he liked to remain at the hotel for several hours before heading home. All in all, it was an odd place.

The cafeteria was lighted by an abundance of fluorescent bulbs, so you nearly forgot that there were no windows and that you were dining in a basement. But there was no rich carpeting or marble floor, only white-speckled linoleum that never looked clean. Just past the checkout register, there was a bank of milk and juice dispensers, where you could take what you wanted for free. There was also a free shoeshine machine. At one end of the room hung a collection of bulletin boards, known as the Information Center, where union notices were posted, as well as pictures of the employees of the month, so named because they had excelled in customer courtesy or work productivity. Anyone whose picture made the board seemed to make it a point to wander through the cafeteria a little more deliberately and to choose a table in a more central location than he or she might otherwise do. Employees understood this little ritual and showed their deference by offering hearty congratulations. That was true except for the cynical old-timers who never turned up on the board and, with their attitude, never were likely to. They just snorted when one of the winners went by, and they tried their best not even to notice who was up there this month.

On the back wall of the cafeteria hung various awards the hotel had won. There was also a plaque testifying to the devotion of John Christaforon, who worked at the hotel for sixty-five years before finally hanging it up in October of 1978, once he hit the age of seventy-nine. As far as anyone could tell, he held the longevity record, and no one expected it to be broken. Christaforon began his Plaza career when he was only fourteen. For many years, he was a night chef, though he later switched to days and was a server in the cafeteria. Just about everyone who knew him had admiring things to say about him.

The cafeteria was where the gossip of the hotel was exchanged, and you could quickly tell which groups had the best dope—they would be bent close to one another, talking excitedly, while watching the other tables out of the corners of their eyes. A few of the

diners seemed to have such dynamite material that they were practically at the point of delirium. Many of the luncheon arrivals had
uniforms drenched with sweat. Some of the maids were complain-
ing that they were hopelessly behind with their work; too many
guests were dawdling in their rooms rather than getting up and out
so the sheets could be changed and the bathrooms scrubbed. "Some
of these guys are just lying there on their ass hour after hour," one
of the maids complained to a companion as she downed a robust
portion of veal cutlet. "I'd like to quickly open the door and hurl
in a stink bomb. That would get the louses out of there in one hell
of a hurry."

"I guess that's right," her companion said.

Planted at a table against the back wall was an Italian who I
knew loved long and argumentative discussions. Apparently he had
managed to find a couple of other employees who were willing to
tolerate him during their lunch hour. Both of them were totally
occupied with their meals, their idea presumably being that the
sooner they got rid of the food the better it would taste. Meanwhile,
the Italian's arms were flailing about at a pretty good clip. Twice
they almost took out a passing tray, but he was too smitten by his
own oratory to notice. I had seen him in the cafeteria often, morning, afternoon, and evening. It was a good place for him to hold
court, I supposed.

WHEN I finished eating, I cruised through the laundry, which was
working overtime to meet the needs of the king and queen. Lenny
Labonia was in his office with his wife and young daughter. He had
come by to make sure everything was running smoothly.

"They're sending down a lot of stuff," he said. "A lot. We just
got a call from the king's staff with some suits. The guy said, 'This
is for the king of kings.' He got a little carried away. So far, we've
been getting the clothes back the next morning by eight if we get
them at night. The stuff that comes in during the day, we get back
to them in an hour and a half. We're giving them a royal job. I
check all their clothes to make sure they've been done right. Everything has looked very good."

"What's been coming in?" I asked.

"Mostly all-white shirts," Labonia said. "No prints or anything. The guy's definitely conservative. I guess you have to be in that line of work. That's good, though, from my standpoint. Whites are easier to press and get clean."

"How are the clothes?" I said.

"The man's got some nice suits. Mostly dark ones. Here's a few right here. A dark blue. A dark gray. Good quality stuff. No question about it. The kind you'd expect on a king."

6

As part of his weekend duties, Howard Hardiman was supposed to inspect at random one guest room other than the one he was staying in. While things were slow, he grabbed a room key and invited me to tag along. "I kind of like this routine," he said in the elevator. "I get to see a lot more of the hotel than I normally do in accounting. There are all the nooks and crannies, all the stuff going on that I'm usually oblivious to."

Room 629 was his pick for the inspection. It was a two-room suite, with good space. As soon as he came in, despite the dazzling sun, he flicked on the lights to see that they were working. They were. He opened up the armoire and turned on the television. It came to life with a religious broadcast. "I can't understand these guys," Hardiman said. "Who really watches them?"

His hands clasped behind his back, he walked around the room, as if pondering a problem. "You have to look for every little detail," he said. "See here? There has to be a can opener on top of the ice bucket and some stir sticks. Let's see, the opener is here and there are four sticks. That's acceptable."

He strode across the room. It seemed void of offenses. "Uh-oh, here's a problem," he said. "The skirt on this side table is messed up. It's supposed to be out." Hardiman bent over and pulled the skirt out. It hadn't bothered me.

A more glaring offense showed itself in the bedroom. The drapery was missing on one of the windows. The valance was there but not the flowered drapery. Hardiman looked sternly at the window and marked down the problem on a pad. "There are some little things here that are undesirable that you have to live with," he said. "You can see some of the seams in the wallpaper. They could have done a better job at that, but now it's too late."

He opened the closet to make sure that the laundry and dry-cleaning bags were there and that the safe had its key in it. You never knew what you might find on one of these tours. When Harvey Robbins was inspecting a room once for an arriving VIP, he unlocked the safe and, to his amazement, found $200,000 worth of jewels glittering inside. It hadn't even been the previous tenant who had left them. By then, the jewels had been in the safe for four nights and two other guests had occupied the room. Robbins might have boarded the next plane for Peru, but instead he turned the jewels in. The woman they belonged to didn't call about them for five weeks.

"Okay, things are looking good," Hardiman said. "They're looking quite a bit better than my place in Brooklyn."

In the bathroom, Hardiman ran his fingers over the counters to check for dust and fished around in the basket of amenities to make sure they were all there. "Some people think toothpaste should be in the package," Hardiman said. "I guess I would go along with that."

After pulling out the skirt on a table in the bedroom, Hardiman was done with his inspection. "A few small things," he said, "but basically an acceptable room. We could put a guest in here and hold our heads high."

7

WOMAN in early middle age, her tallowy blond hair waving, walked by the Palm Court with her dog, which was yipping frantically. "Silence, Brutus," she reproved the dog. "Show some respect or Mommy won't bring you here ever again."

The scolding did no immediate good. Brutus continued his yipping, though perhaps a little less frantically.

"Oh, Brutus," the woman sighed. "You really test Mommy's patience."

The extent of the pet presence in the Plaza was not widely realized. On some days, however, one might be led to believe that the hotel was really a large pet shop, since there were so many animals wandering amid the chandeliers and mink coats. Most hotels frowned on the idea of pets staying in their rooms (the Pierre, however, also admitted them). The Plaza's long-standing unwritten rule was to welcome—or at least tolerate—all "small" animals. The informal definition of "small" was dogs weighing less than twenty-five pounds, which would put the cutoff about at the level of a cocker spaniel. The definition, though, stretched remarkably, depending on the significance of the guest (or pet). If the king of Zaire wanted to bring a rhinoceros to the hotel, the hotel would not object. If Rin-Tin-Tin wanted a suite, he could have it. In fact, a seventy-pound cheetah once stayed at the hotel under the supervision of the wife of the president of Kenya.

Where the hotel did draw the line was at pets accompanying their owners to one of the dining rooms. Other arrangements had to be made. There was one couple who, virtually without exception, ate dinner every Friday in the Edwardian Room. They came with their poodle. They also came with a baby-sitter for the poodle. While they dined, the baby-sitter and the poodle sat in the lobby and listened to the music from the Palm Court. The dog was fond of show tunes.

There had been times when as many as thirty-five dogs lived at the Plaza. Like their owners, they tended to be exceptionally well dressed and well fed. One English-born Sealyham always walked with cotton socks on his feet because his owner was convinced that the sidewalks might hurt his paws. For many years, the Plaza even offered special meals for dogs—a breakfast was available that consisted of cornflakes, lukewarm milk, the yolk of an egg, and cottage cheese; a dinner could be had of raw, lean chopped beef, beef broth, spinach, and a roast-beef bone.

Over the decades, so many pets had come for stays that quite a few of them had gained enough renown that their exploits continued to be recounted by hotel personnel long after their departure. One of the most famous dog guests was a Boston bullterrier owned by Mrs. Benjamin Kirkland of Philadelphia. He was trained to fetch jewels. Each evening, he accompanied a maid to the office to collect a leather case containing the jewels his owner planned to wear that evening. He would then obediently carry it back to her in his mouth.

At times, the pet policy had made for more than just a curious atmosphere. Soon after the hotel opened, Princess Lwoff-Parlaghy, one of the world's best-known portrait painters (she did Kaiser Wilhelm six times), moved in. She had a deep animal enthusiasm. When she visited the circus one day, she became attached to an adorable lion cub, which she eventually obtained and brought to the Plaza. The rather nervous manager cajoled her into renting a separate room for the cub and convinced her that keeping a trainer around was a smart idea. She named the lion General Goldfleck Sickles. He did once sneak out into the third-floor corridor and had a look around, but he didn't eat anyone. Otherwise he pretty much hung around the room and took it easy. After three years, the lion suddenly died. A funeral service was held for him in the hotel.

When he was in town, Lassie always liked to stay at the Plaza. He had checked in on a number of occasions, the last time being in 1978, when he was making some appearances to promote his new film, *The Magic of Lassie,* which was opening at Radio City Music Hall. (I say "he" because Lassie was always a male dog, even though the character was female.) He rode about town in a limo and stayed in a $380-a-day suite. A Pinkerton guard trailed him on his excursions to protect him against vicious and stray dogs (people he didn't worry about that much). For his meals, he got sirloin steak in a silver bowl from room service. (He always elected to dine in his room.) According to employees who served him, Lassie was quite a good guest. His trainer tipped rather well.

Some pets, though, could be annoying. A few years ago, Purina staged an audition in the hotel to pick a cat to star in one of its pet-food commercials. Twenty-seven cats showed up. Neither Purina nor the owners came particularly well prepared. The concierge desk had to send out for twenty-seven litter boxes, a bunch of box liners, fifty pounds of kitty litter, and twenty-seven scoopers.

Guests had brought goats to their rooms. One person arrived with a raccoon. A young, amply endowed woman, with a waist that seemed to measure about six inches, used to strut around the lobby with a snake wrapped around her neck like a necklace. Most of the bellmen didn't bother watching the snake. They had their eyes trained slightly lower.

Some guests, perhaps due to the onset of loneliness, acquired pets once they arrived at the hotel. Soon after checking in, one Argentine man dispatched a bellman to purchase a twenty-five-gallon tank and an assortment of tropical fish. "The guy wanted the whole works," the bellman said. "He wanted the colored rocks and a few plants and a rock mountain. He even had to have one of those plastic deep-sea divers with those big helmets. Yeah, he was really insistent on the diver."

8

THE Oak Room was finished with lunch and empty except for Fred Cristina. He had his tuxedo on and his hair neatly in place, even though it was a couple of hours before the dinner guests would arrive. He sat in the back of the room, behind a pillar, in one of the leather booths.

Some of the waiters were old, acrid fellows who laughed bitterly at the pampered guests. Cristina, who had perhaps served more meals in the Oak Room than any other man, was just as cheerful and upbeat as ever. You would probably have to be to build up the kind of longevity record he had. In all, he had worked at the hotel for forty-nine years.

He had short white hair and was tall, with a squeaky voice and an agitated manner, as if he were always about to pluck a fly out of someone's soup. "I watch the late movie and I see all the stars," he told me. "I used to see them all here live."

He shook his head. "We used to get all Hollywood people, presidents, the best. Now it's more commercialized. The traveling businessman. And a lot of groups. One week it's all Italians. Then the next week it's all Australians. For a while, we got a bunch of Japanese groups. England. France. Germany. It's not that I don't like it. I love my job. But it's a changing world. I miss the stars."

It was pleasant sitting in the darkness of the back of the room.

The place was quiet except for an occasional passing employee reporting for duty. Cristina was feeling relaxed and put his feet up.

"My first job was at a French restaurant on Fifty-fifth Street," he said. "I was there four months and then I came to the Plaza, and I'm still here forty-nine years later. I've always been in the Oak Room. It's like I was born to work this room. I started out as a busboy and became a waiter in a year and a half. That was fast. It used to take four years then to become a waiter, but I was ambitious. I was a great busboy. I worked long hours and I cleaned those tables fast. You had to bus cocktails, the whole menu. While I was a busboy, I began to learn the menu. It used to change every day. Now the menu is seasonal. It stays the same for months. There's nothing to learn. But it used to be murder. That menu killed a lot of waiters."

He reflected for a moment, then continued, "I was a waiter for quite a few years. Then I became a captain. As a captain, you were in charge of a station and so many waiters. The captain took the order and carved anything. The waiter served. They got rid of the captains in 1977. Now it's just waiters and managers. The manager seats you, and the waiter takes it from there. After the captains were eliminated, I became a wine steward for a couple of years. I was put in charge of the bar. Then I became maître d' a few years ago. I'm basically in charge of the place at night. I seat people and I do a lot of service. I know plenty of people and they want special things, and I'll have them made for them. In other words, I'll go off the menu for my regulars. And I work the door. I greet people. I cover every angle of this room."

He leaned forward and lowered his voice. "Get this story. Milton Berle was here one day and I went over and said, 'Hello, Mr. Berle, what is your pleasure?' I don't know what made me say that. And he said, 'Marilyn Monroe.' I thought he was kidding. And then she walked in. They were having dinner. I should have made a note of what she ate, but I was so excited about seeing her that I didn't notice."

I asked Cristina what made a good waiter.

"Names," he replied right off. "You have to know the names. I know hundreds of names. And the important thing is the service. You should remember what a steady guest likes, what he doesn't like. You should know what he likes as a cocktail. Then when the guest comes in, you say, 'Do you want the usual?' When I was a waiter, I used to write this down and memorize it. And you keep your eye on every table. Each waiter here works nine tables at a time. Back when I did it, we had six. But in my time, it was hard being a waiter. I had to serve everything off the silver. Now it all comes on the plate. It's easy. You just serve the plate."

His eyes got wide. "Basically a good waiter has to like his job. That's what makes a good waiter. I wanted to be a waiter so bad it hurt. We had a cocktail list this thick." He spread his fingers as wide as they could go. "You had to know so much. Now you don't have to know as much."

A couple of tieless and coatless men headed for the Oak Bar. Cristina jerked his head up and watched them with a child's bewilderment.

"I used to see George Cohan," he said. "Ethel Merman hung out a lot. Mary Martin. Now it's a different story. There's not the same sort of star today. Over at that bar you see people in jeans. They used to dress. Ray Milland was here. Charlie Chaplin. John Wayne. They were great actors. Now a guy makes a movie with a lot of violence and blood splattered all over the place, and he gets five million bucks. Forget it. That's no actor. The actors are on the late movie."

9

HE banquet for the king and queen of Sweden was supposed to get under way at nine-thirty, but no one seriously thought the event would start on time. Before coming to eat, the couple was attending a concert at Carnegie Hall. The slowness with which the entourage progressed through the New York streets made it unlikely that they would manage to follow any schedule very closely.

Every chair at every table that could be squeezed into the Grand Ballroom had been spoken for—six hundred of them—and there were an additional three hundred people being seated in the nearby Terrace Room. To make them feel more a part of the event, closed-circuit television cameras had been set up in the ballroom. During the dinner, they would be snapped on and played through monitors in the Terrace Room so the diners there could watch the king and queen eating in the other room and hear the speeches later on in the evening.

The entrance foyer to the ballroom had reached a peak of crowdedness. A pianist, harpist, flutist, and bassist were playing classical music. People were eddying slowly, gawking at each other and at the high-ceilinged room. A clutch of tuxedoed men, their faces as starched as their shirt collars, gathered around the ballroom entrance. Two of them shuffled past, looking as if they had just strained a tendon, holding up a parade of people behind them.

One of the guests struck up a conversation with me. He said that he was a middle-level manager at a large corporation that did a lot of business in Sweden, hence his presence. "Not every night do you see a king," he remarked. "But if you ask me, this whole thing is running too late. And I had a ferociously bad night last night. Believe it or not, I've got to be in the office tomorrow. Telexes to do." We chatted of this and that. He had milky eyes. The man seemed slightly perplexed about the affair.

There were a great many Secret Service men on the floor. They walked about in the disorder. Like the guests themselves, they were got up in black tie. In an affair this large, it was hard to keep track of who was not a threat and who might well be. Thus, to help out, hotel officials who would be wandering in and out of the kitchen were "pinned"—that is, they were given small metal pins to affix to their chest pocket that meant they had been afforded security clearance. The pin being used in this instance was a white circle with a horizontal blue streak that contained the letter G.

Marty Walsh, an imperturbable former Brooklyn street cop dressed nattily in a conservative tuxedo, was the site man for the U.S. Secret Service, meaning that he was basically running the security operations. He was a pleasant, slightly smiling man who might have been taken for a delicatessen owner. He was in a corner of the room, making a circle on the floor with his toe.

"Any incidents so far?" I asked him.

"No," he said. "I wouldn't tell you if there had been. But nothing has happened. It's been smooth so far."

He said that the Plaza was better to patrol than most hotels, because the security force was professional and competent. "The hotel wasn't built with security in mind," he said, "but no hotel is. They have entrances and exits all over the place for fire reasons and it makes it hard for us to control who comes in."

He drew another circle with his toe and said, "At these events, we trust the hotel staff to take care of the different pieces. If they don't and they fall apart, we have to pick up the pieces. Like tonight, there was supposed to be someone here to check tickets. There isn't. That's not a security problem, though, because we treat everyone here as the general public. That means everyone is a potential risk."

"What if someone looks fishy?"

"We assign a team to him and watch him very closely," Walsh said.

"How can you tell?"

"Most of us were cops," Walsh said. "We can smell it. The way someone walks. The way they carry themselves. You know."

Walsh said he was looking forward to a pretty easy night, but he knew you could never totally relax at one of these affairs. Back in 1970, Chiang Kai-shek's son, Chiang Cing-kao, was coming through a revolving door at the Plaza on his way to a luncheon appearance when a Taiwanese fired a pistol at him. Luckily a detective grabbed the would-be assassin's wrist an instant before the gun went off, causing him to miss. The bullet left a hole the size of a half-dollar in the glass door. The man was a member of a movement dedicated to overthrowing the Nationalist regime that ruled Taiwan. "Long live Formosa; long live Taiwan; down with Chiang Kai-shek!" he cried as he was dragged away in handcuffs. The apparently unruffled Chiang went on to his luncheon and later drove to Chinatown for dinner.

Inside the still-empty ballroom, a woman was cleaning the podium while a man tested the public address system by repeating over and over: "Ladies and gentlemen, please rise for their majesties."

I was pinioned between several jabbering Swedish women. One of them gave a barking laugh. "I can't wait to see how her hair is fixed," she remarked. "I hope she wears it up."

As the time ticked away, a monumental sort of tedium set in. Pools of irritability formed. Where were they? When would we eat? At ten, word came that the king and queen were on their way. People were asked to go to their tables, and so like a vast swarm of insects they moved into the Grand Ballroom. It took a bit of determined jostling to get seated.

A shifty-eyed female photographer attempted to move into the ballroom, and Walsh and Hoyt blocked her way.

"I'm from the press," she said. "I just want to get some pictures inside."

"You'd better wait out here," Walsh said. "Unless you've got a ticket."

"I've seen her before at these things," Hoyt whispered to Walsh once the woman had backed away. "I don't think she's affiliated with anyone. She may be some sort of groupie."

"Let's keep her out," Walsh said. "I think I'll put a man on her, too."

A fair number of the guests remained around the entrance, wishing to greet the royal couple. An excited murmur arose when, at ten thirty-two, the king and queen finally arrived. He was wearing a tuxedo, and the queen had selected a striking light blue gown. Her cap of blond hair was pinned up. They paused for some photographs and then plunged through the crowd, grabbing hands.

Inside the Grand Ballroom kitchen, the food was being readied for delivery. Socrates Alexander was standing there with his wife, watching over things. The menu consisted of a first course of snow grouse mousse, along with a spring salad and white asparagus soup, followed by poached halibut with crevettes and morels, dill sauce, and fleurons of Swedish caviar. Dessert was hazelnut crown cake filled with lingonberry parfait and coated with raspberry sauce. To wash the food down, the guests would get Mondavi Fumé Blanc with the first course, Mondavi Chardonnay with the entree, and Mondavi Moscato with dessert.

The importance of the event dictated that Reiner Greubal himself be present. The king and queen had brought their own chef with them to make sure that their meals were spiced just right and also to ensure that no one tried to slip some poison into their food. He was Werner Vogeli, a round-faced, cheery man, and he stuck close to Greubal.

The banquet waiters queued up in a human production line, and when Klaus Steinke, the banquet headwaiter, gave the signal, they began scooping up the opening courses and moving hastily out to the floor. They neither walked nor ran, but trotted. I noticed that two plates had been specifically earmarked for the king and queen, who were served first, and Vogeli had requested that a touch more vinegar be poured on their helpings. Alexander said to me, "Some heads of state have their own stewards and they come into the kitchen and pick out a meal at random because if something were made special for them it might be tampered with. The same with wine. They pick out a bottle at random from a case. But with the king's own chef here, nothing can happen."

"No more than four at a time," Klaus Steinke yelled at the waiters. "Four at a time." He kept repeating the injunction over and over, as if it were the first day for all of the waiters.

Chef Greubal, meanwhile, was barking his own instructions: "Don't let the vinegar drip off. Hold the plate straight."

"Don't fight over it, boys," Steinke said.

One of the waiters reached for a plate that was not yet ready, and Greubal snapped at him, "Don't touch that plate."

Another waiter grabbed it. "Leave that alone, dammit," Greubal shouted, "or I'll throw the plate in your face."

The soup went out. More wine. Plates clanked, silver crashed, glasses were raised in incessant toasts.

Then the fish was readied. It was eleven-thirty.

Alexander said, "We're running behind. They poached the fish at the last minute. Often we would work ahead, but not for this party. Meat is a lot easier. Normally we could serve an entree to a group this size in an hour and a half. But the chef is taking his time with the sauce."

Greubal was ladling sauce onto the servings of fish from a tremendous pot, and an assistant was placing mushrooms on the plate. Then the waiters took them. The lateness of the hour was shortening tempers.

"Where's the sauce on this one?" a burly waiter asked Greubal.

"There is none," Greubal said.

"Why not? Where's the sauce?"

"Take it," Greubal snapped.

"How come there's no sauce?" the waiter persisted.

"Because there is none," Greubal shouted.

"Why not?"

"Will you shut up or I'll stop right now."

"I just wanted to know the reason," the waiter said.

Greubal hurled down his ladle. "Get out of here!" he screamed. The waiter finally slunk off.

Alexander took a walk through the ballroom and returned to the kitchen to report, "They seem to be enjoying the food. I watched the plates. They're cleaning them pretty well."

A waiter came in. "I have a guy who doesn't eat fish. What else you got?"

"I've got chicken," the chef said. He opened an oven and slid out a tray with chicken on it and plopped a piece on the plate for the waiter.

The ballroom was extremely noisy. People would often follow circuitous paths to the restrooms in order to get a peek at the king and queen. One rosy-cheeked woman who had made a few too many trips and come a bit too close was shooed off and given a warning by one of the Secret Service men. The waiters passed constantly among the tables, refilling glasses of wine the moment they were even partially empty.

Dessert went out a little after midnight, followed by coffee (some of it Sanka) and a few pots of tea. After all the food was gone, the chef ordered a prime rib dinner for Vogeli to have in his office.

The king rose and strode to the podium. A silence fell over the room. He looked out at the audience evenly and, in faltering English, delivered his remarks. Most speeches are inevitably disappointing, and this was no exception. He spun it out properly, but with no intimations of importance or humor. He said that they had enjoyed a wonderful stay. "Let us dedicate this evening in particular to the Swedish and Swedish English in the cultural fields," he said dryly. "The queen and I wish to thank you all. This evening we will have to remember New York by forever more. I would like to say thank you and good luck for the future."

There were great cheers, and then people began to scatter. The king and queen lingered for a short while to chat with guests before making a well-regulated escape to their suite upstairs. Tomorrow it was off to Detroit.

People stood, transfixed. Others danced. A three-piece band in the outside entryway—a saxophone, drums, and electric piano—played the soft rock tunes you hear in Ramada Inn lounges. In short order, the area was aflutter with dancers. A young chestnut-haired woman in a plum mini was going at it rather dramatically, while her partner was just going through the motions. A crowd had collected to watch her.

The banquet waiters, finally done with their exercises, milled around in the kitchen and helped themselves to the remaining coffee. A few of them were dabbing sweating foreheads. One fellow was doing knee bends, getting the kinks out of his legs.

A strapping, snub-nosed waiter offered me a cup. "Go on," he said, extending the cup in his big-knuckled fingers. "Take some coffee. Nobody else is going to be drinking it tonight." He sat down on a table and heaved a big sigh. "Some banquet," he said. "I tell you, if you want to know about a hotel, put on a jacket and run your ass off with us. You've got pressure on your arm and pressure on your chest. You've got to make you sure you don't spill gravy or sauce on someone's gown. These people are paying a lot of money. Would you want something spilled on you? I wouldn't. I've done it a few times, but never intentionally. I knew one guy who used to spill a little something on purpose at every banquet he worked. He said he liked to see how people reacted. One woman told him, 'Ooh, that was really neat.' He didn't last long in this job. It's a tough job. You see the way we walk. It's not leisurely. It's not a stroll in the park. They want these things over by a certain time. It's a case of how long someone can sit without their fanny getting uncomfortable or without having to keep running to the bathroom. You run your ass off in this job."

SUNDAY

1

THE doctor was needed and came over the first thing. A crisp, sunny spring day was developing, but the mopey woman on the eleventh floor was not in the mood to notice it. Waking up with a queasy stomach at three in the morning, when the hotel was tomblike, she had phoned the front desk. She was immediately given the name of the regular doctor and, putting through a call to him, awakened him at home.

On hearing her symptoms, the red-eyed doctor was not particularly pleased to have had his sleep cut short. All too often this would happen. He would be awakened in the middle of the night by some snooty person, and the symptom would turn out to be something foolishly trite that not only didn't need immediate medical attention but didn't even need nonimmediate attention. Groggily, the doctor posed a few questions. Was she dizzy? Was she vomiting? No, she said, but she felt she might throw up at any second. The doctor politely told her to try to get some rest and to check back with him at a more civil hour.

When he failed to hear from her later on in the morning, the doctor called her room. She told him she had thrown up and was afflicted with diarrhea. The doctor said to sit tight; he would be right over.

When he got there, he found a stone-faced, sharp-featured woman in her fifties who was visiting from New Zealand. He had barely had time to put his black bag down when she began moaning that she must surely be a victim of food poisoning. The doctor was dubious. Though he maintained his own internal medicine practice not too far from the hotel, he regularly treated the hotel's under-the-weather guests. Time and again, he had encountered people with stomach problems brought on by one virus or another, and yet they believed that something they had eaten in the hotel had to be the source of their distress. The doctor knew very well what they were doing. They were hoping to embarrass the hotel so that it would offer not to charge them for their room. (Yul Brynner, however, apparently really did come down with trichinosis in 1974, after he ate some spareribs at Trader Vic's. The incident took the shine off his enthusiasm for the place, and he proceeded to file a $3 million damage suit against the restaurant, which, four years later, was settled out of court.)

In answer to the doctor's gentle questions, the woman said she had ordered a chef's salad from room service and she thought the meat in it had tasted a little peculiar. That alone told the doctor that food poisoning was highly improbable. Often it stems from a dairy product—curdled cream or rotten eggs, for instance—but rarely from meat. What's more, if there was bad food in a hotel as large as the Plaza, the odds were that a half-dozen complaints would have come in rather than just one.

Investigation showed that the woman had a slight fever and other symptoms suggestive of a virus, though otherwise she was in good shape. He scribbled down a prescription for some Compazine, but the woman, who was familiar with the drug, said she didn't want to take it. Rather, she said she wanted to get an antibiotic. ("She was convinced that she had bacteria in her and she wanted to get rid of it with a blast of antibiotics," the doctor said later. "But a virus doesn't respond to antibiotics and they can cause more diarrhea and even vaginitis.") The doctor said he couldn't prescribe that, and if she didn't want the Compazine, he advised her just to steer clear of dairy products and to drink plenty of liquids to avoid dehydration.

The woman grudgingly thanked him and paid his bill of $150, his standard charge for coming to the hotel (if he had to arrive in the middle of the night, he tacked on an extra $50). He wanted the fee settled on the spot, since there were times when he had agreed to send bills to a guest's home address and had been stiffed. Now and then, a guest gave him a hard time about his fee, which always puzzled him. "Here are these people who are staying in a hotel where it costs five dollars for ice from room service," he said. "You'd think they would realize that my bill might be in three figures."

On his way out, the doctor stopped briefly at the front desk and informed the attendants that the woman on the eleventh floor had a virus and that should she lodge a complaint about food poisoning, they should not take it seriously.

This had been the doctor's second call of the week. The other one had also been relatively minor. On Tuesday, a man in the shrub business who was vacationing in New York had phoned after waking up with acute discomfort in his back. His worried wife took a quick look and found an outbreak of lesions. The doctor confirmed that he had contracted a case of shingles. He prescribed some ointment and an analgesic to alleviate the pain. "Anyone can get shingles inexplicably," the doctor said. "It often comes from stress. This was getting into the busy season for the nursery business, and so he might have been under a lot of pressure worrying how many shrubs he was going to sell and how well the fertilizer was going to move."

All in all, this had been a pretty lackadaisical week for the doctor, nothing like his rougher ones. Just last week, he had gotten a particularly harrowing call. At two in the morning, he had picked up the phone and a woman with a pronounced drawl had briskly announced, "I'm from the South. I'm staying at the Plaza and I have a headache. What are you going to do about it?"

Not inclined to rush out of bed to remedy a headache, the doctor told the woman he would see her in the morning. He shrugged at what he figured was another nutty case and returned to sleep. But when he stopped by her room, she was staggering about in a way that made it clear she had been drinking and possibly had taken drugs as well. The hotel staff had been having its own share of difficulties with the woman. For one thing, she was continually calling room service and insisting on being served by black and Jewish waiters. She phoned one of the lobby managers and told him that she would like him to come up at any time; she was his to do what he wanted with. The manager had rapidly decided that there was nothing he wanted to do with her other than help her check out.

The woman was unable to answer the doctor's questions sensibly, and so he rooted around in her purse until he discovered a card from a detoxification center down South. He called the center and was told that the woman had been enrolled in its program there and had left without any notice. She began murmuring about a nasty divorce she was going through and a custody battle and about maybe ending her miseries by taking her life. "This woman had her problems," the doctor said later. "I mean, she really had her problems. It wasn't just one bad day." He felt she was a danger to herself and called a psychiatric center and had her committed. In following up on the case, he learned that she had been discharged the next day and had apparently returned to the detoxification unit.

The strangest case the doctor ever encountered at the hotel occurred some time ago. An assistant manager telephoned to report a guest who had been acting most peculiarly in the lobby. She was a woman in her early thirties who had planted herself in the lobby and had been standing motionless in the same position for hours. Various staff members had approached her to see if anything was wrong. She didn't answer. They tried to assist her to her room. She wouldn't budge. She appeared to be in a trance. Finally, the staff coaxed her into a wheelchair and got her to her room, where she sat unmoving.

When the doctor arrived, he tested her himself. He asked her a few things, but she was totally unresponsive to the questions. He lifted one of her arms above her head. It remained there. He moved her head. It stayed fixed in its new position. The doctor was viewing something he had seen but once before in his life, and that was when he was still a medical student: a classic case of catatonic "waxy flexibility." It was an extremely rare form of catatonia, he said, in which you could move any parts of the person's body, virtually twist him or her into a pretzel, and the person would stay in that shape. In searching through her purse, the doctor found the number of her sister, who lived in another state. When he reached her, she told him that her sister had been under psychiatric care and had traveled to New York to seek help from a specialist there who she was convinced could cure her. Apparently, she had yet to make an appointment, however. The doctor had her taken to Roosevelt Hospital, and she eventually wound up being returned to her home.

Medical services at the Plaza, like many other services, had passed through several phases. For a long spell, the hotel had a house doctor who lived and worked out of a second-floor suite. Presumably he was a capable man with a black bag. Presumably patients found his manner reassuring. Presumably there were relatively few complaints to management about his performance. I say "presumably" because most memories of the doctor dated from his later years at the hotel, when his behavior had taken a bad turn. These were the days when he was best known for his friendship with a bottle and his trembling hands. Because he lived in the hotel, he was available on a moment's notice if someone took ill. As the years wore on, that moment grew longer. Most of the time, when there was a call for him, he was working out at a health club. Also, the doctor became a bit goofy. Too often, when he was required he would be plastered. A couple would call and say their baby was ill. He would recommend that they give the infant an aspirin and put him to bed. One of the hotel operators had a lifelong souvenir of his incompetence. She broke her finger dancing with her brother and went to see him for the repair. He set it crooked and she has never been able to straighten the finger again.

One afternoon the current doctor had cause to open the resident doctor's bag when he was unavailable and there was a pressing need for some supplies. He was taken aback by its contents. Among other things, he had a supply of testosterone, a male sex hormone that athletes sometimes use to build up their muscles. "I couldn't imagine why he would ever have call for that," the new doctor said.

"There were a bunch of other things you would rarely need. What you do need are antihistamines and Compazine to stop nausea and vomiting. That's the number-one thing in the hotel because of drinking or stomach viruses. He didn't have that. The bag seemed as if it had been used to death and then left to collect dust." The man was sent elsewhere.

Upon his departure in the early 1980s, the hotel arranged a system under which any of a half-dozen doctors would be made available to sick guests. The setup did not work; since any one of those doctors might be called by a guest only once or twice a month, he wouldn't bother hanging around during holiday weekends or other off hours. Even during customary business hours, the doctors were loath to make house calls. The trips took too long for the remuneration they received and disturbed their office patterns. Thus guests found they might be forced to dial three or four, or even all six, doctors before finding one available to treat them. The hotel therefore felt it necessary to arrange to have one doctor in particular who would virtually always be able to respond to calls.

The present Plaza doctor was a young, quietly confident man who had offices on a fashionable Upper East Side street. He was a chipper man with short auburn hair and a pacific nature, and was quite sensitive to the needs of his patients, as long as they refrained from middle-of-the-night calls for the sort of indigestion that two Rolaids would cure. He preferred to go incognito. An internist and lung specialist, he also moonlighted as a concert pianist when he shucked his black bag; he made his Carnegie Hall debut in 1979. Around the yearly parade of sicknesses, he squeezed in one or two concert performances.

In all senses, he was glad to be the Plaza doctor. His reasoning was straightforward: he needed the business. "I'm still building up a practice," he said. "I've got a hundred thousand dollars a year of overhead. That means I have to earn that much before I qualify for food stamps, and so I need all the business I can get. I will go over to see whoever wants me to be there. I'd rather have patients knocking down my door and coming here, but until that happens, I'm glad to have the Plaza."

On the average, the doctor got two to five calls a week from Plaza guests. Most of the complaints were relatively minor, if not mindless. Someone had forgotten his or her blood-pressure pills and needed a new prescription. Someone had the sniffles. They could sometimes be more complicated. A hooker had rolled a guest and drugged him. A woman had suffered an ectopic pregnancy. A child's appendix had burst. Overdoses—accidental and deliberate —were not totally unknown. He had never, however, treated a stab or a gunshot wound. "I did have a guy who got drunk enough that when he was having an argument with his girlfriend he slammed his fist into the wall and needed stitches." Sometimes the guest was merely looking for a referral. A cap had fallen out of a tooth. Was there a good dentist around? "The most common things," the doctor said, "are stomach flus and vomiting, colds and earaches, headaches and dizziness, and minor injuries like stubbed toes, lacerations, and puncture wounds. I've never had a broken bone, except for one broken toe." Five or six times a year, something would be serious enough—usually a heart attack—to require hospitalization. Whether the complaints were big or small, the doctor behaved gingerly. There was no telling Plaza guests that they were being stupid.

"When guests get sick, they all assume there is a hotel doctor," the doctor said. "And they all assume that he's sitting in the hotel lobby with a desk just like the concierge desk. When a call comes to the desk, he bounds onto the elevator in five seconds flat. It's really pretty ridiculous."

Before he began to service the Plaza, the doctor used to pick up extra work from a partnership that made house calls to most of the midtown hotels. With fair regularity, he would be in and out of the Helmsley Palace, the Pierre, and the Waldorf—curing dizzy spells, heart palpitations, hangovers. One conclusion he had come to was that Plaza guests call doctors ten times more frequently than guests at the other high-priced hotels. "They seem to have much more of a luxury attitude," the doctor said. "They want to be pampered, which is why they're at the hotel, and so they call for just about anything. Maybe a quarter to a third of the calls are totally bullshit, nonsense stuff that you shouldn't bother a doctor for. Most people have the feeling that whatever they have will pass. The abdominal pain will pass. The vomiting will pass. Most people will not say, 'I'm vomiting. Where's a doctor? Get him here on the double.' But the Plaza people are like that. They're a pampered class. I don't know how else to put it."

The doctor arranged his schedule so that he had an open slot once every hour and a half in order to accommodate the hotel. In five years, he said, he had never kept a hotel guest waiting for more than twenty minutes. To ease his workday, he kept his doctor's black bag at the hotel. Its resting place was the fur vault off the front office. "It weighs about fifteen pounds and I'll be damned if I'm going to lug it around," he said. "I rarely make house calls to my private patients, so I don't really need it."

Apart from the necessary fees that he earned from the Plaza affiliation, the doctor liked the change of pace. The hotel also was a far better source for cocktail-party tales than his private practice.

His favorite story was this one. One Saturday, the doctor got a call from a guest who said he had a rash on his face. When he showed up at the guest's room, he found a small, ruddy man who looked to be in his twenties and an older man, probably in his forties, who was standing in the corner puffing on a cigarette. The younger man had the rash. Most of the talking, though, was done by his friend in the corner. He claimed the slight man was one of Australia's leading jockeys. He identified himself as a Swiss banker. He was cool, aloof.

Listening to this, the doctor examined the man, determined that he had a mild dermatological problem, probably from being out in the cold, and prescribed some medication for him. As he wrote out the prescription, the older man wondered if he could ask something. He mentioned that they had had a hooker up to the room Friday night. He thought the hooker might have drugged them, because he fell asleep and woke up missing a Rolex watch with a diamond on it and $30,000 in cash. What kind of drug might she have given him? The doctor said there was no way he could be sure and left.

Later that day, the doctor received a call from the Swiss banker. He said he had picked up the medication for the jockey from the pharmacy at Fifty-eighth Street and Sixth Avenue, and he was wondering if the doctor could find out if the hooker might have gotten the drug from there. The doctor told him that New York was a big town; it wasn't Geneva. There was no telling where she had obtained her drugs. He had never been to the pharmacy, he said, and didn't know where hookers bought their accessories.

The following day, the Australian jockey was on the phone, saying he wanted to see the doctor in his office. When he showed up, the doctor noticed that his rash had cleared up completely. He had brought along a stack of pictures of horses and of him clutching trophies, apparently to resolve any doubts the doctor might have that he was indeed a champion jockey. "Then he mentioned that there was going to be a race at Belmont and they were going to fix it," the doctor said. "But they needed some money. They were looking for investors who could get together two hundred thousand dollars. He said I would make a ten-times return or something like that. Needless to say, I wasn't interested. It was also becoming crystal-clear to me that he had rolled his friend and then suggested that the hooker did it. He was that kind of con artist. I thought that was it with him. But for four or five days he persisted in calling me from different bars around town, until I instructed the answering service not to take the calls. I'm sure the rash was just a pretext to get acquainted with a doctor. He figured I had money to burn and would surely invest. Well, not this doctor. No way."

2

"EY, is there anybody on duty here? I got something to put in." An icy blonde with chiseled features stood at the window of the safe-deposit room. She said she had some jewelry to leave; what about taking it?

Bill Dougherty, the assistant manager on duty, accepted her bag of baubles and handed her a key.

"They'd better be safe there," the woman said curtly.

Dougherty brushed the remark off distractedly, like someone brushing off lint. "Oh, indeed they will be," he said.

The safe-deposit boxes were tucked away in a sterile metallic room behind the assistant manager's office, adjacent to the front desk. For anything left in one of the boxes, the hotel was liable up to a maximum of $500. The boxes were the safest places in the hotel. Except on one notable occasion, nobody had ever ripped off a box. In August 1972, five robbers smashed open five safe-deposit boxes at the Plaza and made off with more than $45,000 worth of jewelry belonging to jewelers who had come to town for a convention. Waving pistols, the robbers shooed twenty-one hotel employees and bystanders into a small office, broke open the boxes, gathered up an emerald tiara and other pieces, and took off. The robbers were a strange crew. During the operation, they consistently addressed their hostages as "sir" and "madam." The night auditor, who was one of the captives, said afterward, "They were the politest people I've ever seen—for crooks." (They were also pretty slippery, for they were never caught.)

Guests were unpredictable about what they chose to leave in the boxes. "We've had the works, everything from shotguns and handguns left here," one of the assistant managers said. "One woman always locks her fur coats in a closet we have here. People leave theater tickets. Traveler's checks. Jewelry, of course. Liquor. Plane tickets. Train tickets. Bus tickets. I can't think of too much that hasn't been left here, short of somebody's kid. Some people have funny ideas about what's important and what's not. One guy put a rabbit's foot in one of the boxes. I guess it meant a lot to him. We've had amplifiers and guitars stored there by members of bands. Another guy left a pencil in a box. One of those ordinary wooden pencils. I haven't any idea why. We don't question motives. I guess he was extremely fond of it." Whatever they leave, guests store things for free. If they lose a key, though, the hotel assesses them a $75 replacement fee.

3

STOOD outside the Fifth Avenue entrance to watch the king and queen of Sweden depart. Luggage had been coming down in seemingly endless droves from their rooms. I had been told that they had managed to sneak in a bit of shopping while they were here to add further to their belongings.

Their stay, according to reports from their staff, had been pleasant, if a bit tiring, and letters of thanks would arrive for the management in subsequent weeks. From the hotel's perspective, it was gratifying that nothing embarrassing had occurred in view of the royal couple. About three hundred people were now packed around the entrances, each of them staking out a square of pavement to catch a parting glimpse. When they emerged, the obligatory clapping began. The king was in a suit and the queen had on a full-length mink coat. It was nippy out.

Malin Hammer, filling in for Jeffrey Flowers and Hud Hinton, thanked the couple for coming and said she hoped they had had a good stay. They assured her that they had. Elizabeth Allen, standing a few feet away, snapped some pictures for Hammer to have as remembrances. There was no time to dawdle, though. A limousine waited outside to take them to the airport.

After they had settled into the backseat of the limousine, an old curly-haired woman moved forward out of the crowd. The omnipresent Arthur Hoyt intercepted her: "Please stay back until they leave."

"I'm Swedish," the woman said. "I just want to wave."

"Okay," Hoyt said, "but stay back a little."

The car began to pull out. The woman waved. The queen, spotting the woman, waved back.

Once the car had sped off, the Secret Service kept the floor closed to outsiders while they poked through the Presidential Suite in case the couple, like so many travelers, had left anything behind. They didn't find a thing.

s I walked into the lobby with Hoyt, he told me about a scam he had just put a stop to. "A damned sneaky one, too," he said. "I caught this baby just in time."

He got on to it, he said, in a purely coincidental way. He was having something to eat in the cafeteria when he overheard some employees talking enthusiastically about Michael Jackson coming to the hotel. Hoyt was pretty surprised. If a popular singer was checking into the hotel, especially someone likely to attract about fifty million groupies, he would always be one of the first people notified. And yet he hadn't heard a word. When he got done disposing of his tray, Hoyt went upstairs and inquired at the front desk. "Sure enough, there was a booking for Michael Jackson," he said. "I also found out that an advance man named Wade had checked in. He apparently had made the reservations. I discovered that he had ordered a limousine and quite a bit of room service and put that on his tab, which he had told the front desk to bill directly to Motown Records.

"This was smelling fishy to me, so I called Motown and they said Michael Jackson was with Epic. Now this was really stinking. I phoned Epic and asked if Michael Jackson was due to come to New York. No way, they said, he was in Los Angeles and had no plans to come east. So I waited for Mr. Wade to return to his room. When he finally did, he was accompanied by these three big guys who were supposedly security men for Michael Jackson. As it turned out, Wade had just got back from the Salvation Army, where he had bought uniforms for the men. He was going to rip off the hotel for all he could. So I had him arrested on charges of larceny by fraud. It's too bad. A lot of the staff were looking forward to serving Michael Jackson."

5

HERE were a great many women in the hotel. I counted a line seventeen deep outside the lobby ladies' room, and the queue behind the ropes at the Palm Court was twenty-six long, and only one of those waiting was a man. I didn't know what to make of this, except to suppose that Sunday afternoon was a prime gathering day for a certain class of women and the Plaza was a prime spot at which to do the gathering.

I wandered over to the concierge desk, where one of the women, with a thick braid of hair down her back and an incipient potbelly, approached Nolacarol Murfee and asked where she might go to get her hair done today. Like most others in the city, the Plaza hairdresser was not open, leaving women in need of emergency hair work in a tizzy.

"Go to Larry Mathews on Madison Avenue," Murfee said right away. "He's open seven days a week. He used to be open three hundred and sixty-five days a year, twenty-four hours a day. But there's not that much hair business, so he's cut back to normal business hours, except he's still open seven days."

"Is he really good?" the woman asked. "If my hair's going to be wrecked, then I'll just wait. I don't want to take big risks."

"Well, I've never been there myself," Murfee said. "But guests have been quite satisfied with him."

"Okay, then," the woman said with a little shrug. "I'll take my head over there."

I fell into conversation with a couple and their daughter, tourists from Texas. They were in town to see some sights and some shows. The husband, a short rubicund man, said he was in the diesel maintenance business. His long-lashed wife said she was in the home maintenance business.

They told me they had had a nice stay and were impressed by the hotel. "We'd heard a lot about it," the husband said. "It's what we would have thought. Really fancy-dancy type of operation."

"We're going to eat at the Oyster Bar tonight," the wife said. "Then we've got play tickets. We saw the Statue yesterday and were up at the Empire State Building."

The daughter, who was thirteen, was looking monumentally bored by the conversation. The wife looked a little doubtful. "To be perfectly frank, Eileen isn't crazy about the Plaza," she said. "She's used to staying in Hyatts and Sheratons with those bland rooms but indoor swimming pools. She loves to swim. She couldn't believe it when she found out there was no pool here. So she's sulking."

"I'm not sulking, Mother," Eileen said.

"Okay, you're reflecting, then."

6

"ELL, I'm just about ready to wrap things up," Howard Hardiman said cheerfully as he took a final walk around the hotel, seeing if anything was happening.

Only a few scattered complaints had come in over the weekend. The most vocal had been from a man in 611 who was upset about having to wait for a car for nearly an hour. The unavoidable cause was a parade on Fifth Avenue, but the hotel still went ahead and picked up his garage charges.

I asked Hardiman how things had gone on his checklist.

He said he had tried the phone service by calling and leaving a message for himself. "I hate to say it, but I think they recognized my voice," he said. "The message was delivered promptly."

A small adventure had resulted when he had hunted for ice at around eleven-thirty the night before. The closest ice machine was on the floor above his room. From experience, he knew where it was, though, for some reason, there was no sign directing people to it. When he came out of his room to fetch the ice, he bumped into two women helplessly wandering the halls, ice buckets in their hands. They couldn't find the machine. Hardiman led the way and apologized for the missing sign. That failing went on his report.

On Saturday Hardiman had had lunch in the Oyster Bar and dinner in the Oak Room, then ordered a late sandwich and ice cream from room service. "No problems," he said. "I might have gotten a little special attention, because they knew I was the manager on duty. In the Oyster Bar, I noticed that all the smoking seats are in the front of the restaurant and so nonsmokers have to walk through a bit of a smoke haze to get to their tables. I think they should consider a circulation system or reconfigure the seating. In my room, there was a phone in my bathroom that wasn't working. I'll be noting that. I have a couple of suggestions to make, too. I will question whether there ought to be toothpaste in the amenity package, but I will also question whether sandalwood is the proper fragrance for a shampoo. I think it may be too masculine. All in all, though, this will be a pretty good report. There have been times when I couldn't be as positive. Once I checked in and found a vacuum cleaner sitting in the middle of the room and the room was still really dirty."

He walked into the Grand Ballroom, which was being set up for some sort of Monday meeting. Hardiman picked up a silver spoon from the floor and took it into the kitchen, now spotless. All the windows were open to get the staleness out. He peeked into the Savoy Room, where the Japan Consulate General had established a temporary office. Hardiman had been puzzled by it. No one ever seemed to come by. There were several facsimile machines, and a sole Japanese man was sleeping in a chair with his feet propped up on a table. "It's hard to figure out what that's about," Hardiman said. "Strange. Very strange."

Down in the subbasement, Hardiman dropped in on the chief engineer, who was on the phone with John Petrolino asking him what his wife's panty-hose size was. So that he wouldn't get ideas, the chief engineer explained to Hardiman that his son's mother-in-law's brother was a panty-hose salesman and had given him a load of panty hose, too many for his wife to use, and he was trying to find women to offer some to. "Having a hell of a time unloading it all," he said. "Don't women need this stuff all the time?" When he got off, he told Hardiman he'd better take a look along Fifty-eighth Street because there was garbage heaped out there from last night's banquet and it looked miserable and stank.

On the way outside, Hardiman spotted a bulb burned out in the

Fifth Avenue lobby and marked that down for the benefit of the building department. When he got to the Fifty-eighth Street side, sure enough, there were eight black bags of garbage tossed in a pile, looking awful. Hardiman shook his head unhappily. "Okay," he said, "we're going to have to get stewarding on those."

The hotel was winding down, dissolving into the lazy slowness of Sunday evenings, when many rooms were available. Tourists were heading home to the suburbs or wherever they were from, tongues already tasting the tales to tell of the eclecticism of a day in New York. Their departure was a proclamation that a week was ending. Employees were breathing easier, glad that guest needs had diminished. Outside, a wind whipped the flags.

Hardiman punched the elevator button. He would go to his room to pack, then return to the lesser splendor of his home in Brooklyn. "All in all, not a bad weekend," he said. "A good one for me. And a good one for the hotel."

7

A s dusk set in, activity at the front desk began to perk up a bit. Some new arrivals took the places of departing guests. Transitions went swiftly. Phones were ringing. Computer printers were chattering. A guest checked in from London. Someone from West Germany paid $1,827.42 and checked out. A man from Munich checked in. A couple from Brooklyn checked out.

"Front, please," an attendant called, looking for a bellman.

A man wanted to change 50 marks to dollars. The result was $27.77. A sour-faced man from Philadelphia paid $484.56 and checked out. Two women from Quebec checked in. A man from Maine checked out.

A woman on her way back to her home in Italy came up to the desk. She had on a knobby green sweater.

"Leaving the hotel?" one of the attendants asked.

"Yes," she said. "Right away. Actually, I left yesterday. I missed my plane. All my luggage was checked at the airport. I had my boarding pass and they bumped forty-five people."

"Wow," the attendant said. "I hope you have better luck today."

"Thank you."

She asked for change for $20.

The attendant said, "Did you enjoy your stay with us?"

"Yes," she said, "I really did."

"Well, thank you for staying at the Plaza," he replied. "I hope we see you again."

The Rudnitskys, after a one-night stay, were checking out. Much more than most guests, they had seen the best and worst of the Plaza. They had occupied a pleasingly spacious park-view room and had eaten well in the hotel, and yet there was no balance at all on their bill. The hotel was picking up the tab. The last time the couple had been here, the hotel had fouled up.

On that Sunday night, the previous December 13, Robin Rudnitsky stood at the front desk at midnight in her wedding gown, being told that there was no reservation for her and her husband, Gary. They were shocked, irritated, disappointed. More than six months earlier, they had arranged with Harvey Robbins for a honeymoon stay to precede their flight to Hawaii. The then Miss Kelz had stopped by several times to check with Robbins that everything was going according to plan. She had been assured that it was. And now there was no room.

Gary Rudnitsky rolled his eyes at his new wife. This was the only detail she was supposed to have taken care of. He had dealt with the wedding at the Tammybrook Country Club in New Jersey. He had dealt with the arrangements for the three-week trip to Hawaii. All she had had to do was handle a single night at the Plaza.

After the couple spent twenty minutes or so waiting around sulking, the attendant found the Rudnitskys a room, but not one with a park view as had been expected. They were lucky it was Sunday, when occupancy wasn't too high, or they could have been forced to go to another hotel, and Kelz had had her heart set on the Plaza. In planning the night, she had visited all the top hotels in New York—the Waldorf, the Regency, the Plaza Athénée, the Pierre—but it was the Plaza that had captivated her.

Mrs. Rudnitsky, a real estate broker for Williams Real Estate Company, and her husband, a New York dentist, had met at a disco club in the city. ("That's not typical for me," she said. "I never met anyone else at a disco club.") For some time, she had been coming to the Plaza's hairdresser, and through him she had been introduced to Harvey Robbins, who told her he would personally take care of her arrangements. How the foul-up had happened was still unclear. Robbins thought the name had been misspelled when it was typed into the computer.

When they returned from their honeymoon, Mrs. Rudnitsky stopped by and paid a call on Robbins. He was greatly annoyed about the mistake. He told her that he would like them to return at their convenience for a free night and a free dinner in the Edwardian Room. This Saturday was good for them, so they took it.

They checked in late Saturday afternoon, took a walk down Fifth Avenue to look at Trump Tower, had a knish on the sidewalk, and then returned to their ninth-floor room overlooking the park to dress for dinner. In the Edwardian Room, they found the service and the food quite to their liking. The trio performing there, by sheer coincidence, made Mrs. Rudnitsky's visit memorable because they played "I Wish You Love." That was the song her mother always sang, and whenever she heard it she thought fondly of her.

This morning, they had slept late. When they got up, they watched the movie *Wall Street* in their room, finding it rather entertaining. Then they ordered a room-service brunch of impressive cholesteric dimensions, packed, and checked out.

"This more than made up for last time," Mrs. Rudnitsky said. "It was a lovely weekend for us. Absolutely lovely. Now I'm hoping my husband surprises me on our anniversary with another night here. I'd like to make this a real habit. You know, once a year, as long as we live, to come and spend a night at the Plaza."

EPILOGUE

EVER since Donald Trump bought the Plaza (on his way to buying up the rest of the world), there has been a great deal of conjecture about what his ownership will mean for the hotel. Similar speculation invariably engulfed previous sales. In the months following this latest transaction, a mixed picture has been developing. Fortunately, the quiet elegance of the hotel has still been very much in evidence. No mirrors have been mounted on the ceilings of rooms. More amazingly, Trump has somehow managed to restrain himself from putting his name on the building. The place has, in fact, improved in some cosmetic ways. More stylish English and French furniture and accoutrements have steadily been supplanting the rather drab contemporary pieces in the guest rooms. As some of the suites have been reworked, they have been named after famous families, such as the two-bedroom Vanderbilt suite on the fifth floor, which is available to anyone who cares to part with $4,000 a night. The hotel is being kept cleaner and various services have been added. Guests can get their shoes shined free of charge, the towels are fluffier, and room amenities have been enhanced.

Plans for some ambitious alterations, most of them in tune with the hotel's traditions, are moving ahead. Trump intends to construct three layers of posh suites, largely duplexes and triplexes, on the top three floors of the hotel, which will be leased to regular tenants for a minimum of three years. In addition, a restoration is scheduled for the Fifth Avenue lobby—a dropped ceiling will be removed to reveal the original ornamental plaster ceiling—and the outside marquees are to get new glass roofs. Some of the ground-floor shops are being converted for new tenants, and an oriental restaurant and spa is being talked about for the vacated Trader Vic's space. A champagne porch is going to be built over the front desk, as well as a business center offering secretaries and fax machines to fulfill the communications needs of traveling businessmen. And so it is likely that the ping of hammers and ring of drills are going to be heard in the hotel for some time.

Staggering media hype has greeted the supposedly bold new era the Trumps are ushering in at the Plaza, for Donald and Ivana Trump are nothing if not accomplished at orchestrating hype. The reality, it seems to me, is that the Plaza is also losing something. Among many members of the staff, there has been deep displeasure over what they see as the suffocating way in which Mrs. Trump has been presiding over the hotel, for suddenly virtually every action requires approval from her or one of her associates and no longer are department heads entrusted with the sort of authority they have been accustomed to. At one point the hotel preposterously ran out of light bulbs because the buildings department hadn't gotten approval to buy replacements. More and more, the strong family feeling that existed under Westin appears to be fading. A number of the top people with long tenures under Westin have come to believe that Mrs. Trump, despite her previous stint as the chief executive of the Trump Castle Hotel and Casino in Atlantic City, is rather unqualified to be running a big luxury hotel.

By the beginning of 1989, quite a few of the people I had met at the Plaza were working elsewhere. The hourly staff has remained virtually intact, though most of the department heads are gone. Some departures were the consequence of the itinerant nature of the hotel industry, but most resulted either from the Trumps' dissatisfaction (Mrs. Trump told me she felt many of the Westin people were incompetent) or because managers were unhappy under the Trump management philosophy, which struck them as a more mean-spirited approach than was prevalent under Westin. Thus a new chef is overseeing the kitchen, and there is a new director of security, a new front-desk manager, and a new building superintendent. In the late summer of 1988, Jeffrey Flowers left as managing director and became president of the Clio Group of Companies, a Japanese enterprise scouting for American hotel properties. Hud Hinton, overdue for a hotel of his own, was promoted to his position. Near the end of the year, however, Hinton accepted the general manager's job at Westin's Arizona Biltmore, a classy five-star resort hotel in Phoenix. Mrs. Trump assumed his title. Like some others, Hinton had found himself stifled by the stubbornly heavy-handed rule of the new boss. "Mrs. Trump feels as if she has all the answers, and she just doesn't think she needs any assistance," Hinton told me during one of the last conversations I had with him. "Working in a nonparticipatory environment isn't very rewarding." One downcast former department head I spoke with echoed the feelings of others when he described the situation as "an awful nightmare that I'm glad I woke up from."

What lies ahead for the Plaza? Some speculation has already begun to circulate that Donald Trump will tire of his new toy within a few years and probably peddle it to some other rich investor. After all, Trump paid a great deal more for the hotel than he could ever recoup from its operating profits—and he is a man who cherishes money almost as much as he does power. If the Plaza is ever put on a make-the-space-pay basis, it will find itself in a parlous state. Part of the hotel might then become converted to condominiums or the entire building might turn fully residential. But who knows?

If nothing else, I have learned that it would be sheer foolishness to try to formulate any hasty predictions about the Plaza. It has developed such a resilient personality and is so often capable of the improbable. Instead of paying too much attention to the fortune-telling going around, I prefer to imagine that there will always be the maids making up the beds and peeking underneath for forgotten shoes, the concierges chasing down whole fresh chickens, the bellmen working on ways to cadge an extra dollar from a guest, all of them refusing to be overly disturbed by the changing world around them and betting that the Plaza's luck will never run out.

About the Author

SONNY KLEINFIELD is a reporter for *The New York Times* and the author of seven previous nonfiction books, including *The Hidden Minority, Staying at the Top: The Life of a CEO,* and *A Machine Called Indomitable.* He has also contributed articles to *The Atlantic, Harper's* and *The New York Times Magazine.* He lives with his family in New York City.